RESTLESS

RESTLESS

Popular Music, the Christian Story, and
the Quest for Ontological Security

DAVID J. GILLARD

◥PICKWICK *Publications* • Eugene, Oregon

RESTLESS
Popular Music, the Christian Story, and the Quest for Ontological Security

Copyright © 2022 David J. Gillard. All rights reserved. Except for brief quotations in critical publications or reviews, no part of this book may be reproduced in any manner without prior written permission from the publisher. Write: Permissions, Wipf and Stock Publishers, 199 W. 8th Ave., Suite 3, Eugene, OR 97401.

Pickwick Publications
An Imprint of Wipf and Stock Publishers
199 W. 8th Ave., Suite 3
Eugene, OR 97401

www.wipfandstock.com

PAPERBACK ISBN: 978-1-6667-1189-9
HARDCOVER ISBN: 978-1-6667-1190-5
EBOOK ISBN: 978-1-6667-1191-2

Cataloguing-in-Publication data:

Names: Gillard, David J.

Title: Restless : popular music, the Christian story, and the quest for ontological security / David J. Gillard.

Description: Eugene, OR: Pickwick Publications, 2022 | Includes bibliographical references and index.

Identifiers: ISBN 978-1-6667-1189-9 (paperback) | ISBN 978-1-6667-1190-5 (hardcover) | ISBN 978-1-6667-1191-2 (ebook)

Subjects: LCSH: Popular music—Religious aspects—Christianity | Popular music—History and criticism | Popular music—Social aspects | Bauman, Zygmunt, 1925–2017

Classification: ML3921.8 G55 2022 (paperback) | ML3921.8 (ebook)

01/27/22

All Scripture quotations, unless otherwise indicated, are taken from the Holy Bible, New International Version®, NIV®. Copyright ©1973, 1978, 1984, 2011 by Biblica, Inc.® Used by permission of Zondervan. All rights reserved worldwide.www.zondervan.com The "NIV" and "New International Version" are trademarks registered in the United States Patent and Trademark Office by Biblica, Inc.®

Figure 10. Silver, D., et al., Dendrogram of 'Music Worlds.' Used with authors' permission.

Figure 14. Woodhead, L., 'No Religion' and religion by age. Used by permission, The Journal of the British Academy.

Figure 19. Marsh C., and Roberts, V., The Magisteria-Ibiza Spectrum. Used by permission Baker Academic, a division of Baker Publishing Group, copyright © 2012.

Figure 20. Brown's Hierarchical View of Musical Semantics. Used by permission, Stephen Brown, "Introduction" in Music and Manipultion. Oxford: Berghahn, copyright © 2006.

With thanks to Professor Christopher Partridge
for encouragement and guidance.

Contents

Introduction		1
1	Sociological Expressions of Restlessness	16
2	Restless Society Expressed within Popular Music	56
3	Christian Belief and Secularisation	88
4	Lyrical Content, Transcendence, and Shalom	112
5	Music and Emotion	147
6	A Theology of Emotion and Popular Music	188
Bibliography		219
Discography		237

List of Figures

Figure 1. New Order, 'Restless'	20
Figure 2. New Order, 'Restless'	21
Figure 3. Jonas Blue, 'Fast Car'	62
Figure 4. George Ezra, 'Don't Matter Now.'	63
Figure 5. George Ezra, 'Don't Matter Now'	63
Figure 6. Lily Allen, 'The Fear'	64
Figure 7. Avicii, 'Wake Me Up'	65
Figure 8. Radiohead, 'Burn the Witch'	69
Figure 9. Sia, 'Cheap Thrills'	70
Figure 10. Silver et al., Dendrogram of 'Music Worlds'	74
Figure 11. Pharrell Williams, 'Happy'	81
Figure 12. Robbie Williams, 'I Love My Life'	83
Figure 13. Black Eyed Peas, 'Where Is the Love?'	99
Figure 14. Woodhead, 'No Religion' and Religion by Age	102
Figure 15. Black Eyed Peas, '#WhereIsTheLove'	108
Figure 16. The Verve, 'Bittersweet Symphony'	109
Figure 17. Henderson, 'Ghost'	126
Figure 18. Scenes from Drake's 'God's Plan'	128
Figure 19: Marsh and Roberts' Magisteria-Ibiza Spectrum	157
Figure 20. Brown's Hierarchical View of Musical Semantics	179
Figure 21. Florence and the Machine, 'Big God'	190
Figure 22. Florence and the Machine, 'Big God'	196

Introduction

WESTERN SOCIETY, IT CAN be argued, is suffering from an epidemic of existential restlessness. Structurally, restlessness is expressed towards institutions, especially concerning the abuse of power. Politically, the surprising results of the 2016 'Brexit' referendum, the 2017 British General Election, and even the 2016 American Presidential election have been interpreted as examples of such dissonance.[1] I encounter existential restlessness daily in my role as a parish priest, when individuals, reflecting on their lives, ask me profound questions about the meaning of life or the reason for suffering. Social dis-ease and existential dissonance can be seen in the rise in the number of individuals who feel lonely or who struggle with self-esteem issues, anxiety, and depression—especially amongst adolescents and young adults.[2] This restlessness is evidenced in Western popular culture, notably so within popular music.[3]

Why do members of Western liberal democracies not feel at ease with themselves? How can the institution of the Church, the historic Western provider of a discourse offering ontological security, speak more effectively into such dis-ease? These issues lie at the center of the concerns informing this book. In particular, three unrelated concerns led me to undertake this work. Firstly, I feel frustration with the continual arguments within the institutional Church around identity. Despite significant research concerning Western societal change these internal arguments affect the ability of the Church to tell its story of divine love, simply evidenced in the decline in church attendance.[4]

Secondly, I play and listen to music which I find both therapeutic and invigorating. I remember hearing OneRepublic's 'Counting Stars' (2013)

---

1. E.g., Fox, "Post-Truth Politics?"; Patel, "UK Democracy."
2. E.g., Girlguiding, "Girls' Attitudes Survey."
3. E.g., Partridge, *Mortality and Music*.
4. Church of England, *Statistics for Mission*, 18.

playing 'back to back' with Ella Henderson's 'Ghost' (2014) on a national commercial radio station. Imagery from both videos came to mind, making me think that in this ostensibly secular age such radio programming should not be occurring. How is it possible for there to be such public reference to God while Christian socialization is declining? Lastly, I remember entering a music shop in London and hearing a short chord sequence played on a synthesizer. It felt like the sound had somehow penetrated my being. This serious encounter with music[5] simply and profoundly moved me. I did not equate this with a religious experience, but the sound left its mark on me. How could that be so? What did the feelings of excitement and fulfilment elicited in that moment really mean? To a large extent, this book is a critical reflection on these concerns.

1. Method

This research brings together three different fields of study: popular music studies, theology, and sociology. I am writing primarily from a Christian theological perspective, while seeking to ground that experience with sociological insight which largely reflects the Marxist tradition. In using Marxist analysis as a theoretical tool, I am interested primarily in understanding the significance of the hegemonic forces which shape and structure society. Perhaps needless to say as a Christian priest, the book is not a Marxist analysis of religion *per se*.[6] Rather, the primary sociological lens through which I examine society and consider the Church's response to contemporary culture is that provided by Zygmunt Bauman in his work 'liquid modernity'.[7]

Of course, while there are different approaches and sociological models that could be used, it is recognized that none are absolutely perfect, and all have their strengths and weaknesses. They are tools that help us more easily to understand a range of social phenomena and processes. Many years ago, in 1977, Oliver Whitely developed Robin Gill's work in *The Social Context for Theology* to address the following questions: 'Accepting the premise that theologians make certain assumptions about persons, societies, and cultures, and about how human beings behave, what models taken from sociology might provide a basis for theological reflection?

From the theological side, the question is: What understandings of persons, societies, and cultures are implicit in the ways in which sociologists

---

5. E.g., Gabrielsson, *Strong Experiences*.
6. E.g., Dawson, *Sociology of Religion*, 40.
7. Bauman, *Liquid Modernity*.

attempt to describe and explain the behavior of human beings?"[8] While he suggested four models that might be used by Christian theologians, it is clear that the situation is complex, and that the scholar needs to be discriminating in the approach taken to a particular area of sociological enquiry. After looking at a number of approaches, it became clear that the sociological work of Bauman around what he theorized as 'liquid modernity' offered the best way forward. Again, I do not claim that it is the only way forward and others, such as Christopher Partridge,[9] have made more use of cultural sociological approaches. The notion of liquid modernity and Bauman's analysis of ontological security, therefore, has been central to the analysis of popular music and society in this study.

This book is written by an Anglican theologian with a critical eye towards the Church *in* England. As such, it provides a broadly emic, theological analysis of its missiology. It asks why the Church's discourses are not as well received by wider British society as they might be. That said, although written with the institutional church in mind, arguably the conclusions of are also applicable to wider society, in that this is reflection on popular music and contemporary ontological security in British Society.

Throughout the following pages there is frequent reference to 'the Christian story.' Specifically, the term is taken from 'narrative theology.'[10] The term is used of the Christian faith understood as a revealed history of human redemption as related in the Bible. 'Telling' the Christian story is the relating of that biblical message to everyday life. So, for example, John Colwell's analysis of Christian Ethics is entitled *Living the Christian Story*—the application of Christian principles to everyday life.[11] While the Church itself holds a number of views as to the nature of the Christian story and how it should be told and lived, it is not the concern of this book to evaluate these or to take sides in theological debates.

Why is it so challenging to socialize individuals into Christian discourse when our use of popular music suggests that spiritual issues, even traditional doctrines are still plausible? This would suggest that if we were to consider why popular music is such a positive platform to express spirituality we may be able to gain fresh insights into this problem. Here, popular music, as distinct from euroclassical music, is mass produced, often for heterogeneous groups of listeners. This is possible due to both technological and commercial processes, which Philip Tagg notes is "subject to the laws of

---

8. Whitley, "Sociological Models," 331.
9. Partridge, *The Lyre of Orpheus*; Partridge, "Religion and Popular Culture."
10. See Fackre, *The Christian Story*.
11. Colwell, *Living the Christian Story*.

'free' enterprise, according to which it should ideally sell as much as possible of as little as possible to as many as possible."[12]

It should be noted that, what one draws from a piece of music, whatever its genre, is necessarily subjective. However, as Diana Raffman notes, music holds an ineffable quality. Or, more precisely, as she describes her cognitive approach, music holds a "multileveled scheme" of ineffabilities, be that structural ineffability, where a listener's knowledge of the musical structure is unconsciously enacted, feeling ineffability, which is drawn from the tonal quality of the piece, or nuance ineffability, where musical representations are unconsciously picked up on.[13] This makes music very adept at expressing feelings that we would not, in other circumstances, be able to verbalize. Music can profoundly affect our sense of self. Clearly, the choice of music that this book draws on is subjective. Songs used are not particular favorites, rather they are simply to be found within the public domain and are, in that way, representative of aspects of popular culture. The choice of songs and any comments drawn from the internet are to illustrate particular sociological points. Broadly speaking, songs are favorable to the Christian tradition.

A differing approach could be to interrogate songs which are antithetical to Christian belief. Yet a question this book seeks to address, while there are popular songs which are very warm towards the Christian tradition, suggesting, therefore, a wider openness to become socialized into the Christian story, why is the Western Church not as effective in maintaining its membership as in the past? What prevents people outside the Western Church from drawing more freely on its discourses to resource feelings of ontological security?

Having, therefore, considered the nature of liquid modernity, in particular how it challenges what the psychiatrist R. D. Laing observes is our need for ontological security,[14] or what John Bowlby identifies as the need for a "secure base,"[15] we will explore how we are using popular music to both still feelings of existential restlessness and to express an ongoing need for spirituality in both its transcendent and immanent forms. We will recognize the 'turn to the self'[16] and, in particular, the need to resource the immanent self. Of course, transcendent expressions of spirituality do, for many, hold

---

12. Tagg, *Analyzing Popular Music*, 4.
13. Raffman, *Language*, 2.
14. Laing, *The Divided Self*.
15. Bowlby, *A Secure Base*, 25.
16. E.g., Partridge, "Occulture and Everyday Enchantment," 318; Houtman and Aupers, "The Spiritual Turn," 315.

validity. Yet, while the institutional Church does reference the turn to the self,[17] it is not framed as part of our need for ontological security and a secure identity. Rather, the rise of immanent spirituality remains "a challenge for churches with their transcended frames of reference."[18] In other words, the institutional church struggles to understand why such societal change has occurred and how to respond to it.

The reason for drawing on mainstream popular music is that, as we will see, it reflects how most of us in everyday life make sense of the world around us.[19] While popular music is subject to the laws of free enterprise, its lyrical content and emotional quotient connect authentically with those who purchase them.

Clearly, there are songs that are antithetical to Christian belief (e.g., Metallica's 'Leper Messiah,' 1986). While these, of course, reflect opposition to Christian discourse,[20] the focus of the book is to interrogate why some in society hold a more positive view of Christian belief and yet are unwilling to draw more fully on the Christian story. We will draw on comments made by fans and listeners, primarily placed on YouTube, as to how they are making use of these songs to shape their own sense of identity while resourcing their pursuit for ontological security.

Our need for ontological security begins at birth.[21] Indeed, some musicologists have noted this with reference to the theory of communicative musicality,[22] in that early forms of communication between adult and infant are proto-musical in nature.[23] A comparative view is also found in Jonathan Baylin's and Dan Hughes' work with attachment theory and traumatized children.[24] This highlights why our musical encounters are so valuable. Our ontological security is not simply a cognitive issue, where we intellectually ascribe to a particular discourse—whether religious or not. Discourses which offer ontological security contain an emotional component which humans draw on throughout their lives in order to feel secure. Likewise, we can draw on the stimuli within popular music as we seek to navigate our way through life. Stimulated by both the emotional quotient of the music and also any lyrical content, popular music is a significant component in

---

17. E.g., Moynagh, *Church for Every Context*.
18. Moynagh, *Church for Every Context*, 86.
19. See DeNora, *Music in Everyday Life*; DeNora, *Music Asylums*.
20. See Partridge, *The Lyre of Orpheus*.
21. E.g., Bowlby, *A Secure Base*.
22. E.g., Gratier and Apter-Danon, "The Improvised Musicality," 301.
23. E.g., Dissanayake, "Root," 22.
24. Baylin and Hughes, *Neurobiology of Attachment-Focused Therapy*.

the construction of everyday ontological security. The book also explores this allegorically, framing the disconnect between Western society and the Christian story as that of the relationship between a traumatized child and her primary carer.

This is not to suggest that the Church can surreptitiously use popular music to enchant the lives of the people it wants to reach, rather, it is to argue that, it creates spaces where what Baylin and Hughes term as "affective-reflective dialogue"[25] can take place. As such, we can encourage those who experience existential restlessness to consider their feelings alongside any rationale argument being made for Christian belief. Again, this is to recognize the importance of our feelings in our decision-making processes.

The global COVID-19 pandemic struck while preparing this for publication. The pandemic has heightened feelings of existential dis-ease and has affected how we have been able to consume popular music. As such, the theme of this book is particularly relevant today. That said, the pandemic is not a major focus in what follows. However, our need for music as a resource to managing feelings of disorientation caused by the pandemic reinforces the conclusions that are drawn. Much more reflection is needed on how our use of music has helped us to deal with the effects of the pandemic, but some initial observations can be found at the end of the penultimate chapter.

2. Rationale and Literature Review

Western society has undergone significant change over recent decades. For example, Robert Putman notes how "most Americans today feel vaguely and uncomfortably disconnected," becoming more individualistic than in past generations.[26] Ulrich Beck argues that capitalist society seeks to limit the risks felt by such societal change,[27] while Manuel Castells[28] notes the networked and fast-paced nature of this individualized society. Bauman's work considers the fluid nature of society alongside the insecurity and ambivalence this all brings.[29]

Having said that, he also does not seem to be able to identify a solution to such feelings of existential angst. Indeed, he makes the point that

---

25. Baylin and Hughes, *Neurobiology of Attachment-Focused Therapy*, 118.
26. Putman, *Bowling Alone*, 402.
27. E.g., Beck, *Risk Society*.
28. Castells, *Communication Power*.
29. E.g., Bauman, *The Individualized Society*; Bauman, *Community*; Bauman, *Identity*; Bauman, *Culture*.

restlessness is an inevitability of our present situation.[30] He partly traces this to the end of the Western reliance on the Christian discourse as a source of ontological security,[31] heralding an era of greater social freedom. Yet, the result has been a reoccurring cycle of restlessness as individuals struggle to find identities which feel secure.[32] Amongst Bauman's critics, Raymond Lee contends that society continues to remain "solid" around issues of religion, race, and class. Yet, he notes how Bauman's view provides a "poetic but partial sketch" of society today.[33] Such a poetic paradigm of fluidity will provide a helpful way to explore Western existential restlessness.

Bauman's model provides a more 'bottom-up' understanding of society's functioning over models suggested, for example, by Beck or Anthony Giddens.[34] Their work illustrates how many negotiate and seek to maintain our capitalist driven hegemony. Bauman, drawing on his Marxist past, is more critical towards the effects of society on the individual. His desire to honor the ethical relationships formed between one another[35] provides a more nuanced understanding of lived experience and the restless feelings this generates. Of particular interest are his views that society found a sense of freedom in moving away from the Christo-centric telos which for so long offered Western society ontological security.[36] Yet he has also noted the human struggle for certitude that this break has generated.[37] Bauman's work has been used effectively by theologians such as Pete Ward.[38]

A further significant viewpoint is held by Michel De Certeau, who asserts that we tactically articulate resistance to hegemony by utilizing the art we encounter around us.[39] Such thinking is mirrored in the groundbreaking sociological work of Paul Willis, who argues that we are now all "cultural producers."[40] These viewpoints support the view that we all actively engaged in bricolage, eclectically picking from the cultural artefacts we find around us in order to shape our identity. Here, the argument will be that we use popular music and the scenes they represent to resource our search

---

30. E.g., Bauman, *Community*, 3.
31. E.g., Bauman, *Liquid Modernity*, 23.
32. E.g., Bauman, *Community*, 3; Bauman, *Culture*, 24.
33. Lee, "Modernity, Solidity and Agency," 662.
34. E.g., Giddens, *Modernity and Self-Identity*.
35. See Bauman, *Liquid Modernity*, 77.
36. E.g., Bauman, *Liquid Modernity*, 23.
37. E.g., Bauman, *The Individualized Society*, 142.
38. E.g., Ward, *Liquid Church*.
39. Certeau, *Practice of Everyday Life*, 37.
40. Willis, *Common Culture*, 145.

for ontological security. Importantly, we do this not because we can, but because we need to. As Bauman rather sardonically asserts,

> We are all like game hunters now or told to be hunters and compelled to act like hunters, on the penalty of eviction from the hunting world; and in case we don't repent and correct our ways, the penalty may mean relegation to the ranks of the game itself.[41]

This is different from the postmodern viewpoint, which, while echoing the ever-changing nature of the nascent state,[42] focuses on the simulacrum and the dominance of the surface without substance.[43] Rather, here, the argument is that our cultural engagement, especially with popular music, is highly significant.

Yet, the reasons behind such bricolage do not sit comfortably with the institutional Church. As Linda Woodhead points out, many British people feel "alienated" from the Church.[44] Instead, the Church places "more emphasis on distinctive language, piety and moral purity"[45] rather than speaking into this restlessness. There are those within the institutional Church who view its missionary zeal as embattled yet effective.[46] Andrew Rumsey, for example, argues that there continues to be value in the Anglican Church's parish system, while at the same time noting how "loss of power usually equates to loss of place."[47] Research additionally highlights the difference between aspects of the Church's espoused theologies and those operant within the wider body of its membership,[48] all of which further accentuates this alienation and longer-term concerns around socialization into its discourses.[49]

Alongside the institutional church, of course, is the movement known as the Emerging Church,[50] which Phyllis Tickle describes as "the Great Emergence,"[51] a reformation of new, progressive forms of ecclesiology. However, as the language of emergence indicates, this movement is relatively small in number. Diana Butler Bass, for example, has argued that

41. Bauman, "Education in Liquid Modernity," 307.
42. E.g., Lyotard, *The Postmodern Condition*, 79.
43. Baudrillard, *The Consumer Society*.
44. Woodhead, "The Rise of 'No Religion,'" 256.
45. Woodhead, "The Rise of 'No Religion,'" 257.
46. E.g., Davison and Milbank, *For the Parish*.
47. Rumsey, *Parish*, 187.
48. E.g., Ward, *Liquid Ecclesiology*, 100; Hawkins and Parkinson, *Reveal*, 13.
49. E.g., Woodhead, "The Rise of 'No Religion,'" 254.
50. E.g., Tickle, *Emergence Christianity*; Marti & Ganiel, *The Deconstructed Church*.
51. Tickle, *Emergence Christianity*, 25.

"where Christianity is now vital, it is not really seen as a 'religion' anymore. It is more of a spiritual thing."[52] While there are problems with this type of analysis, the point is that her views, and those of many others, reflect the turn-to-the-self in Western culture. Bass continues: "the root of many people's anxiety about church [is] that religion is the purveyor of a sort of salvation that does not address their lived struggles."[53] In other words, even an emergent church struggles to speak effectively into the restlessness that people feel.

It is worth mentioning here the 'Mission-Shaped Church' initiative,[54] which has focused on the need for a greater contextualization of the Church within culture.[55] 'Pioneer ministers,' as they have become known, seek to evangelize within our fluid societies. Cathy Ross, for example, observes that pioneers hold "a certain amount of theological homelessness" alongside "the gift for not fitting in."[56] However, rather than being a gift, this simply emphasizes that the institutional church *does not fully understand* why individuals hold such feelings of existential restlessness. Indeed, while well-resourced at its conception, the Mission-Shaped Church initiative has fallen out of favor, with resources increasingly being placed in more established forms of evangelization which tend to focus on a specific evangelical-charismatic model of church growth.[57]

Alongside this Paul Heelas and Linda Woodhead have argued that, within wider society, the turn-to-the-self has reframed how individuals view religion and spirituality. That is to say, individuals seek meaning in their lives through means other than those provided by traditional religion.[58] Their qualitative work, of course, focused on the "holistic milieu"[59] rather than on popular music. Nevertheless, it applies directly to the significance of popular music in society. For example, drawing on the comments left on internet platforms such as YouTube we will see how our contemporaries are continuing to resource the subjective turn, yet, I want to argue, also expressing a need for transcendent belief. Woodhead has subsequently researched

---

52. Bass, *Christianity after Religion*, 7.
53. Bass, *Christianity after Religion*, 182.
54. E.g., Moynagh, *Church for Every Context*.
55. Moynagh, *Church for Every Context*, 51.
56. Ross, "Pioneering Missiologies," 31.
57. E.g., Hailes, "A Time to Plant."
58. Heelas and Woodhead, *Spiritual Revolution*, 156.
59. Heelas and Woodhead, *Spiritual Revolution*, 156.

the growing trend of 'nones'—i.e., those who identify as holding no religion, but who are open to resourcing the self.[60]

In the final analysis, some use popular music to not only manage their existential restlessness, but also to broadly express positive comments towards Christian belief and practice. Yet despite the Church investing in its evangelistic methods, the juxtaposition between the felt belief expressed through popular music culture and the rational arguments for belief articulated by the Church remains. While Pete Ward points out how "modern conversion requires rationalistic discourse plus a rational response,"[61] our use of popular music suggests an over-reliance on rational thought. Such rational argument is not widely interpreted as the offer of hope that the Church seeks to extend. Rather, it pushes away many who are expressing their angst in a differing form of language, that of emotion. Our emotional responses have historically been frowned upon by the Church,[62] yet, existential restlessness is, by its very nature, emotional. The expression of such angst in popular music is, by its very nature, emotional.

One of the key areas interrogated by this book, therefore, concerns how we might draw on our understanding of popular music and of emotion to help bridge the gap between the rational language favored by the institutional Church and the emotive langue used by wider society to express its existential angst. There has been little work done in this area that fundamentally addresses the issue. For example, while Marcus Moberg has written about how popular music is specifically being utilized within the Church in an attempt to connect young people with its teachings, albeit in a very traditional manner,[63] the methodology he reports has had limited success. In contrast, Graham St John's work amongst the electronic dance music scene (EDM) emphasizes how, from his observations, many draw existential meaning from the scene.[64] This type of work, which has little interest in Christianity, is actually much closer to my own research. What can we draw from this type of socio-cultural analysis that will help the Church to be better placed to tell its story?

---

60. Woodhead, "The Rise of 'No Religion.'"
61. Ward, *Liquid Ecclesiology*, 113.
62. E.g., Riis and Woodhead, *Sociology of Religious Emotion*, 15.
63. Moberg, "Popular Music Divine Services."
64. E.g., John, "An Overview"; John, *Tecnomad*; John, *Global Tribe*.

Scholars such as Moberg,[65] Clive Marsh and Vaughan Roberts,[66] and Rupert Till[67] assert that popular music is used to express something of our ultimate concern. Chris Partridge has written extensively on the relationship between popular music and religion,[68] showing, for example, how we are making use of popular music to express constructions of the sacred and the profane.[69] Significantly, he theorizes the importance of music-generated affective space to human meaning-making.[70] Within such affective spaces evoked by pieces of music we can begin to make sense of our sense of who we are. The effect of this can be amplified through our use of music, which Partridge describes in terms of a prosthetic technology.[71] Music is used in everyday life to manipulate emotion and, indeed, physical responses. Again, while he says very little about Christian mission, my concern is how this type of work might be practically drawn upon to tell the Christian story?

Gavin Hopps explores the opportunity for the "re-enchantment of contemporary culture."[72] This is an interesting argument which connects, to some extent, with what I want to explore in this book. However, again, he says little about how the Church might draw on the resources provided by popular music. Closer to my own work is that of the American theologian Jeff Keuss, who argues that young Christians are able to positively draw from the ever-changing nature of popular music in order to help them to make sense of belief in the modern world.[73] However, he fails to address the principal concerns of this thesis: existential restlessness and ontological security.

More usefully, the British theologians Marsh and Roberts explore whether our use of popular music can encourage Christian belief.[74] They helpfully visualize how the fluid nature of society influences our sense of self through what they term their *Magisteria-Ibiza Spectrum* (Fig. 19). However, while their work focuses on *how* we may use popular music as a spiritual resource in everyday life, it reflects how the Church negatively perceives our

65. Moberg, "Popular Music Divine Services."
66. Marsh and Roberts, *Personal Jesus*.
67. Till, *Pop Cult*.
68. E.g., Partridge, *The Lyre of Orpheus*; Partridge, *Mortality and Music*; Partridge, "Psychedelic Music."
69. Partridge, *The Lyre of Orpheus*.
70. Partridge, "Emotion," 31.
71. Partridge, *The Lyre of Orpheus*, 196; Partridge, "Emotion," 31.
72. Hopps, "Theology," 91.
73. Keuss, *Blur*, 37.
74. Marsh and Roberts, *Personal Jesus*; Marsh and Roberts, "Religious Practice (Part One)"; Marsh and Roberts, "Religious Practice (Part Two)."

present age as 'pick and mix,' where one uses sources of music as a form of escapism. While I have some sympathy with this approach and understand why they have taken it, I am arguing, more specifically, that, to follow Bauman, we are forced to consider identity issues, not because we want to, or even because we can, but because we *have to* in order to survive. I am seeking to address something much more fundamental than choice, something that music seems to address.

This brings us to music and emotion and to a key contribution of this research. A link between music and 'survival' can be drawn from what Mlaya Gratier and Gisele Apter-Danon term as "communicative musicality."[75] We are hardwired from birth to find ontological security from our principle carers through ways that can be considered as musical, for example, in a mother speaking *motherese* to her infant. A relationship can be seen between such proto-musical expression and feelings of ontological security.[76] When that "secure base"[77] is not successful, individuals can find themselves dealing with significant attachment issues, that is, particular difficulties in how we form relationships with others.[78] Our feelings of ontological security are linked not only to how we may rationally make sense of such a discourse, but, to draw from our earliest experiences, the proto-musical feel of it, too.

Baylin and Hughes make an interesting observation that trauma therapies are moving away from 'top-down' approaches, where the focus has been on "rational, conceptual areas of our brain" to a 'bottom-up' process, where trauma is *felt* within the body. Whether conscious or not, this reflects how we are now viewing cultural formation, as a bottom-up, felt response to hegemony, emphasizing, again, that we have become over-reliant on cognitive approaches to wellbeing and that greater weight needs to be placed on felt outcomes.

The use of attachment theory in this manner is, I would argue, not pushing Bowlby's original theory too far. Indeed, religion-as-attachment research is gaining ground as an important area of enquiry.[79] This humanistic understanding explores how we are able to attach to unseen figures (e.g., God) as much as those who are significant attachment figures to us.[80] Pehr Granqvist and Lee Kirkpatrick note that while religion can cause

75. Gratier and Apter-Danon, "The Improvised Musicality," 301.

76. See Dissanayake, "Root," 22; Nagel, *Melodies of the Mind*; DeNora, *Music Asylums*, 45; Baylin and Hughes, *Neurobiology of Attachment-Focused Therapy*, 16.

77. Bowlby, *A Secure Base*, 12.

78. E.g., Bowlby, *A Secure Base*; Baylin and Hughes, *Neurobiology of Attachment-Focused Therapy*; Laing, *The Divided Self*.

79. I.e., Granqvist and Kirkpatrick, "Attachment and Religious Representations," 933.

80. Granqvist and Kirkpatrick, "Attachment and Religious Representations," 917.

physiological issues, "the representation of attachment to a God perceived as a reliable safe haven and secure base may confer the kinds of psychological benefits associated with secure interpersonal attachments, especially in times of personal trouble, when other attachment figures are insufficient or unavailable."[81] However, as I have already noted, I do not view religion from, for example, a Marxist perspective as a primal human projection. Such modelling, though, can provide fresh ways to understand how we can view our relationship with God within liquid modernity.

What this highlights is that, regardless of taste, our musical engagement draws from our earliest experiences of life and our fundamental need to feel secure. This, of course, is enormously significant, in that such early experiences subsequently shape how we make sense of who we are as adults. This identifies an area for research regarding how such musicality, not only shapes our worldview, but also how such processes shape how we make sense of any discourse that may offer us ontological security, such as that provided by Christianity.

Finally, one of the principal thinkers to consider the relationship between music (primarily classical music) and theology is Jeremy Begbie. He has also commented on Christian belief, emotion and music,[82] noting its ability to shape who we are. "When we claim that God was in Christ to reconcile us to himself . . . as the risen human, our representative, he can concentrate, shape and reshape our emotional life in the likeness of his."[83] While this is explored in relation to music, my concern is that this overestimates where the vast majority of people are. It is, not to put too fine a point on it, ivory tower theology. It fails to take into account the social forces that shape society today, particularly around telling the Christian story.

Struggling individuals do not engage in this level of theological reflection. Rather, most of us are simply working through unacknowledged existential angst in the best way that we can on a daily basis. This, I want to argue, is, for many people, evident in their listening habits. The practical outworking of this is to provide a stage someway before Begbie's theological analysis, that in reflecting on the emotional responses engendered by popular music, including those evoked by music videos, we can help close the gap between felt and rational knowledge in order that something of the Christian story can be communicated to liquid moderns.

Our need for ontological security is not simply a cognitive issue. People don't listen to a song and then commit themselves to a particular

---

81. Granqvist and Kirkpatrick, "Attachment and Religious Representations," 934.
82. Begbie, *Resounding Truth*, 294.
83. Begbie, *Resounding Truth*, 303.

discourse. Rather it holds an emotional component which can be affected by differing stimuli, including popular music. This is not to suggest that popular music is always an agent of enchantment *per se*. Rather, to draw on what Baylin and Hughes term as "affective-reflective dialogue,"[84] it is able to create spaces where such affective-reflective conversation can take place. Again, we are seeking to make connections between the 'felt knowledge,' such as that evoked by angst, and the rational language of the Church which may, for some at least, offer reconciliation, shalom, peace.

In short, the book explores the ways in which the legacy of the Enlightenment has problematized the telling of the Christian story. With this in mind, it explores how popular music manages angst and expresses ontological dissonance, which can then be addressed by the Christian story. It explores the significance of the close relationship between emotion, religion, and popular music.

3. Overview

The first chapter sets the context for the analysis. It considers how liquid moderns express their existential needs. It also discusses the ways in which ideological forces prevent the Christian discourse from being heard clearly.

In chapter 2 we will see how these key existential concerns are being expressed within popular music. We will do this by considering how popular music can provide sociological insight which demonstrates our need for ontological security. We will also explore how, to some extent, the ways in which it resists a critical secular hegemony that questions traditional Christian constructions of a divine Other. We will look not only at the lyrical and musical content of selected compositions, but also at accompanying official video material. This will help us to consider the wider symbolic value of popular music in society. This is to acknowledge that music is consumed, not simply audibly, but also via multi-platforms such as YouTube and Spotify. It is to also reimagine the medieval phrase *ut pictura poesis*. That is to say, the discussion interrogates the similarity in emotional and heuristic affect between the visual, aural and poetic based arts.[85] Our engagement with the symbolic nature of the songs we listen to or watch holds a high emotional quotient that affects our sense of ontologically security.

It is clear that our understanding of spirituality and the religious has evolved considerably in recent years. Chapter 3 will look at how the Church has responded to the loss of its hegemonic power. We will again consider

---

84. Baylin and Hughes, *The Neurobiology of Attachment*, 118.
85. Braider, "The Paradoxical Sisterhood," 168.

how some of these themes are reflected in song and video (and, as such, disseminated within society). This will further reinforce a significant point developed in the first two chapters, namely that there is still an ontological need to make sense of that which they feel they experience yet cannot see.

Chapter 4 will look at how the contemporary consumption of popular music reflects aspects of how we use the function of religion to express our need for ontological security. Chapter 5 will develop this further by considering how we engage emotionally with music, even in elementary ways from before birth. We will see how our use of music acts as a 'reward' in the brain, which we may begin to interpret as security.

Chapter 6 will draw these themes together, considering the pedagogical opportunities that popular music offers the Church to share its discourses, particularly our use of affective space,[86] and how our emotions are integral in taking decisions which affect our ontological needs. We will see that as we reflect on how music affects us we can gain fresh insight from the discourse that is being told within that space. We will term the purposeful formation of such reflective space as 'creative space for spiritual reflection' (CSSR). We will reinforce the opportunities provided through the use of such space by examining how the analogy of a traumatized child needing to reconnect with a caregiver may help a restless liquid modernist to reconnect with the Christian discourse, drawing links between playfulness and that of beauty, between acceptance and socialization into belief, curiosity and poetics and, lastly, empathy and wisdom.

Finally, we draw together a theology of emotion and popular music, so bringing together fresh insights to our understanding of the relationship between religion and popular music. More particularly, this will provide an applied theological contribution in how the Christian story might be discussed within liquid modernity. Finally, on the basis of the spheres of enquiry, a theological approach to popular music is suggested.

---

86. Partridge, *The Lyre of Orpheus*, 43–47.

1

Sociological Expressions of Restlessness

WESTERN SOCIETY HAS WITNESSED significant transformation over the past sixty years.[1] The growth of consumerism and liberal pluralism—that is the presumption that individuals may live their lives as they see fit within a broad range of life choices[2] and their own values are seen as holding no particular hierarchy of significance in relation to others[3]—has run in parallel with huge technological advances. This has resulted in a diversification in the number of sources from which we draw ontological security. For example, the holistic milieu[4] includes a wide range of activities that reflect the subjective nature of what is on offer, from yoga to channeling. Alongside this lies the consumeristic hope that the latest large purchase may bring deep satisfaction. Such discourses and the structures that support them are hegemonic and have usurped the earlier hegemonic discourses provided by Christianity with its message of salvation and eternal security in heaven. The Church must now tell its story about ontological security alongside a range of other stories.

This diversification in narratives from which we seek to draw security exists despite our time being heralded as a period of secularization.[5] One

---

1. See Brown, *Death of Christian Britain*; Bruce, *God Is Dead*.
2. Galston, *Liberal Pluralism*, 3.
3. Galston, *Liberal Pluralism*, 5.
4. E.g., Heelas and Woodhead, *The Spiritual Revolution*, 156; Redden, "Religion," 651; Lynch, *The Sacred in the Modern*, 4.
5. Bruce, *God Is Dead*.

should expect to see a decline in the number of narratives of non-secular meaning making as we adjust to a secular understanding of reality. Yet, instead, society has experienced an ever-increasing level of angst, the response to which is often to turn to the non-secular. For example, we can see how popular music explores aspects of what may lie beyond the horizon of our dominant secular lifeworld, including the ongoing possibility of transcendent encounters with the divine.[6]

Concerning this angst *per se*, we will see that Bauman in particular has explored this, although he is not alone in his observations. Ulrich Beck, for example, discusses the notion of a "risk society"[7] in which people manage social, political, economic and individual risk without the monitoring or protection once offered by traditional institutions.[8] Risk society for Beck is about capitalistic control.[9] Likewise, Manuel Castells[10] views the West as a networked society where power relationships have been transformed through globalization and where digital networks are viewed as "the fundamental symbol-processing system of our time,"[11] the speed of which may accentuate feelings of dis-ease.

The point is that dramatic and complex sociological change affects not only our individual pursuit of ontological security but also how traditional institutions such as the Church frame the telling of their particular narratives. This should not all be conflated into a discussion about secularization (to be discussed in the chapter 3), in that the increase in the number of spiritual offers found within liquid modernity simply expresses the continual need of humans to make sense of who they are in the face of constantly shifting socio-cultural forces. There are two points here: (1) Having lost its hegemonic hold, the Church currently provides only one of many discourses that seek to satisfy our need for ontological security. This means that the decline in recent years of church attendance, which are significant, should not be viewed through the lens of secularization alone, rather that wider social and hegemonic forces are at work. The trends for attendance in Anglican churches for 2019 show that whilst 10 percent of churches have experienced statistically significant growth, 41 percent have experienced significant decline while the remaining 49 percent remain around the same levels.[12] (2)

---

6. See Partridge *The Lyre of Orpheus*; Partridge, *Mortality and Music*.
7. Beck, *Risk Society*, 14.
8. Beck, *Risk Society*, 5. See also Knowles, "Signs of Salvation."
9. Beck, *Risk Society*, 5.
10. Castells, *Communication Power*.
11. Castells, *Communication Power*, 4.
12. Church of England, *Statistics for Mission*, 18.

Our present societal model is not able to provide a cogent answer to feelings of restlessness. This is not simply a theological issue, it is a sociological and psychological concern as well. Unresolved restlessness can lead to serious psycho-social issues.

The decline in Western church attendance does, however, highlight a crisis in the number of individuals becoming socialized into Christian belief. Some scholars, such as Steve Bruce[13] and Callum Brown view this as the beginnings of an existential crisis for the Western Church:

> It freed me and British popular culture as a whole from the relentless misery of an inescapable Christian discourse which governed virtually all aspects of self-identity and expression, community-regulated leisure and domestic life (and to an extent economic life too.[14]

Brown's observation pinpoints a significant fact that is often overlooked in the traditional secularization debate, where the decline in religious belief has long been interpreted as society modernizing and growing up. Rather, the significant issue is that of liberation from *restrictive* socio-cultural practices. This suggests that, rather than religious belief declining as modern societies 'mature' and no longer feel able to believe in the existence of God, the decline is as much about a need for social freedom: the praxis of religion is seen as being socially too restrictive. Such sentiment is reflected in The Stooges' 2007 song 'The end of Christianity' which notes both how former grand narratives no longer hold, especially that of Christian belief.

Yet, as we will see, the fact that there are so many non-derisive references to the Christian story within popular music highlights that it is still a discourse that makes some sense to many Westerners. In other words, the decline of Christian commitment can be attributed to a broader change in social practices as society becomes shaped by the hegemony of liberal pluralism.[15] Within this hegemony the divine can still be spoken of, but in a different way to that of past generations. There becomes a point when its discussion becomes hegemonically restricted. This highlights that a much broader framework of ideological forces are the reason why Christianity has fallen out of favor. This chapter will highlight those forces which prevent the Christian discourse from being listened to clearly.

This, broadly speaking, theoretical chapter will explore three key themes: (1) liquid modernity, (2) ontological security and emotions and (3)

---

13. Bruce, *God Is Dead*, 74.
14. Brown, *Death of Christian Britain*, 200.
15. See Woodhead, "Rise of 'No Religion'"; Galston, *Liberal Pluralism*.

popular culture. While focusing on Bauman's liquid modernity, we will also consider aspects of Jürgen Habermas' notion of lifeworlds as that highlights some of the key ideological forces which restrain the Christian discourse within liquid modernity. Having unpacked these terms we will be in a position to see how popular musical culture expresses Western society's existential incongruence as well as how we are using popular music culture to resource our expression of ultimate reality, which we will see in chapter 2.

1. Liquid Modernity

In 2016, despite both the group's longevity and success, New Order released the song 'Restless.' It simply speaks of a deep discomfort and unhappiness with life which is expressed as restlessness. Whether Bernard Sumner, the band's lyricist, is reflecting his own sense of dis-ease or simply observing the everyday world he inhabits is not clear. What does seem clear is that his thinking is not wholly out of step with current research.[16] Being the first new material for ten years,[17] one might have expected a more upbeat, triumphal lyric. Why should a pop-group which has had significant commercial success sing about a deep unhappiness with life?

Even if one agreed with Theodor Adorno's views on popular music and societal control—"From this darkest of perspectives, then, commodification converges with totalitarian manipulation in the destruction of all cultural value, the promotion of conformism and the retardation of individual development"[18]—one still has to make sense of the negativity of the lyrics and what that may say about society today. The song lyric's language does not reflect a feeling of control in life, while its accompanying video portrays the video's protagonist not able to escape events which overtake him: it is the language of feeling paralyzed. It reflects a lack of agency, an inability to know how to think and act in the face of massive change. New Order are, of course, older individuals who have enjoyed financial success. Yet they still suggest that they are affected by personal and societal restlessness. At one level, this cannot be surprising. Humans have always sought to make sense of their lot in life with many in each generation declaring "Everything is meaningless" (Eccl 1:2). Yet, as noted above, the song lyric and its accompanying video captures something of the *zeitgeist*.

---

16. See Fitzpatrick and Sharry, *Coping with Depression*; Partridge, *Mortality and Music*, 97–136.

17. Young, "New Music."

18. Adorno, *The Culture Industry*, 53.

Concerning the video material accompanying the song, there is a mixture of images drawn from mythic and fantasy discourses, focusing mainly on the Arthurian 'sword in the stone' myth (following T. H. White's influential popular rendering of the story in 1938). This is significant, in that engaging with a mythical narrative can help one explore values and identities through archetypal figures.[19] As such, the video provides a genre in which the viewer is able to explore their own values and concerns.

The mythic narrative is introduced before the song begins through the opening image of a bloodied Arthurian character lying on the ground. The video flows into a *cinéma vérité* styled scene[20] where a group of present-day young people are documented sealing a letter with their own blood thus setting the contrast between the present and the archetypal figures within the myth. When viewed against the lyric of the inner-self feeling down the scene conveys a sense of emptiness with which the young people wrestle. This flows immediately into an enactment of the sword in the stone myth where a physically dominant character unsuccessfully attempts to remove the sword from the stone. This character is later seen wearing a simple crown, symbolic of the authority he holds. His place at the stone is then taken by the Arthurian character who removes the sword and, according to the myth, is, as such, invested with the authority to be king (Fig. 1). Having said that, as the video develops that authority is challenged.

Figure 1. New Order, 'Restless'

19. Lyden, *Film as Religion*, 58.
20. See Loughlin, "A Theological Introduction," 7.

A new scene is then introduced where the young people attend a rave, although this is interspersed with images of the character wearing a crown controlling the lead female character. Two strands of imagery then become juxtaposed: (a) a gluttonous medieval banquet and (b) the crowned character presiding over it. However, the food is contemporary fast-food, which is gorged and wasted, accompanied by lyrics describing the superficiality and desire at the heart of consumer society: the hope for both material possessions and an attractive soul-mate. Yet the female character, looking longingly at the Arthurian character, is wearing a crown of thorns (Fig. 2), which is of course, imagery associated with the crucified Christ in Western culture. A raven, often symbolic of mortality walks along the banquet table while a lyric questioning how much sustenance is truly needed is sung, emphasizing the emptiness and pointlessness of the banquet—thus indirectly challenging consumerist hegemony. Interestingly, a similar theme is developed by Trent Reznor or Nine Inch Nails in his song 'Hurt' (1994), which was then covered from a conspicuously Christian perspective by Johnny Cash near the end of his life.

Figure 2. New Order, 'Restless'

As the narrative of New Order's 'Restlessness' progresses, the protagonists, Arthur and the woman, become sexually involved, finding fulfilment in their union. Yet their passion and escape are interrupted by a demonic figure looming menacingly towards the foreground, closely followed by Arthur and the woman, who are relentlessly bombarded by waves. This suggests, perhaps, a clash of values. The protagonists battle the forces of consumerism which they have little chance of escaping. Hence, the 'restlessness' and angst of which New Order sings, and which many of our contemporaries recognize,[21] can be read as a critique of the excesses and fragility of the hegemony of capitalism, drawn out not just in the imagery, but also in the lyrical content, too.

The video draws to a close with Arthur and Guinevere riding on the backs of two horses into an open field, into the freedom of the natural world. Whether wittingly or not, it speaks of a common theme in contemporary spiritual discourses, namely a Romantic longing for the natural, which are often expressed within popular music.[22] That said, the opening image of the bloodied Arthur must raise the possibility that such freedom was not attained, which, again, as is Reznor's song, reinforces restless feelings of futility, longing, and meaninglessness.

Bauman captures this in his analyses of societal change. He explores it through the metaphor of 'liquid,' in that society is now free-flowing, restless and, therefore, not stable. In introducing the expression 'liquid modernity' Bauman makes the point that he does not equate it with terms such as 'postmodernity', 'late modernity', 'second' or 'hyper' modernity.[23] While he examines sociological analyses of postmodernity, with which liquid modernity has sometimes, erroneously, been compared, he is critical of their narcissistic outlook.[24] Indeed, he became frustrated with the "rubbish written in the name of name of postmodern theory"[25] and the lack of engagement with the moral challenge posed by the individual in relation to the Other.[26] Hence, liquid modernity is not a catchall term covering differing philosophical traditions. Rather it identifies a significant move in society away from producing goods to consuming them:[27]

> We presently find ourselves in a time of "interregnum"—when the old ways of doing things no longer work, the old learned or inherited modes of life are no longer suitable for the current *conditio humana,* but when the new ways of tackling the challenges and new modes of life better suited to the new conditions have not as yet been invented, put in place and set in operation. . . . We don't yet know which of the extant forms and settings

---

21. Partridge, *Mortality and Music.*
22. I.e., Bossius et al., "Introduction," 7; Marsh and Roberts, *Personal Jesus,* 126.
23. Bauman, *Culture,* 11.
24. Beilharz, *Socialism and Modernity,* 177.
25. Bauman, *Postmodern Ethics,* 135.
26. Smith, *Zygmunt Bauman,* 24, 152; Bauman, *Liquid Modernity,* viii; Davis, *Freedom and Consumerism,* 27; Davis, "Bauman's Compass," 184.
27. Smith, *Zygmunt Bauman,* 118.

will need to be "liquidized" and replaced, though none seem to be immune to criticism and all or almost all of them have at one time or another been earmarked for replacement.[28]

While sympathetic to Bauman's critique of certain discourses around postmodernity, viewing them as nihilistic and lacking a focus on the ethics of relationships,[29] there are two areas of postmodern theory which have been used to understand popular music. Firstly, the use of signs. For example, Jean-François Lyotard views popular culture as a site where "anything goes," where taste is seen as irrelevant and money is viewed as the only valuable sign.[30] Likewise, Baudrillard's discussion of the simulacrum and the dominance of the surface without substance.[31] However, while there is, of course, evidence of this within popular musical culture, there is also evidence that our relationship with the symbolic has taken on added depth. It is not simply 'surface.' It is our engagement with such symbolism that we "saw up and make fit."[32] We construct an identity that provides a limited level of ontological security. Indeed, we will shortly consider the cultural omnivore theory, whereby it is noted how past musical lines of demarcation have themselves become more fluid, so enabling individuals to draw on a far wider pool of sonic symbols to express the need for ontological security.[33]

However, a point where "liquid modernists" and postmodernists would agree is captured by Stephen Crook, Jan Pakulski and Malcolm Waters. They note that the level of societal change means that it is no longer possible to predict where the trends of modernity are leading. As such, we are entering a "new historical configuration,"[34] which can only further reinforce the level of restlessness as unique to our period of time. We can perhaps think of this in terms of an experience of what Alvin Toffler famously called "future shock."[35] Rapid change over a short period of time leads to significant disease and insecurity: ontological angst. St. Vincent's 2017 song, 'Fear the Future' captures this dilemma in seeking answers that will bring security, while also being fearful of the response, bluntly worried for the future. Likewise, but in a broader sense, in evoking the image of "liquid," which is constantly flowing into new formations, Bauman is expressing

28. Bauman, *Liquid Modernity*, vii.
29. E.g., Bauman, *Postmodern Ethics*, 135.
30. Storey, *Cultural Theory and Popular Culture*, 196.
31. Baudrillard, *The Consumer Society*.
32. Bauman, *The Individualized Society*, 142.
33. E.g., Peterson and Kern, "Changing Highbrow Taste," 904.
34. Crook et al., *Postmodernization*, 1.
35. Toffler, *Future Shock*.

how the structures that govern society constantly change, which, in turn, provokes feelings of restlessness and cognitive dissonance that individuals must now negotiate.

Specifically related to these feelings of restlessness is Bauman's critique of religious belief and religious power.[36] In commenting on the communal telos that once provided Western Europe with ontological security (i.e., Christian belief), he notes the following: "With such beliefs out of the way, we humans found ourselves "on our own," which means that from then on we knew of no limits to improvement and self-improvement other than the shortcomings of our own inherited or acquired gifts, resourcefulness, nerve, will and determination."[37]

However, Bauman's thinking on the divine became more nuanced, recognizing that there is ontologically more than he can account for sociologically. For example, he views religious language in the public sphere as enriching.[38] Yet, he is concerned that in using the language of God a higher authority becomes evoked which cannot be objectively critiqued. Hence, he speaks of the "blind arrogance" of a single truth and his desire to be agnostic towards polytheism.[39]

In contemporary Western societies, there are no longer *prescribed* religious discourses that individuals are expected to assent to or a communal telos for individuals emotionally to gather around. Yet society's new found freedom from such discourses becomes, as Bauman emphasizes, a fate we must deal with rather than a simple range of consumeristic life choices that we now make.[40] The fate with which we must deal is the need to attain ontological security without which one feels fearful and restless:

> Whichever was the case, human nature, once seen as a lasting and not to be revoked legacy of one-off Divine creation was thrown, together with the rest of divine creation, into a melting pot. No more was it seen, no more could it be seen, as 'given.' Instead, it turned into a task, and a task which every man and woman had no choice but to face up to and perform to the best of their ability.[41]

For Bauman, our understanding of identity stems from the formation of nationhood. Yet, when that identity loses its 'natural' feel so "'identification'

---

36. See Ward, *Unbelievable*, 14–17.
37. Bauman, *Liquid Modernity*, 23.
38. Bauman and Obirek, *Of God and Man*, 44, 56.
39. Bauman and Obirek, *Of God and Man*, 2.
40. Bauman, *Liquid Modernity*, 34; Bauman, *The Individualized Society*, 46.
41. Bauman, *The Individualized Society*, 142.

becomes ever more important for the individuals desperately seeking a 'we' to which they may bid for access."[42] The need for identity comes from the desire for security.[43] Here, the ability to fulfil a secure life project requires "'confidence to dwell in disorder' and the ability to 'flourish in the midst of dislocation.'"[44] How may this be achieved?

Steph Lawler's work on identity supports key aspects of Bauman's thinking. She speaks of individuals creating a narrative identity[45] that is shaped by both autobiographical information and how this is interpreted in relation to others.[46] It is through the stories we share with others that our identities become located and the confidence to dwell in disorder is found. Lawler notes that "identity needs to be understood not as longing 'within' the individual person, but as produced between persons and within social relations."[47]

Although we will return to this, it's worth noting here that popular music, often referred to as "the soundtrack to life," functions in this way, providing a meaning-making accompaniment to our personal narratives. It creates affective spaces within which we can imagine our histories and think about our lives. Hence, when we hear a particular song that is significant for us, memories are evoked, which often inject meaning into particular situations. Songs, moreover, may stimulate thoughts about the passage of life, the people we have loved and lost, the times that meant something to us, and, of course, the inevitability of death.[48]

This all helps us to understand the significance of music in relation to the social construction of identity. The socially constructed identity is Bauman's "postulated self."[49] However, for now, we simply note that identity construction is not what it once was and popular music is an increasingly part of it. As Pablo Vila has observed in New York and Buenos Aires, "the variegated identitarian uses music has for young people in Latin America usually escape the perception many people have of Latin American music they know."[50] This is true of all societies, including British society.

---

42. Bauman, *Identity*, 24.
43. Bauman, *Identity*, 29.
44. Bauman, *The Individualized Society*, 39.
45. Lawler, *Identity*, 25.
46. Lawler, *Identity*, 26.
47. Lawler, *Identity*, 19.
48. See Partridge, *Mortality and Music*.
49. Bauman, *Identity*, 15.
50. Vila, "Introduction," 1.

Music is far more significant in identity construction and in the articulation of values and concerns than is often realized—certainly by many theologians, clergy, and laypeople in the Church.[51] The broader point however is that, while no doubt always a complex issue, in past generations one simply 'knew one's place' with the security that such a rigid social structure brought.[52] This is not the case nowadays. Such a significant societal change will inevitably bring feelings of restlessness. Ole Riis and Linda Woodhead have suggested how this "leads to an increasingly subdued and self-conscious emotionality (with outbursts of spontaneity and intensity), a high valuation of the emotionally 'cool' and controlled (with a longing for greater authenticity and openness), and a strong attachment to, and quest for, people, institutions, and symbols to which it is possible to give wholehearted and trusting commitment, despite growing cynicism and distrust."[53] Hence, now, a key societal value is that of wanting authenticity. We can begin to see here *why* popular music becomes a key cultural text to consider. David Machin, for example, notes how "The discourse of authenticity is at the heart of the way that we think about music."[54]

In the final analysis, Bauman was downbeat in his understanding of creating a secure identity within liquid modernity. Culture "consists of offers, not prohibitions; propositions, not norms."[55] Or, as he describes it more sardonically, "progress, in short, has moved from a discourse of the shared improvement of life to a discourse of personal survival."[56] He argues that the ending of religious discourses, which historically provided the source of ontological security, has forced individuals to face the "task" of moving away from an insecure "*de jure*" identity which is not robust enough to deal with the complexities of late-modern life, to pursuing a secure "*de facto*" identity.[57] This is a narrative identity which is purposefully pursued and factually expressed through narrative, symbolism and lifestyle in order to feel at peace with the world. Identity becomes the pursuit of authenticity. It holds an ontological value. It concerns the expression of ultimate concern.

However, Bauman notes that individuals fail to attain the longed for security out of fear that the new identity will simply fail to provide it.[58]

---

51. See Keuss, *Your Neighbor's Hymnal*.
52. Bauman, *Identity*, 45.
53. Riis and Woodhead, *Sociology of Religious Emotion*, 176.
54. Machin, *Analyzing Popular Music*, 14.
55. Bauman, *Culture*, 13.
56. Bauman, *Culture*, 24.
57. Bauman, *Liquid Modernity*, 23.
58. Bauman, *Community*, 3.

In turn, the fear of commitment means that individuals experience further restlessness so forcing them to attempt to find a further *de facto* identity that could provide security.[59] The cycle begins again, restlessness is increased and so on. Yet, such feelings of restlessness must be resolved for individuals to feel at peace with themselves.[60] This is the restless conundrum that must be resolved. Bauman does assert that political help is required to actualize a secure transition, but, he concludes that the inability of individuals to commit to identity projects means that restlessness will remain.[61] His reasoning for this lack of commitment will be further explored below.

While there is much in Bauman's thinking that clearly describes how our society is functioning, the argument here is that it is still possible to find an identity that is ontologically secure enough to deal with all of life's situations. In being free of the communal hold of a religious discourse one is simply subject to a differing set of hegemonic forces. By their nature, such ideological forces remain hidden until society begins to notice and challenge them. Popular music, being typically transgressive,[62] not only challenges mainstream religious discourses, but, we will see, also does not shy away from resisting dominant secular ideas.

There is much to be learnt from Bauman's work and it is clear that the restless nature of a fluid society will express this in some way through its cultural artefacts. However, what Bauman does not significantly unpack is how liquid modernity deeply affects one's emotional sense of self. To understand the depth that our emotions affect our quest for ontological security, the book combines three perspectives, two of them explicitly countercultural (and as such challenging to contemporary hegemonic perspectives), namely those provided by Abraham Maslow, R. D. Laing and Anthony Giddens. The following discussion will additionally define two significant and related terms that are central to this: "ontological security" and "ontological reality."

2. Ontological Security and Emotions

We have noted that Western society exhibits an existential dis-ease and we will subsequently see how this is expressed in the symbols and narratives used in popular music culture, such as in the Norah Cyrus song 'Sadness' (2018). Such restlessness reflects a lack of individual ontological security, where one's sense of self, one's identity and one's 'place in the world' feel

---

59. Bauman, *Community*, 3.
60. E.g., Festinger, *Theory of Cognitive Dissonance*, 2; Laing, *The Divided Self*, 39.
61. Bauman, *Culture*, 69; Bauman, *Liquid Modernity*, 39.
62. See Partridge, *The Lyre of Orpheus*.

fluid, unfixed, insecure. As Cyrus sings, following on from three years of some form of therapy, while she is responsible for her own actions and attitudes she still needs to deal with the seeds of discomfort that she carries. What we have not noted is the emotional pressure such restlessness exerts. Understanding how important our emotions are in relation to our pursuit of ontological security will also help us to understand how valuable our emotional encounter with popular music can be.

Maslow and Laing

Maslow identified what he viewed as a universal set of human needs which he arranged in a hierarchy of pre-potency. The base level of an individual's physiological needs must be met before the next level can be achieved. Once attained, an individual can then deal with the needs of belongingness and love, the fulfilment of needs for self-esteem and the possibility for self-actualization.[63] Within his base-level need for physiological security he identifies the following: "The tendency to have some religion or world-philosophy that organizes the universe and the men in it into some sort of satisfactorily coherent, meaningful whole is also in part motivated by safety-seeking."[64]

Of particular note here is that Maslow's theory suggests a need for a coherent metanarrative that can help make sense of the breadth of life's experiences. Whether one views the present age as late modern, postmodern or liquid modern, the new found absence of such a metanarrative is significant. From Maslow's perspective, the formation of a secure understanding of how the universe is organized significantly contributes to subjective wellbeing.

Maslow's theory has been critiqued for not taking into account the socializing effects of differing cultures.[65] That said, there has also been a renewed interest in a universal understanding of human need which incorporates this. Ed Tay and Louis Diener observe that a "balance in life is desirable," whereby one will seek to attain subjective well-being in different and contrasting areas of one's life (i.e., work life, home life).[66] This is to describe the pursuit of ontological security as holding a multi-layered aspect and of the opportunity for it to feel unstable at different levels of our sense of self. Likewise, in exploring how differing psychoses develop Laing first noted the need for each of us to experience a "primary ontological security," which

---

63. Maslow, *A Theory of Human Motivation*, 6.
64. Maslow, *A Theory of Human Motivation*, 16.
65. I.e., Tay and Diener, "Needs and Subjective Well-Being," 354.
66. Tay and Diener, "Needs and Subjective Well-Being," 358.

may occur when an individual is able to "sense his presence in the world as a real, alive, whole, and in a temporal sense, a continuous person."[67]

Aware that ontology drew from a long philosophical tradition, Laing used the term "ontological security" as it "appears to be the best adverbial or adjectival derivative of being."[68] Laing is clear that such a psychopathology, with its pursuit of helping others to attain a secure sense of being, presupposes a 'psyche,'[69] which has sometimes been referred to as one's soul, or life-force.[70] The point is that Laing notes that primary ontological insecurity occurs when one feels there is a partial or almost complete absence of primary ontological security.[71]

In other words, the absence of security in our lives causes a need to resolve feelings of dissonance. Interestingly, this is the theme of the Fleet Foxes' song 'Helplessness Blues' (2011), where the singer recognizes he has no sense of knowing his place in the world with a hope that resolution may eventually occur. Ontological security emphasizes the ability of an individual to understand their place in the world. This is done within relationships with others. This is a point, as we will see, which is drawn on by Habermas in his discussion of "lifeworlds." Laing notes that insecurity may stem from a sense of feeling insubstantial, of not feeling "genuine, good, valuable."[72]

Again, this is where popular music is often life affirming having a positive influence on a person's sense of wellbeing and their construction of a positive identity.[73] A good example of this is Gloria Gaynor's "I Will Survive," often used by people to articulate meaning and reconstruct self-affirmation following the pain of a destructive relationship. Again, as Partridge argues, the message of *memento vivere* is nowhere better summed up than in Monty Python's "Always Look on the Bright Side of Life" (written by Eric Idle). Consequently, it has consistently been one of the most popular of funeral songs, often *the* most popular.[74] It allows individuals to make sense of life—even if from an atheistic perspective—in the face of Sisyphean meaninglessness.

The point is that feelings of cognitive dissonance require resolution and often popular music is used as a technology for that purpose.[75] Lawler notes

67. Laing, *The Divided Self*, 39.
68. Laing, *The Divided Self*, 39.
69. Laing, *The Divided Self*, 24.
70. See Tillich, *Systematic Theology*, 3:24.
71. Laing, *The Divided Self*, 42.
72. Laing, *The Divided Self*, 42.
73. E.g., Gabrielsson, *Strong Experiences*; DeNora, *Music Asylums*.
74. Partridge, *Mortality and Music*, 35.
75. E.g., Partridge, *The Lyre of Orpheus*, 196.

how one's sense of identity tends to be "explicitly invoked only when it is seen as 'being in trouble'"[76]—when there is a need to declare "I will survive." She raises the concern that feelings of dissonance can distort those parts of one's identity which remain secure when under stress (e.g., the identity of being a father may be secure, whereas at the same time one's identity as a husband may become strained). Certainly, when the meaning of one's existence feels ontologically insecure there is a need to take steps to repair or reconstruct one's sense of identity in order to restore meaning. In other words, it is not simply enough to *acknowledge* that one feels restless. One needs ultimately to find resolution in order to live life more securely and fully.

Ontological Insecurity

In seeking to understand feelings of dissonance, Leon Festinger noted how an individual's set of opinions and attitudes will normally hold a level of internal consistency.[77] Inconsistencies that have the potential to make an individual feel uncomfortable will generally become rationalized.[78] For example, while a smoker may recognize the health risks of smoking, the dissonance may be reduced by accepting that the enjoyment gained in smoking outweighs its risks. Festinger noted, though, that when that rationalization does not occur one may endure psychological discomfort which tends to motivate a person to reduce the dissonance in order to achieve consonance. In addition an individual will actively avoid both situations and any information that may increase feelings of dissonance.[79] However, when dissonance is not resolved it can affect one somatically as well as psychologically in one's subconscious dream life.[80]

To relate this to stories that seek to 'organize the universe,' when opinions and attitudes are questioned, such as when belief in an afterlife becomes implausible, the cogency of the wider story that supports that belief must be questioned and altered in an attempt to establish some level of internal coherence. Gradually, however, the story may become vulnerable to new knowledge, leading to increased restlessness. Eventually, a new story is required.

The overall point is that, an individual's pursuit of a secure identity in the modern world is rarely a superficial consumerist choice. Rather it

---

76. Lawler, *Identity*, 1.
77. Festinger, *Theory of Cognitive Dissonance*, 1.
78. See also Fishbien and Ajzen, *Belief*, 41.
79. Fishbien and Ajzen, *Belief*, 2; see also Csikszentmihalyi, *Flow*, 37.
80. Ward, *Unbelievable*, 95.

is a significant meaning-making project, which involves the whole self, including the psychic self and the integration of the social and the symbolic aspects of identity too.[81] The lifestyles and behavior of participants of the 'underground' rave scene, particularly prior to the formation of the Criminal Justice and Public Order Act (CJA) 1994, also reflect the depth of this meaning-making project. By expressing both their dis-ease with the political structures of the day and reimagining an alternative world-order through the dynamics and aesthetics of the dance floor,[82] early members were keen to acknowledge the 'whole of life' nature of the genre.[83] As Mark Angelo, co-founder of Spiral Tribe (who are making music as SP23) records on his blog:

> The outlawed Spiral Tribe Sound System: a collective of people who staged large, free and unlicensed, dance parties across Britain and Europe. That is until the British government accused myself and others of being the ringleaders of a new rebellion—a rebellion so dangerous in its appeal and popularity that it required a new law to criminalize it.[84]

Equally, such feelings of dissonance are also evident within hip-hop. This genre is particularly recognized as providing a political voice for, primarily, young disempowered black people in a manner that expresses both dissonance and a hope that may one day be resolved.[85] We will consider this genre in greater detail in chapter 4.

At its more extreme end Laing notes how when ontological insecurity is experienced, the individual will be preoccupied with "preserving rather than gratifying" themselves.[86] This point is developed by Jonathan Baylin and Dan Hughes, who, through their work with traumatized children, have likewise noted what they term as "self-provisioning."[87] This is the result of an infant not attaining a "secure base" with their principle care-provider.[88] They note, too, how children growing up in threatening environments focus particularly on threatening sounds, while more musical, higher pitched sound is ignored or suppressed. Of note, though, is how such musical

81. Woodward, "Identity and Difference," 12.
82. John, *Tecnomad*, 194.
83. E.g., Fritz, *Rave Culture*; Sylvan, *Trance Formation*.
84. Angelo, "Waywardtales."
85. Bailey, "Existentialist Transvaluation," 38; Railton and Watson, *Music*, 20; Peddie, "Music," 32; Miller et al., *Religion in Hip Hop*.
86. Laing, *The Divided Self*, 42.
87. Baylin and Hughes, *Neurobiology of Attachment-Focused Therapy*, 45.
88. Bowlby, *Secure Base*, 21.

trauma can be overturned "like learning a second language."[89] In referencing Nigel Osbourne's work on music and the brain,[90] they note his description of music as a hotline to the subcortical brain, and the brain's limbic and deep motor systems, which moves and mobilizes people without having to pass through higher, reflective brain regions first.[91]

Baylin and Hughes conclude that music is "definitely a powerful activator of the brain, usually in positive ways that enhance the sense of safety and engagement with life."[92] The point here is that there are clear links between the sound of music and safety making, that is, resolving feelings of dissonance; of music's ability to influence our decision-making, with, in some circumstances, some sounds bypassing lengthy discursive activity concerning safety. This is to suggest that we are influenced by the feel of the sound of safety. We will see in chapter 5 how music can help construct an asylum, a socially constructed space in which individuals may make use of music to make more sense of who they feel they are.[93]

Very deep feelings of insecurity can lead to feelings of "engulfment," the result of not feeling understood, loved or of being seen.[94] It may also leave one feeling empty. Shawn Mendes sings of the immensity of this in 'In My Blood' (2018), where he speaks of giving up, of therapeutic help not being successful and yet he knows he must carry on in life.

Yet, while one may recognize this, such feelings of emptiness can feel so paralyzing that one is left powerless to move on. To recall Bauman's thinking, this could explain why some individuals are simply unable to commit to an identity as the fear of moving on from feeling empty simply feels one with dread.[95] Restlessness develops into paralysis. Laing's work supports this view demonstrating that such a negative position can become a vicious circle. The more one seeks to maintain that sense of empty autonomy, by purposefully keeping an other's ontological status at distance, so one's own ontological security becomes further decreased.[96] When such positive attachments are unable to be achieved and utter detachment and isolation is felt, then an individual may, as Laing describes it, form "clam- or vampire-like" attachments in order to facilitate one's survival. In the extreme, one

---

89. Baylin and Hughes, *Neurobiology of Attachment-Focused Therapy*, 16.
90. Osbourne, "Music for Children," 331–56.
91. Baylin and Hughes, *Neurobiology of Attachment-Focused Therapy*, 246.
92. Baylin and Hughes, *Neurobiology of Attachment-Focused Therapy*, 246.
93. DeNora, *Music Asylums*, 47.
94. Laing, *The Divided Self*, 43.
95. Laing, *The Divided Self*, 45.
96. Laing, *The Divided Self*, 52.

can feel unembodied.[97] Again, music can both reflect and perpetuate this. For example, feelings of engulfment are also expressed within The Police's 'Canary in a Coal Mine' (1979), where Sting's experience of life is expressed through the image of the bird miner's carried in a cage while working, aware that the bird could very quickly succumb to poisonous gasses.

Likewise, the Goth subculture is a particularly good example, in that the music articulates a gradual turning in on oneself and the cultivation of morbidity.[98] Donna Gaines's ethnographic study of American youth cultures in the 1980s, found that, as part of an interest in transgressive music and discourses, many "dead-end kids" expressed a sense of helplessness and despair, which led to morbidity and, particularly, to a fascination with violence and self-harm.[99] For Laing, as no doubt for many of the youths in Gaines's study, becoming aware that one's dependency on another is a requirement for ontological security, is a necessary step forward. Again, as Partridge discusses, music sometimes helps in this process, sometimes it exacerbates the problem. Or, as Daniel Levitin notes, lyrics which some may view as challenging, even dangerous in character, can act as a point of comfort, bringing solidarity in face of a social challenge.[100]

Laing's work, alongside that of Maslow's, emphasizes the need for positive relationships with others, especially from our first care-givers, while it also emphasizes that without a secure narrative base to work from ontological insecurity will occur at many levels of the self. Insecurity is a situation that needs reparation. This must frame the question as to whether that secure base requires the secure attachment to a discourse that explains the reason for *being* in the world. I would answer in the affirmative. This is to consider the word ontology from a theological/philosophical point of view (see below).

Giddens and Reflexive Modernity

Giddens developed Laing's understanding of ontological security as an integral aspect of what he terms reflexive modernity. His work is of particular value as it helps to explain how those he views as late moderns may side-step particular narratives that may threaten our sense of self. He asserts that this

---

97. Laing, *The Divided Self*, 53.

98. See Partridge, *Mortality and Music*, 97–136; Hodkinson, *Goth*; Healey and Fraser, "A Common Darkness," 12.

99. Gaines, *Teenage Wasteland*.

100. Levitin, *The World in Six Songs*, 129.

refers to the confidence that most human beings have in the continuity of their self-identity and in the constancy of the surrounding social and material environments of action. A sense of the reliability of persons and things, so central to the notion of trust, is basic to feelings of ontological security; hence the two are psychologically related. Ontological security has to do with 'being' or, in the terms of phenomenology, 'being-in-the-world.' But it is an emotional, rather than a cognitive, phenomenon, and it is rooted in the unconscious.[101]

To summarize Giddens' theory, in a "post-traditional" society, where family ties have become eroded, we must now reflexively negotiate the narratives we encounter in order to make sense of the world around us, seeking an identity which reduces feelings of risk and threat.[102] As he describes, "the reflexive project of self involves an emotional reconstruction of the past in order to project a coherent narrative towards the future."[103] His work expresses both the growing fluid nature of society, reflecting Bauman's thinking, but he is also aware of the wide variety of narratives that we draw on in order to frame our sense of ontological security. In other words, he helps us to understand why we trust certain discourses and not others. Exploring the feeling of trust, Giddens notes that its opposite, "chaos," is "the loss of a sense of the very reality of things and of other persons," which engenders an individual's pursuit of security.[104] He notes how this sense of trust is formed in childhood.[105]

Our late-modern approach to listening to music reinforces Giddens' point of how we draw on many differing narratives in order to attain security. While an older song, Rush capture something of this in 'Digital Man' (1991) which expresses that reflexive behavior of drawing on what information you need to feel secure amidst ongoing societal change. Our approach to listening is now far more fluid than that of past generations, where music consumption was bound by issues of class[106] and of maintaining hegemony.[107] Now, however, we may well still favor particular musical genres, but we are much more open to cross cultural and musical divides, reflecting the Cultural Omnivore theory.[108] We will consider this further in the following chapter.

101. Giddens, *The Consequences of Modernity*, 92.
102. Giddens, *Modernity and Self-Identity*, 36.
103. Giddens, *The Transformation of Intimacy*, 102.
104. Giddens, *Modernity and Self-Identity*, 36.
105. Giddens, *Modernity and Self-Identity*, 37.
106. See Bourdieu, *Distinction*.
107. See Clarke et al., "Subcultures," 101.
108. See Peterson and Kern, "Changing Highbrow Taste," 904.

As reflexivity forms an integral part of how liquid moderns negotiate particular discourses we will turn to a slightly more nuanced definition of reflexivity. Barry Sandywell notes:

> For reflection in the modern rationalist or empiricist tradition a true theory ideally discovers and describes the natural world 'as it is'; reflexivity, on the other hand, deconstructs the (con)textual formations and aporetic modes of evidence constituting experience as a prior field of practices (for example, where 'language' and 'communicative experience' are unexplicated resources for reflection they are deconstructible topics for reflexivity).[109]

Or, as he describes it more succinctly, "reflexivity attempts to provide a reasoned account of the social practicalities by which 'reference' to worlds are textually constructed by powerful groups and interests."[110]

Such reflexive opportunity has been viewed by some as the preserve of late modernity,[111] as so many more choices are now available to us. Yet, others, such as Margaret Archer, assert that society has always been reflexive.[112] Archer, though, draws helpful attention to the importance of the individual's inner world where "reflexivity is defined as the regular exercise of the mental ability, shared by all normal people, to consider themselves in relation to their (social) contexts and vice versa."[113] It is driven by the internal conversation of the self: "self-talk,"[114] or to use Bauman's terminology, our interiority.[115] People become reflexively drawn to listen to those songs which help them to self-talk, reflectively side-stepping those songs which do not reflect their inner conversations.

While Maslow's hierarchy of needs draws attention to very practical aspects of wellbeing, for example shelter and food, it is the inner self that is in need of ontological security. The narratives, images, sounds we reflexively engage with, including the popular music we listen to, inform that 'self-talk' and in so doing, begins to influence the discourses that ultimately shape who we are. This can, as we will see, be fast-tracked in what Alf Gabrielsson terms "strong experiences with music"—SEM.[116] Discourse, here, is the

---

109. Sandywell, *Reflexivity*, 7.
110. Sandywell, *Reflexivity*, 8.
111. E.g., Beck, "The Reinvention of Politics," 3.
112. Archer, *Making Our Way*, 25.
113. Archer, *The Reflexive Imperative*, 2.
114. Archer, *Making Our Way*, 2.
115. Bauman and Raud, *Practices of Selfhood*, 36.
116. Gabrielsson, *Strong Experiences*, 2.

language used to express and to construct meaning and to interrogate the structures of the world, of inner thoughts, beliefs and feelings.[117]

Archer further observes that our reflexive activity has become focused around the discourses held by smaller groups of people. In other words, it is to these smaller networks of individuals who we particularly trust and turn to as a source of authority to judge which discourses we listen to. Archer evidences these more focused discursive conversations particularly in young people who express "meta-reflexivity," a focused form of self-inspection often centred on a critique of action within wider society, such as supporting social or political causes.[118] Such meta-reflexivity is typically inferred in popular music, especially in music that espouses political or ethical view-points.[119]

Emotions and Security

However, reflexive negotiation should not be viewed as simply a cognitive process. Our emotional response plays an equally significant part in our decision making, as Maria Carey notes in her 1991 song 'Emotions.'[120] The function and purpose of our emotions has long been a focus of study with two distinct fields dominating, namely those represented by Charles Darwin's functional approach[121] and William James's analysis of emotional states.[122] Debate continues as to whether our cognition leads to us feeling our emotions or, whether different stimuli create emotions which we then cognitively engage with.[123] James brought this into focus in his work with Carl Lange. Their formative James-Lange theory suggested that our emotions are caused by bodily sensations, such that we cry and then feel sad, rather than feeling sad and then crying. This is in contrast with the Cannon-Bard theory, whereby the quality of emotion is driven by the level of stimulation sent from the brain to parts of the body.[124]

Such debate continues. For example, Lisa Barrett comments that her work "suggests the counter-intuitive view that the variety in emotional life extends past the boundaries of events that are conventionally called

117. Fairclough, *Analyzing Discourse*, 124.
118. Archer, *The Reflexive Imperative*, 31.
119. See Martinelli, *Give Peace a Chant*.
120. Rolls, *Emotion and Decision-Making*.
121. Darwin, *The Expression of the Emotions*.
122. James, *The Principles of Psychology*.
123. See also Robinson, *Deeper than Reason*.
124. Colman, "James-Lange Theory."

'emotion' to other classes of psychological events that people call by different names, such as 'cognitions.'"[125] In contrast, John Elster, in his work on addiction, argues that our emotions inform our cognitive reasoning which is largely triggered by the beliefs and cultural values we hold.[126] This thesis is largely supported by Ole Riis and Linda Woodhead, in what they term as "psycho-physical sensations."[127] A further approach is that of *emotional cultures*, whereby, rather than biological responses, feelings could be spoken of simply as cultural and social responses.[128] One thing we are assured of is that our emotional responses inform our meaning-making, especially around religion and spirituality.[129]

While these differing approaches indicate some confusion about how to understand the significance of emotions, Edmund Rolls has provided some clarity. Certainly his own position helps us toward an understanding of (1) the value of our emotions in our decision making processes, (2) how feelings of confidence affect our decision making, and (3) the effect of symbolism in our decision making. These will, therefore, be considered with (4) Rolls' reductionist views on consciousness.

(1) In contrast to the more complex approaches noted above, Rolls' functional model provides an accessible way to understanding how our emotions affect our decision making and how that helps us to feel ontologically secure.[130]

He argues that we respond to our emotions and motivational states as rewards and punishers which ultimately shape our behaviors:[131] positive stimuli, which produce states of pleasure, positively reinforce a behavior, while the opposite stimulus acts as a punisher that we seek to avoid.[132] Wolfram Schultz affirms Roll's thinking in noting that: "The foremost function of the brain is to assure individual survival and gene propagation for ultimate evolutionary fitness. To this end individuals need to acquire specific substances for their bodily functions. The substances come in foods and liquids and require effort to obtain. They are called rewards and support

125. Barrett, "Variety Is the Spice of Life," 1284.
126. Elster, *Strong Feelings*, 2, 98–108.
127. Riis and Woodhead, *A Sociology of Religious Emotion*, 6.
128. Riis and Woodhead, *A Sociology of Religious Emotion*, 24.
129. I.e., Corrigan, "Introduction," 7.
130. See also Levitin, *The World in Six Songs*, 89.
131. Rolls, *Emotion and Decision-Making*, 45.
132. Rolls, *Emotion and Decision-Making*, 3.

learning, approach behavior, decision making and positive emotions like pleasure, desire and happiness."[133]

Levitin also notes that the brain is biased towards "security-motivation."[134] Significantly, Anne Blood and Robert Zatorre reinforce Rolls' model by looking in particular at music and emotional responses such as the 'chill' or 'shivers-down-the-spine.' Using tomography they were able to show that, as the intensity of heightened positive emotional experiences increase, so cerebral blood flow also increases to parts of the brain that communicate reward. These are areas in the brain known to be active during episodes of euphoria, alongside parts of the brain that are associated with determining survival. As they note, "This finding links music with biologically relevant, survival-related stimuli via their common recruitment of brain circuitry involved in pleasure and reward."[135]

Notably, the response to music that was felt to be unpleasant or dissonant was markedly different. Such music can stimulate those areas of the brain which would normally respond to feelings such as fear as well as euphoria is significant. Music is seen to induce feelings that, while not being in the same frame as those which drive our physical survival, show it to be beneficial to our physical and mental well-being,[136] so helping us to frame feelings of security. Significantly, the brain processes the sounds and narratives of music in the same manner that it processes all other information. While we will look at further aspects of how we emotionally respond to music in Chapter 5, this does emphasize again how valuable popular music can be in communicating feelings of security.

(2) Rolls additionally notes that we must feel confident as we appraise a decision-making situation.[137]

The greater our feeling of confidence, so the more reinforced our decision making becomes. This highlights that our decision making is significantly affected by our emotional responses, which is in contrast to the enlightenment rationale of limiting the value of our emotions, which were felt to be too subjective.[138]

---

133. Schultz, "Updating Dopamine Reward Signals," 229.
134. Levitin, *The World in Six Songs*, 200.
135. Blood and Zatorre, "Intensely Pleasurable Responses to Music," 11818.
136. Blood and Zatorre, "Intensely Pleasurable Responses to Music," 11823.
137. Rolls, *Emotion and Decision-Making*, 417.
138. E.g., Frei, *Eclipse of Biblical Narrative*, 141; Damasio, *The Feeling of What Happens*, 39.

We can see how such feelings of confidence do affect our decision making by again turning to the dance floor. Sally Sommer picks up on the need to feel confident when summing up the importance of the feel of the venue, the vibe of the place where people gather to play music and to dance, noting:

> Of all the formal qualities that constitute the essentials of House, nothing could be more ephemeral or more powerful than the vibe, the defining building-block of the Underground-House scene. The vibe is an active communal force, a feeling, a rhythm that is created by the mix of dancers, the balance of loud music, the effects of darkness and light, the energy. Everything interlocks to produce a powerful sense of liberation. The vibe is an active, exhilarating feeling of 'now-ness' that everything is coming together—that a good party is in the making. The vibe is constructive; it is a distinctive rhythm, the groove that carries the party psychically and physically.[139]

The dance-floor's soundscape, alongside its symbolic representation and discursive conversations, begins to act as a Promised Land. As the collective dance, they transcend themselves forming, if only fleetingly, a moment of corporate confidence where the world is as it should be. This is particularly relevant with those genres which seek to influence political opinion, such as aspects of EDM and Hip-hop. This confidence helps individuals to embody the alternative narrative, drawing it into their collective narrative. Such embodiment occurs as we process these external images and conversation and our private feelings, which we then draw into our longer term consciousness's.[140] This also highlights both the corporate and aesthetic quality of our decision making.

(3) Here, we also begin to see how such feelings of confidence and security are further affected by our reaction to the symbolic. Gabrielle Starr reinforces aspects of Rolls' thinking in noting the power of our reactions to symbolic imagery, such as those found on the dance-floor.

She, too, observes how our reactions tap into the brain's reward mechanisms, arguing that such imagery helps to both integrate and remake knowledge at both a conscious and unconscious level.[141] Riis and Woodhead, who fa-

---

139. Sommer, "C'mon to My House," 73.
140. Damasio, *The Feeling of What Happens*, 36.
141. Starr, *Feeling Beauty*, 92–99; see also Rolls, *Emotion and Decision-Making*, 39.

vor Damasio's more complex understanding of emotions, are also keen to emphasis the transformative value of symbols.[142] This, they note, becomes visible in considering the dialectic between self, society and symbol such that "Individuals carry 'in their hearts', and sometimes on their bodies, symbols that have uniquely personal emotional resonances: an icon, a talisman, a form of dress, a vial of holy water, a lock of hair, images of ancestors, photos, and so on. Such objects may assist personal emotional cultivation that reinforces collective emotion or offers an escape and an alternative, or both."[143]

While Roll's work reflects how our brain and bodies react as individuals, Riis and Woodhead and Jari Kiirla[144] also seek to understand how our emotions affect us collectively, drawing on aspects of Durkheim's thinking of 'collective effervescence.' In highlighting the term Emotional Energy (EE), they see a collective positive EE which becomes shaped and reinforced through collective ritual action.[145] Symbols, therefore, become items which can act as a magnifier of collective emotions, such that Riis and Woodhead note how "symbols mediate, express, and shape social relations, and can take them in new directions." Here, symbols "signify beyond their mere appearance or use by establishing relationships between the objects or events they bring together as complexes or concepts. These connections are not entirely arbitrary, contrary to some forms of post-structuralist semiotics, but are enshrined by established authority, tradition, ritual practice, local convention, and so on."[146]

As such symbolism may exert agency at an individual, group and societal level, or all three.[147] We can note here, too, Riis and Woodhead's definition of religious emotions as "those emotions that are integral to religious regimes and hence to their social and cultural relations."[148] The key point here is that the symbolic will also affect the intensity of our decision making. We should include in this what we may draw from the symbolic content included in popular music videos. We will see this in greater detail in chapter 4 when considering how our use of popular music helps is to function as individuals.

142. Riis and Woodhead, *Sociology of Religious Emotion*, 15, 26.
143. Riis and Woodhead, *Sociology of Religious Emotion*, 8.
144. Kiirla, "Emotional Energy," 117–29.
145. Riis and Woodhead, *Sociology of Religious Emotion*, 30; Kiirla, "Emotional Energy," 118.
146. Riis and Woodhead, *A Sociology of Religious Emotion*, 41.
147. Riis and Woodhead, *A Sociology of Religious Emotion*, 77.
148. Riis and Woodhead, *A Sociology of Religious Emotion*, 10.

(4) Rolls also highlights the distinctly human ability which he views as being a "part of the large problem of consciousness,"[149] that is the ability to reflect on one's experiences.

This he describes as the Higher-Order Syntactic Thought (HOST) theory of consciousness.[150] While many actions are performed relatively automatically, such as driving a car, Rolls points to particular regions of the brain which are able to process our reflective activity, such as our engagement with symbols, including language. It is our ability to self-reflect which enables us to engage with self-talk.

Rolls notes, too, how reinforcing stimuli can leave our cognitive and linguistic processing feeling overwhelmed. He notes that it is this ability to be strongly moved by drama or reading (or moved by music), which enables us to understand others and, even to predict their behaviors.[151] Yet, we will see in chapter 4 how such overwhelming musical experiences, SEM,[152] can profoundly affect one's outlook on life, with some interpreting such moments as encountering the divine.

Rolls' model also suggests that consciousness, which within the Christian tradition may be thought of as a significant aspect of the soul, spirit, *geist*—that which may carry on beyond death—can be reduced to electrical impulses in the brain. As he notes,

> Conscious feelings of self will be likely to be of value to the individual. Indeed, it would be maladaptive if feelings of self-identity, and continuation of the self, were not wanted by the individual, for that would lead to the brain's capacity for feelings about self-identity to leave the gene pool, due for example to suicide. This wish for feelings and thoughts about the self to continue may lead to the wish and hope that this will occur after death, and this may be important as a foundation for religions.[153]

He does accept that this process may be seen as reductionistic,[154] and that philosophers may wish to argue whether his theory is deterministic.[155] Damasio views such outcomes in a more prosaic manner: "Understanding consciousness says little or nothing about the origins of the universe, the

---

149. Rolls, *Emotion and Decision-Making*, 1, 486.
150. Rolls, *Emotion and Decision-Making*, 484.
151. Rolls, *Emotion and Decision-Making*, 540.
152. See Gabrielsson, *Strong Experiences*.
153. Rolls, *Emotion and Decision-Making*, 507.
154. Rolls, *Emotion and Decision-Making*, 488.
155. Rolls, *Emotion and Decision-Making*, 505.

meaning of life, or the likely destiny of both,"[156] with which I concur. Yet, it is through our emotional functioning as much as our cognitive understandings that we also begin to explore whether something is 'real' enough for it to offer us ontological security.

Ontological Reality

In its philosophical sense, the word 'ontology' concerns 'the study of being.'[157] From a theological point of view, of course, it concerns the "Supreme being" and, indeed, more philosophically, the ultimate nature of being. To use the existentialist language of Paul Tillich, we can think of the divine in terms of "ultimate reality, being itself, ground of being, power of being; and the other, that he is the highest being in which everything that we have does exist in the most perfect way."[158]

The need for individuals to express what they feel is ultimately real is woven throughout popular music. We can, again, return to feelings of authenticity.[159] Some genres may be characterised by their hedonistic outlook, where ultimate reality becomes expressed as living life 'in the moment.' This is a particular aspect of the EDM scene, which St John notes is a genre that is "a vehicle for variant projects of the self . . . the extremes of which evince hopeful and nihilistic dispositions."[160] Of course, not everyone will view the scene in such a manner. Mike Posner describes the paradoxes of the scene through his song 'I took a pill in Ibiza' (2015). He describes how he was listening to Avicii play a set in Ibiza when a fan recognized him, offering him a pill to take. The song describes how high he was as a result, yet also how much older he felt once the effects had worn off. The song explores the perception of the songwriter's life as fulfilled when Posner actually felt alone.[161]

Yet, within the subgenre of Goan-trance, many participants use the music as a prosthetic technology to explore who they are and their relationship to the cosmos—to ultimate reality.[162] In a more generalist fashion, Robyn Sylvan is keen to argue that all "beat-driven popular music and its attendant youth subcultures can be understood as religious phenomena,"[163]

---

156. Damasio, *The Feeling of What Happens*, 28.
157. Hjelm, *Social Constructionisms*, 91.
158. Tillich, *Theology of Culture*, 61.
159. I.e., Machin, *Analyzing Popular Music*, 14.
160. John, *Global Tribe*, 100.
161. See Posner's verified annotation in Posner, "I Took a Pill in Ibiza."
162. John, *Global Tribe*, 18, 101.
163. Sylvan, *Traces of the Spirit*, 5.

operating at "the intersection of the physical and spiritual worlds."[164] Popular music, again, becomes a medium to explore ontological themes.

Now, more than ever, the pursuit of ultimate reality has become entwined with our consumption of popular culture. To follow an aspect of Tillich's thinking, which will be explored in greater detail in chapter 4, this is not to suggest that popular culture is inherently or implicitly religious, rather, that popular culture helps to express our search for ultimate meaning.[165] We turn, now, to our definition of popular culture.

3. Popular Culture

Historically, there was far less opportunity to attain what Bauman terms a de facto identity,[166] with one's social position set in place within the social constraints of Christendom's ideology. This, however, did provide a corporate discourse supportive of ontological security. For example, restless feelings may have been perceived as the result of alienation from God's will: "because you have made us for yourself, . . . our hearts are restless, until they find rest in you."[167] Callum Brown has identified 1963 as the year which saw a clear break with Christendom's ideology. His deduction, drawn primarily by looking at the popular discourses recorded in the newspapers, is that its ideology ceased to hold power as "a means by which men and women, as individuals, construct their identities and their sense of 'self.'"[168] This is where Bauman's fate of identity becomes firmly rooted.

While Christendom was viewed by some as a "symphonia" (harmony) between church and state, acting as an earthly icon of God's kingdom,[169] it can, from a broadly Marxist perspective, also be viewed as an ideology, which, according to Louis Althusser's concept of 'interpellation' is embodied within the individual.[170] Therefore, it can be argued that Christendom's ideology coercively influenced both the individual's imagination and behavior. In this way the language of fulfilling God's will compelled individuals to respond. Christendom's discourse included that of a heavenly hope which provided many with ontological security. An ultimate power controlled

---

164. Sylvan, *Traces of the Spirit*, 12.
165. Tillich, *Systematic Theology*, 1:39. See also Sylvan, *Traces of the Spirit*.
166. Bauman, *Liquid Modernity*, 23.
167. Augustine, *Confessions*, 1.1.1.
168. Brown, *Death of Christian*, 1.
169. Koyzis, "Imagining God," 277.
170. Althusser, *Lenin and Philosophy*, 118.

those events which cause restlessness, such as those concerned with the maintenance of health, security and wellbeing.

Such ideological coercion would subsequently be attempted again in Matthew Arnold's notion of 'culture' as civilization—the hope of individuals bettering themselves through engaging with a morally improving 'culture.'[171] With his deeply held sense of Christian morality and a Victorian hope to see society develop for the better, Arnold viewed such cultural engagement akin to the Christian theological process of sanctification.[172] Here, engagement with the activities of the working classes was viewed as 'anarchy,' understood in terms of sinful chaos. This is to see the use of culture as a 'top-down' form of control. Culture, understood in this sense, should be imposed on society to improve it and make it 'good.' This reinforces the view that culture cannot be considered as neutral, rather, it holds agency. From Bauman's perspective, the concept of 'culture' was not utilized until the eighteenth century, there being nothing before "which even remotely resembled the complex world-view which the word 'culture' attempts to capture."

Now, within liquid modernity, the fluid nature of society has created the opportunity to express a 'bottom up' resistance to towards aspects of hegemony. The greater opportunity there is to 'buy into' the differing offers from the holistic milieu so there must also be the opportunity to critique them and aspects of the wider hegemony from which they come. As we will see below, especially through the work of Michel de Certeau, we may tactically express our feelings of restlessness. Within popular music such tactical resistance can be seen in the lyrical content of certain songs and the style of the genre.

Certeau draws attention to this noting that while very few have the ability to create art that purposefully speaks into a cultural situation, the majority "make do (*bricolent*)" with "everyday art,"[173] redistributing and claiming aspects of the arts' power, its symbolism, for their own purposes. In contrasting the "strategies" used by those who retain power, to those who must use "tactics" to evade those in power,[174] Certeau speaks of the "art of practice,"[175] with the power of art becoming a tactical way of evading those in power: the "art of the weak."[176] As he notes, "Art is thus a kind of knowledge that operates outside the enlightened discourse which it lacks."

171. Arnold, *Culture and Anarchy*.
172. Partridge, "Religion and Popular Culture," 562.
173. Certeau, *Practice of Everyday Life*, 66.
174. Certeau, *Practice of Everyday Life*, 37.
175. Certeau, *Practice of Everyday Life*, 43.
176. Certeau, *Practice of Everyday Life*, 37.

He speaks, too, of individuals having to "make do" with the symbols they come across, "poaching" from differing cultural traditions to expresses their hopes and fears.[177]

Certeau's language of "make do" is certainly softer than that of Bauman's need "to saw up" and to "make fit" aspects of one's identity in order to feel secure.[178] However, it is through this re-appropriation of symbols found in everyday practice, the "reading as poaching," taking aspects of differing texts and reforming them into a fresh text through which individuals begin to express their tactical opposition to those holding power.[179]

Musically, the advent of rock 'n' roll can be viewed as a moment of artistic creation which following generations have subsequently 'poached' in differing ways.[180] Likewise, Dick Hebdige has highlighted the contribution of punk as a musically defining moment on which others have subsequently drawn, speaking of the genre as "a series of spectacular negations of consensually defined musical, sartorial and sexual norms."[181] Simon Frith simply observes how "music is a metaphor for identity," asserting the influence of aesthetics as an experience which we both feel and react with.[182]

This is also a feature of Michel Maffesoli's theory of neo-tribalism, where groups of likeminded individuals draw together to express hopes and fears through appearance and form.[183] Again, this is to emphasize the value of aesthetics as an important component for attaining ontological security. This is precisely why popular music, with its many genres, styles and aesthetics is such a fertile ground for self-expression and for wanting to understand ultimate reality.

Like Certeau, Paul Willis views us as now holding a "common culture" through which we create a "grounded aesthetic." While Willis sees a difference between his grounded aesthetic and the symbolic creativity of established 'high' art, which, being partially funded through Government grants mediates a politicized message, he notes that we are now all "cultural producers."[184] Again, to reflect this particularly onto popular music, Peter Martin notes how the fragmentation of musical style can be linked,

---

177. Certeau, *Practice of Everyday Life*, 66.
178. Bauman, *The Individualized Society*, 142.
179. Certeau, *Practice of Everyday Life*, 165. See also Jenkins, *Textual Poachers*.
180. Middleton, *Studying Popular Music*, 13.
181. Hebdige, *Into the Light*, 212.
182. Frith, "Music and Identity," 109.
183. Maffesoli, "The Return to Dionysus," 32.
184. Willis, *Common Culture*, 145.

specifically, and the "active process of identity construction that is increasingly typical of late-modern, mass consumption societies."[185]

This is not to suggest that individuals are entirely free to draw their identity of choice from popular culture. Agency is countered by hegemony. Hence Certeau sees the need for tactics to outwit the strategy of hegemonic forces. In following Antonio Gramsci' view of the relationship between culture and the economy, the economy may hold the upper, deterministic hand, yet the production of cultural artefacts retains a relative autonomy.[186] This enables Richard Middleton to conclude that cultural relationships and cultural change are not predetermined, but become the result of negotiation, resistance, imposition and creativity. In speaking in particular about popular music he notes how it tries "to put a finger on that space, that terrain, of contradiction—between 'imposed' and 'authentic', 'elite' and 'common', predominant and subordinate, then and now, and ours, and so on—and to organize it in particular ways."[187]

A contrary viewpoint to Certeau (and Middleton) would be that held by Adorno who commented on popular culture, viewing it as a form of mass manipulation that promoted conformism over individual development.[188] As a Jewish individual fleeing the totalitarian regime of Nazi Germany and resettling in America, Adorno subsequently commented that he found what he termed "the culture industry" as providing no greater expressive freedom than in the country he had left.

His thinking, and that of the Frankfurt School, has held a strong influence over many views held concerning popular culture and popular music.[189] Adorno is right to draw attention to how ideological views do interpolate us, yet his particular context, together of living in an age where Fordist views on construction were so prevalent, need to be born in mind when critiquing his viewpoint. Simply, as Rupa Huq notes, people do not uncritically accept what the culture industries may place before them, neither may these industries simply construct a market or produce a consumer.[190]

Rather, to follow Nicholas Abercrombie and Brian Longhurst, we are not passive receivers of culture, but active constructionists.[191] The point here is that while Adorno's views held much capital in his day, and while issues of

185. Martin, "Music," 65.
186. E.g., Day, *Gramsci Is Dead*.
187. Middleton, *Studying Popular Music*, 7.
188. Adorno, *The Culture Industry*, 53.
189. I.e., Huq, *Beyond Subculture*, 46; Stone, *Value of Popular Music*, 78.
190. Huq, *Beyond Subculture*, 163.
191. Abercrombie and Longhurst, *Audiences*, 29.

ideology must still be borne in mind, society has evolved significantly to the extent that popular culture and popular music is now used to express resistance against the dominant hegemony. The argument is that there has been a democratization within society's use of culture that is organically evolving. As Martin notes, "rather than inducing passive conformity, popular music in particular may be effective in facilitating the active assertion of self in the increasingly unstable social circumstances of late (or post-) modernity."[192]

A final point should be made before drawing this chapter to a conclusion. In highlighting how and why we construct meaning and identity from the symbols we find in popular culture, we have begun to note the difference between epistemological and ontological approaches to understanding the world around us.[193] We have also begun to note that our emotional connection with music emphasizes our need for ontological expression, to help us make sense of who we feel we authentically are as a holistic person. This is a significant aspect why our appreciation of popular music should inform our telling of the Christian story today. Habermas' concept of *lifeworld* will help us see more clearly the difference between these two understandings and how the enlightenment turn towards episteme has restricted the promulgation of the Christian story. This will also help to emphasize how valuable music is in giving expression to those things which we feel are of ultimate value to us and, therefore, fresh insight into how the Christian story may be, to use Certeau's terms, tactically told against the strategy of our epistemologically driven hegemony.[194]

Habermas and Lifeworld

If the Enlightenment can be characterised by its pursuit of concrete, rational knowledge, then Habermas concluded that rationality was really to be found in the language games played between two or more actors, where "rationality has less to do with the possession of knowledge than with how speaking and acting subjects acquire and use knowledge."[195] From such a starting point Habermas constructed his theory of communicative action. It is within the framework of explicitly expressed knowledge that a lifeworld (*Lebensvelt*) is formed.[196] Rationality needs to be understood in terms of

---

192. Martin, "Music," 56.
193. E.g., Taylor, *Sources of the Self*, 10.
194. Certeau, *Practice of Everyday Life*, 37.
195. Habermas, *Theory of Communicative Action*, 8.
196. Habermas, *Theory of Communicative Action*, 70.

locutionary acts.[197] Actors will use constative speech acts and argumentation to construct their lifeworlds.[198] In other words, the language games we utilize shape differing levels of the way the Self engages with society.

Habermas notes "the concept of the lifeworld is based on the distinction between performative consciousness and fallible knowledge," whereby his understanding of lifeworld emphasizes that phenomenology is moving away from individual experience to that of communicative action between at least two people.[199] This emphasizes that individuals, in relationship with others, are seeking to make sense of who they are. The fluid nature of society has resulted in a proliferation of opportunities where our locutionary acts will shape and form our sense of identity.

While Habermas argues that cultural values hold no universal value, as norms of action may do, he sees that artistic, musical and literary endeavor should be viewed "as an authentic expression of an exemplary experience, in general as the embodiment of a claim to authenticity."[200] In other words, the cultural objects and texts we 'make do with' both authenticate our lifeworlds and also enable us to challenge them. This places a high value on the cultural objects we engage with. It also highlights an area of ambiguity in Habermas' thinking: if a cultural object is a claim to authenticity, then we are moving towards expressing ourselves ontologically over his preference for episteme.

Yet, to follow Habermas, unless such a cultural object can be epistemologically shown to be true, it must be spoken of only as a *claim* to authenticity. Habermas holds a desire to locate ontological authenticity, yet his reluctance to speak of that in language other than in epistemological claims, runs throughout his thinking. We see that in his reflections on religion and in his key terms of postsecular, postmetaphysical, the lingistification of religion and the public sphere. Habermas' work is influential, especially within secular circles, and his work emphasizes many of the ideological forces at work preventing the Christian discourse from being listened to clearly today.

A key influence on Habermas' religious thinking is what Karl Jaspers refers to as the "axil period."[201] In short, Jaspers deduces that a cognitive development in human development occurred around 500 BC, as evidenced by the rise of religion along similar, although distinct lines in the ancient-near-east. While seeking to be rational Jaspers concludes that "if not empirically cogent and evident" his observations are "so convincing to empirical

---

197. Habermas, *Theory of Communicative Action*, 16.
198. Habermas, *Theory of Communicative Action*, 18.
199. Habermas, *Postmetaphysical Thinking*, 6.
200. Habermas, *Theory of Communicative Action*, 20.
201. Jaspers, *The Origin and Goal*, 1.

insight as to give rise to a common frame of historical self-comprehension for all peoples-for the West, for Asia, and for all men on earth, without regard to particular articles of faith."[202] Jaspers argues that humanity became conscious of Being, seeing both the beauty of the world and, to use his language, feelings of terror and powerlessness against the size of the world.[203] It is this, what he sees as a new rationality, that sets this age apart for time before, where myth became "the material of language"[204] and new forms of religious and ethical understanding were shaped through "spiritualization."[205] Simply, something biological and cognitive occurred to humanity.[206]

Jaspers makes the specific point that he is not arguing that there had been a "direct intervention on the part of the deity" for this action to occur,[207] rather, that sociological factors simply took hold.[208] He argues that "Man cannot endure the fundamental attitude of nihilism," rather, instead humanity "succumbs rather to a blind faith. Such a faith is an immense substitute, is fragile, and suddenly discarded again; it may embrace the most singular contents; it may be, as it were, an empty faith of mere motion. It interprets itself as a feeling of oneness with nature, with world history. It takes concrete shape in programs of salvation."[209]

Yet, however rational Jaspers seeks to be, it could be that society *did* become religiously aware of the divine albeit through sociological developments and has sought to repress such feelings, as to accept that God could exist would be simply too terrifying to consider. That is a key ontological question. Jaspers further concluded that, alongside the positive nature of scientific and technological developments,

> a dialectic of spiritual evolution, impelled by Christian motives, led from Christianity to such a radical illumination of truth that this religion brought about the reversal against itself, out of its own forces. But again this road need not have led to loss of faith. To be sure, dogmatic positions were lost in this transition process of painful and perilous melting down and recasting, but the transformation of Biblical religion remained a possibility.[210]

---

202. Jaspers, *The Origin and Goal*, 1.
203. See also, for example, Bellah and Joas, "Introduction," 1.
204. Jaspers, *The Origin and Goal*, 3.
205. Jaspers, *The Origin and Goal*, 5.
206. Jaspers, *The Origin and Goal*, 14.
207. Jaspers, *The Origin and Goal*, 18.
208. Jaspers, *The Origin and Goal*, 17.
209. Jaspers, *The Origin and Goal*, 132.
210. Jaspers, *The Origin and Goal*, 136.

In contrast, Jaspers mentor, Weber, took a differing point of view. His notion of *occidential rationalis* saw the protestant work ethic driving Western capitalism, leading to the disenchantment of society.[211] Both Weber's and Jaspers' work has been instrumental in framing the arguments for secularization and have a strong ideological influence on late Western religious thinking. However, despite Weber's predictions, and Jasper's assertion of a sudden cognitive development framing the religious imagination, religious discourses are still robust, which Habermas seeks to explain through his term postsecular.[212]

Related to this is the development of what Habermas has termed postmetaphysical. This point is important in our understanding of how a lifeworld functions within liquid modernity. Moving from a philosophical to a sociological understanding, to, now, exploring how religious viewpoints may engage with politics within the public sphere,[213] Habermas is keen to dampen the effects of metaphysical thinking to that which only can be proven epistemologically. Yet, his ambiguity remains. While philosophy, as a "secular intellectual formation . . . turned its back on religion while simultaneously renouncing strong metaphysical claims to knowledge," he is still interested in how "reflection on this repressed background changes the self-understanding of postmetaphysical thinking."[214]

For Habermas, truth claims can be expressed as true or false, while intuitive knowledge about ontological issues, such as belief in God, may only be made explicit when expressed as a description.[215] In other words, the lifeworld should be viewed as our concrete experience in the world.[216] Beyond the lifeworld lies what Habermas sees as the *worldview* within which resides the sedimented narratives that reflect traditional and metaphysical thinking, such as belief in God.[217] While subjective in nature and, therefore, unable to be spoken of as being part of the *lifeworld*, this still permeates our societal discourses.

Thus, we see Habermas wanting to draw together the differences between Weber and Jasper. He acknowledges Jasper's view that religion can play a function in society today in facilitating social cohesion. However, he is agnostic towards religious faith claims as they cannot be expressed

---

211. Weber, *The Protestant Ethic*; Cotesta, "Axial Age and Modernity."
212. Habermas, "Secularism's Crisis of Faith"; Habermas, *Postmetaphysical Thinking*.
213. Mendieta, "Spiritual Politics," 321.
214. Habermas, *Postmetaphysical Thinking*, 5.
215. Habermas, *Postmetaphysical Thinking*, 3–7.
216. Habermas, *Postmetaphysical Thinking*, 3.
217. Habermas, *Postmetaphysical Thinking*, 33.

propositionally as true or false. Yet, as Terry Eagleton comments on Habermas' stance, "There is something unpleasantly disingenuous about this entire legacy, 'I don't happen to believe myself, but it is politically expedient that you should' is the catchphrase of thinkers supposedly devoted to the integrity of the intellect."[218]

Habermas would argue that he is not being disingenuous. Rather, he is simply observing that western religion is undergoing metamorphosis through what he terms a post-conventional orientation. From his point of view, religious ritual and reflection on sacred texts, now devoid of any transcendent engagement with the divine, may provide a resource for societal strengthening, giving both "orientation" and "confidence-building" within the lifeworld—this is his lingistification of religion.[219] Habermas' hope is that, while religions may make exclusive faith and power claims, such views should be articulated in the public sphere in a manner that does not preference them over any other discourse. This is a subtle, yet effective ideology that limits the promulgation of the Christian discourse.

However, within his use of the term public sphere and Nancy Fraser's critique,[220] we also see how this may be challenged. By public sphere, Öffentlichkeit, Habermas is referring to private individuals wishing to express public concerns, ideas of common interest. Drawing on the notion of the eighteenth century coffee houses where the social climbers of the day could share and influence public opinion, Habermas notes that the West still functions with such rationale, enabling hegemonic forces begin to find their equilibrium, though the coffee houses can now include events such as "theatre performances, rock concerts, party assemblies, or church congresses up to the abstract public sphere of isolated readers, listeners, and viewers scattered across large geographic areas, or even around the globe, and brought together only through the mass media."[221]

In critiquing his work, Fraser has noted how Habermas "idealizes the liberal public sphere but also that he fails to examine other, non-liberal, non-bourgeois, competing public spheres."[222] Rather, she notes that society holds differing strata, each which may seek to express their viewpoint, acting as "subaltern counterpublics."[223] These "multiple publics" reflect the fluid nature of liquid modernity, with many competing voices at work straining

218. Eagleton, *Culture*, 207.
219. Habermas, *Postmetaphysical Thinking*, 29.
220. Fraser, *Rethinking the Public Sphere*.
221. Habermas, *Between Facts and Norms*, 284.
222. Fraser, *Rethinking the Public Sphere*, 5.
223. Fraser, *Rethinking the Public Sphere*, 12.

to be heard.[224] Within popular music we can see that there are many genres which can be viewed in a similar fashion.

The development of multiple publics not only reflects the fluid nature of liquid modernity, it is a significant development away from our recent sociological past where youth resistance to hegemony was expected and expressed in musical genres such as the Mods and Rockers of the late 1950s and 1960s. This reflects the subcultural analysis developed at Birmingham University's Centre for Contemporary Cultural Studies (BCCC), which noted that within modernity limited resistance to the dominant culture was allowed. The expectation was that as subcultural members subsequently matured they would integrate themselves into the dominant economic culture.[225]

However, for some, such assimilation has not occurred and these individuals have actively held onto the resistance expressed in their youth, heralding the development of a post-subcultural theory.[226] For some, this resistance is expressed neo-tribally,[227] seen, for example, in movements such as 'Reclaim the Streets.' Here, the practice of articulation can be seen with the multiple publics seeking to reclaim space from what it sees as capitalist encroachment. Its modus operandi is to set up a 'temporary autonomous zone' (TAZ) that celebrates creativity and social autonomy alongside the abolishment of what Curren views as "hollow materialism." It seeks to accomplish this through music and dance, so creating political theatre in order to demonstrate that "another world is possible."[228]

That older people still hold on to the musical attributes of their youth can be interpreted as both a continuation of similar taste patterns into older age as well as a desire not to grow up.[229] Yet, it can also be that feelings of security are drawn from the community that forms around the genre. For some this will reflect a desire to be part of a community that resides outside of hegemony (e.g., the early participants of the underground rave scene; older participants of the heavy metal scene), while for others these post-subcultures operate as a multiple public that will express a particular point of view, such as hip-hop, or in movements such as 'Reclaim the Streets,' mentioned above. The point here, is that such fragmentation is concerned with groups of individuals constructing their own *lifeworld* to make their understanding of the world as ontologically secure as possible.

224. Fraser, *Rethinking the Public Sphere*, 6.
225. Thornton, "Social Logic of Subcultural Capital," 210.
226. See Bennett and Kahn-Harris, *After Subculture*; Huq, *Beyond Subculture*.
227. Maffesoli, "The Return to Dionysus," 27.
228. Curren, *21st Century Dissent*, 181.
229. Bennett and Hodkinson, *Aging and Youth Cultures*, 3.

What is also of interest here is how the strong aesthetic held by these genres helps to reinforce the group's message, helping it to be transmitted across generations. The Christian discourse should be considered as a multiple public alongside the differing discourses of meaning making that are now on offer and the Church should, therefore, tactically remonstrate with hegemony. To draw on the 'Reclaim The Streets' movement, there is a clear aesthetical approach which seeks to publicly challenge views through music and dance, elements of which local church congregations could draw on. As Philip Tagg notes, "music is capable of transmitting the affective identities, attitudes and behavioral patterns of socially definable groups."[230] Equally, that musical cultures and certain multiple publics hold strong aesthetics should encourage church communities to consider their own particular aesthetical content as they seek to help socialize people into belief.

Habermas' understanding of lifeworld provides a helpful model that helps us to understand how the sociological forces that shape liquid modernity are biased towards epistemological understandings of the world around us. This does place the Christian discourse, which seeks to explain aspects that may lie beyond the horizon of the lifeworld, at a disadvantage. It is these ontological aspects of Christian belief which frame the discourse which offers ontological security, that is, to ultimately be at peace with God. We have also seen that subaltern counter publics have a voice that can be shared, which, to follow Certeau, can act as a bottom-up tactical challenge to the wider hegemony of liberal pluralism. Yet, what should be particularly noted is the value of the aesthetical content mediated by these multiple publics in reinforcing their message.

4. Summary

Our starting point has been to note that feelings of restlessness and existential dis-ease are being expressed within popular culture. We are focusing specifically on how this is being expressed within popular music lyrically, sonically and visually through associated videos. Bauman has noted this existential angst, concluding that within liquid modernity such feelings will remain.[231] As he notes, the ending of religious discourse as the key way the West found existential stability has been bitter-sweet. More social freedom may have resulted, yet restlessness abounds. His later thinking did begin to question whether talk focused around God could be helpful, yet he

---

230. Tagg, *Analyzing Popular Music*, 4.
231. Bauman, *Culture*, 24; Bauman, *Community*, 3.

remained concerned that institutional abuses of power, a key aspect that freedom from religious discourses brought, would remain.[232]

Bauman's liquid modernity clearly expresses the fluid nature of society and represents our sociological zeitgeist with the restlessness which results. Habermas' *Lifeworld* adds depth to aspects of Bauman's reflection. Here, we see why Bauman is unable to square his circle of seeing value in aspects of religious belief while aware that society deeply cherishes its social freedoms. For Habermas, this is the difference between concrete *Lifeworld* experiences which are spoken of in terms of epistemological truth and understandings of the wider Worldview which should only be spoken of in terms of hopes and possibilities. Such possibilities cannot be considered as epistemological truth and, therefore, be expressed only as ontological hopes.

Habermas' views help explain, too, that while belief in God has always been a question of faith seeking understanding, the hegemonic need for epistemology and liberal pluralism has placed the Church's discourses in a challenging position to be listened to. By using Bauman's thinking as its starting point (e.g., the fluid nature of society) the Church should be tactically challenging the reasons why restlessness abounds. Not from the starting point of Augustine's "our hearts are restless, until they find rest in you,"[233] rather, by drawing out how these social forces do prevent us from looking for answers to cognitive dissonance beyond our *lifeworld*, meaning restlessness will remain.

Whereas Bauman captures the negative effects of restlessness, Maslow, Laing and Giddens explore the longer term damage which results: that of sociological and physiological dis-ease. I would add theological dis-ease results, too. If restlessness is to subside then adequate answers to these tensions must be provided. Alongside this, Rolls' work on emotion and decision making demonstrates that we are hard-wired to find answers which can help us to *feel* safe. This helps explain why, according to Bauman, we look for identities which may fulfil our existential needs but cannot commit to them[234] either because we feel paralyzed by our feelings of angst[235] or that the offer simply does not *feel* robust enough to offer security.

That existential tensions are being expressed within popular culture further shows that this is a significant issue which requires resolution. Within popular music examples show that such restlessness is expressed symbolically through the sonic nature of the song, its lyrical content alongside

---

232. Bauman and Obirek, *Of God and Man*, 2.
233. Augustine, *Confessions*, 1.1.1.
234. Bauman, *Community*, 3.
235. E.g., Laing, *The Divided Self*, 45.

any visuals seen in accompanying music videos and the discursive conversation that occurs between fans and song writers. We will explore this in the next chapter. Within our consumption of popular music we also see the dynamics of Bauman's liquid modernity at work as individuals seek to "saw up and make fit"[236] from the differing discourses they encounter to create an identity that may bring some relief from restlessness.

We are ultimately asking the question as how best to tell the Christian story within such a fluid society. We will see in chapter 3 that a lot of evangelistic effort is directed towards providing epistemological understandings of Christian belief, albeit that popular music culture would suggest an ontological approach would be more fruitful in helping individuals to respond to the Christian story today. The argument here is that our emotional response to the music we listen to, its sonic qualities alongside the symbolism it may contain, helps us to work out what we feel can offer us ontological security. We will expand this argument over the coming chapters to consider how this should influence our telling of the Christian story today. We will be considering how within liquid modernity the songs we engage with help us to function as individuals living in relationship with others (chapter 4) and how the emotional quotient of a song may cause us to react (chapter 5). Now, to further ground the argument that we use popular music to express our dis-ease with hegemony we will consider eight key themes which represent specific points of restlessness and our need for ontological understandings of the world around us.

---

236. Bauman, *The Individualized Society*, 142.

2

Restless Society Expressed within Popular Music

WESTERN SOCIETY HAS BEEN described above as liquid modern where, beyond Christendom's hegemony, individuals must deal with the fate of identity by "making do" with the narratives and symbols one encounters in order to make one's self feel as ontologically secure as possible. Of course, that said, if one follows Zygmunt Bauman's outcomes it is improbable that such security is attainable. To look at further musical articulation of this restlessness we will examine eight key themes that are often captured in song: (1) restlessness; (2) fear and risk; (3) the need to belong; also (4) the fear of belonging; (5) a need to search for differing symbols to feel secure; (6) a frustrated pursuit of cosmopolitanism; (7) seeking happiness, also expressing narcissism, and (8) exploring further what may lie beyond the horizon of our personal lifeworlds.

As tactical expressions of resistance to hegemony these are as much emotional as cognitive expressions that listeners will connect with at both a conscious and unconscious level.[1] To draw on Edmund Rolls' work, there are moments when our engagement with popular music causes us to react to the emotional quotient of the song as we feel rewarded by what we listen to. Such a reward helps us to express our restlessness and even cause us to feel safe, 'at one' with the world around us, even if that is in a mutual sharing of restlessness with likeminded people. Such reactions, of course, will not be

---

1. E.g., Giddens, *The Consequences of Modernity*, 92.

found in every song. Yet, the point is that popular culture *is* used to express such feelings. The examples provided are made to highlight the sociological points made thus far.

To follow Philip Tagg's rationale, we ought to note that our *analysis objects* are affected by the researcher's "mentality."[2] This is to consider what popular music may say about liquid-moderns positively viewing the Christian discourse. We will also draw on what David Machin terms as discourse schema in order to highlight the social values that underlie the song. Such schema is used to discern and maintain hegemony, yet, it can also be used to identify discourses which seek to resist it.[3]

Some comment is also needed to frame our understanding of music video. While having a relatively short history, early academic work focused largely on music video as a postmodern text.[4] Much of the analysis was focused on the rise of MTV in the 1980s,[5] the technological aspect of video making[6] and the de-centered nature of the narratology of the video.[7] It was argued that it constituted a challenge to our understanding of the relationship between linear time and storytelling.[8] Ann Kaplan noted how this "increasingly reflects young people's condition in the advanced stage of highly developed, technological capitalism evident in America."[9] Andrew Goodwin's view on the early use of video was more nuanced, focusing more on the communicative aspect that it generates: "It is important to establish from the outset that pop music is, and always has been, a multi-discursive cultural form, in which no one media site is privileged. The implication of this for music video analysis is that it becomes impossible to understand the meaning of any individual clip without considering its relation to the wider world of pop culture."[10]

However, with the demise of MTV's original format of playing videos 'wall to wall,' so music videos fell out of favor with music producers. Yet, the rise of YouTube brought fresh energy to the format with what Carol Vernallis terms its "intensified audiovisual aesthetics."[11] She notes the influence of You-

---

2. Tagg, *Analyzing Popular Music*, 7.
3. Machin, *Analyzing Popular Music*, 78–83.
4. E.g., Hebdige, *Into the Light*; Kaplan, *Rocking around the Clock*.
5. Kaplan, *Rocking around the Clock*, 1.
6. Goodwin, *Dancing in the Distraction Factory*, 20.
7. Björnberg, "Structural Relationships of Music," 351.
8. E.g., Chion, *Audio-Vision*, 167.
9. Kaplan, *Rocking around the Clock*, 5.
10. Goodwin, *Dancing in the Distraction Factory*, 25.
11. Vernallis, *Unruly Media*, 9.

Tube on music video: "We can begin to understand today's music video if we consider some of the aesthetic features that define YouTube: (1) pulse, reiteration, and other forms of musicality; (2) irreality and weightlessness (tied to low resolution and the digital); (3) scale and graphic values; (4) unusual causal relations; (5) variability and intertextuality; (6) humor and parody; (7) volubility and condensation; and (8); formal replication of the web."[12]

This developed into a significant relationship between music video and film. Some have linked the intensity of music video, with short clips, quick edits and preference for spectacle with the development of a post-classic/post-Hollywood film style.[13] Vernallis, for example, describes *The Bourne Identity* as such a film which holds its viewer through spectacle over narrative.[14] Barry Langford notes: "By de-emphasizing characterization and narrative in favor of overwhelming spectacle, such films seemingly reversed the evolutionary trend which by the end of cinema's first decade had established narrative as the senior partner in the narrative-spectacle relationship."[15]

Yet, while the characteristics of music video and post-classical film may emphasis spectacle—what Longford terms as the "hyperstimulated"[16]—others have argued that such traits represent us firmly moving into the postmodern condition.[17] For example, Catherine Constable draws this from the negative aspects of violence seen in films by directors such as Oliver Stone and Quentin Tarantino.[18] However, such traits can also be understood as reflecting aspects of Bauman's liquid modernity over the nihilism of postmodern thinking.

Music videos are ostensibly there to promote a song. Vernallis makes the point that the video should not directly tell the story of the song, otherwise it is viewed more like film music. Therefore, music videos are rarely teleological in nature. Indeed, because of the song's structure, the video can be seen as more cyclical and episodic rather than holding a linear progression.[19]

Is it plausible, though, to argue that music video can influence one's decision making and behavior? In developing his term 'filmosophy', Daniel Frampton argues that "the filmgoer can decode to use it as part of their

---

12. Vernallis, *Unruly Media*, 182.
13. Langford, *Film Industry*, 255.
14. Vernallis, *Unruly Media*, 6.
15. Langford, *Film Industry*, 247.
16. Langford, *Film Industry*, 255.
17. E.g., Constable, *Postmodernism and Film*, 2; Toubiana, "The Brain Is the Screen."
18. Constable, *Postmodernism and Film*, 39.
19. Vernallis, *Experiencing Music Video*, 3.

conceptual apparatus while experiencing a film—they would then see the film through this concept. Filmosophy conceptualizes film as an organic intelligence: a 'film being' thinking about the characters and subjects in the film."[20]

We will see further in chapters 4 and 5 how music can move someone, exerting agency over them. Yet, to draw on Frampton's observations, a video can provide opportunity to help explore unknown concepts as the viewer steps inside the imagery of the video, reflexively negotiating its content as it progresses. "The filmgoer experiences film more intuitively, not via technology or external authorship, but directly, as a thinking thing."[21] Starr draws attention to the power of aesthetic experience, which she notes holds an "evolving reward value,"[22] which enables "novel kinds of reward in a process that makes these rewards particularly meaningful for inner life and opens up possibilities for new knowledge, or new ways of negotiating the world."[23] We will draw this into the intentional creation of affective space, a theme we will build on over the coming chapters.

Indeed, our poetic engagement, especially with mixed media enables new ideas to be put together that, outside of the arts, would not be possible.[24] Vernallis observes the following: "In sum, music videos work to interpolate us—engaging us physically as well as prodding us intellectually. They create forms of identification with ideas, values, subjectivities, and bodies."[25]

She further adds that "these clips will help global citizens discover shared rhythm,"[26] so providing us with, as we will see below, material that promotes Bauman's understanding of cosmopolitanism (to be explored below).[27] Perhaps the potential of music video to explore ontological security is best captured in Giles Deleuze's comment about film's

> unexpected ability to show not behavior but spiritual life (at the same time as aberrant behaviors). Spiritual life is not the dream or the fantasy, which have always been dead-ends for cinema, rather it's the domain of cold decision, of absolute determination (entitlement), of a choice of existence.[28]

---

20. Frampton, *Filmosophy*, 7.
21. Frampton, *Filmosophy*, 8.
22. Starr, *Feeling Beauty*, 24.
23. Starr, *Feeling Beauty*, 25.
24. Vernallis, *Unruly Media*, 25, 160.
25. Vernallis, *Unruly Media*, 160.
26. Vernallis, *Unruly Media*, 183.
27. Bauman, *Community*, 56.
28. Toubiana, "The Brain Is the Screen."

The following examples cover several musical genres, making this approach both, to use Tagg's terminology, *intersubjective* and *interobjective*,[29] especially when considering the visual content of accompanying 'official' videos. This, together with Machin's use of discourse schema[30] identifies the rationale by which we may consider the following songs. What we draw from this does hold sociological value over simply the writer showing, to use William James' term, 'overbelief.'[31] With that as our background we can turn to our eight themes.

1. How Popular Music Expresses Restlessness

We have already noted the New Order song, 'Restless,' which expresses a feeling of cognitive dissonance with society at large. A cursory look at comments placed by one YouTube viewer demonstrates how listeners do engage with such symbolic reality: "The song speaks to that which I can't explain. This is what New Order is about. Tapping into forgotten recesses of the human psyche, recognizing and identifying the important aspects of one's life that appear meaningless and mundane on the outside and giving all those inexplicable, repressed feelings a voice, a sound."[32] This, of course, is not what New Order is 'about,' but the fact that this is the way their work is read is significant, reflecting Deleuze's expression of our inner "spiritual life."

A further example of restlessness can be seen in the re-release of Tracy Chapman's song 'Fast Car.' First released in 1988, it was re-recorded in 2015 by the record producer Jonas Blue against an electronic dance music (EDM) house beat, the vocal sung by the British singer, Dakota. The video highlights the narrative nature of identity and the need for social confidence to be able to dwell in disorder.

The song peaked at number 2 in the United Kingdom charts, beating even Chapman's highest position. While cover versions can be more popular than the original song, especially now with the availability of music streaming, the song connected with many differing people as individuals *made do* with the symbolic reality of the song to express inner Deleuzean-styled feelings. The lyric begins as a one-sided conversation between two people where one person seeks to escape their life situation through gaining a lift in the fast car owned by the other person. It is a lyric which explores the need for these two conversationalists to break free from the mundane

29. Tagg, *Analyzing Popular Music*, 10.
30. Machin, *Analyzing Popular Music*, 78.
31. James, *The Principles of Psychology*, 20.
32. See Amanda Laggan's comment in Neworder, "New Order – Restless."

life the singer vocalizes. The protagonist seeks escape from her father's excessive drinking and her job as a supermarket checkout girl. She heads for the bright lights of the city together with her lover, to 'be someone' where the physical connection felt between the pair further adds to her sense of resolving her feelings of dissonance.

In many ways it is a very common form of lyric, a love song where girl meets boy and the world's problems are put to rights, it could be seen as affirmation of Adorno's understanding of popular music as a form of manipulation that promotes conformism over individual development, a way of keeping individuals socially 'in their place.'[33] However, the video visualizes a young lady on a motorbike 'breaking free' and romantically driving through sand dunes. She comes into a rundown town, symbolizing dissonance and disorder, where she passes three cowboys riding by on horseback. A race over the dunes ensues between the three cowboys and the woman. The woman edges ahead but at the top of a dune she falls off her bike. The lead cowboy comes to the rescue and the couple are eventually seen falling asleep together under the stars. As the couple sleep the remaining cowboys come and pull the sleeping friend away back to his restless, humdrum life.

The woman wakes alone. She is upset and on driving back into town she discovers the cowboy actually works as a supermarket checkout operator. She confronts him and returns a blue heart-shaped stone that had been given to her earlier in the video. She leaves the store alone, yet soon discovers the checkout operator has once again become her cowboy. The couple are seen riding, again, into the desert, she on her bike, he, still on his horse (Fig. 3). The video highlights aspects of both Bauman's and Lawler's thinking. The juxtaposition of a biker, three cowboys and a run-down town reflects the experience of feeling 'out of place' in life. Yet, the dissonance held by the lead characters is resolved as, together, they find the 'confidence to dwell in disorder,' their collective identity drawn from the unlikely collaboration of a fake cowboy and a biker girl, so bringing them a fleeting sense of ontological security.

---

33. Adorno, *The Culture Industry*, 53.

Figure 3. Jonas Blue, 'Fast Car'

2. How Popular Culture Expresses *Fear and Risk*

George Ezra wrote the song 'Don't Matter Now' (2017) as a way of expressing his own feelings of anxiety towards the world. He writes of how his feelings of anxiety are reinforced through his reflexive negotiation of the different discourses he encounters. For example, Ezra sings that the overuse of his smartphone has left him feeling restless.' He observes that "People reading headlines but not the article. I am guilty of that." As he notes: "It's good to switch off."[34] He is commenting on the connected nature of living in liquid modernity where news stories are so accessible and where narratives can leave you feeling fearful. The song and video express the need to escape such feelings.

The theme of escapism is captured in the video through scenes of him driving in his car along with his dog (Fig. 4). Vernallis notes that the props used may hold a specific metaphoric quality about them,[35] seen here also in the image of a small hedgehog resting in a cup (Fig. 5). The words 'I woke up like this' are written on the side of the cup, framed against Ezra singing of his need to move away from narratives that make him feel anxious or

---

34. "Don't Matter Now by George Ezra."
35. Vernallis, *Experiencing Music Video*, 104.

fearful. The song has been interpreted by his fan base as "such a summer tune," an opportunity to put life's challenges to one side.³⁶

Figure 4. George Ezra, 'Don't Matter Now'

Figure 5. George Ezra, 'Don't Matter Now'

The issues of connectedness and the speed at which information now travels is echoed in Manuel Castells work where he comments on our "network society." As he contends: "The process of formation and exercise of power relationships is decisively transformed in the new organizational and technological context derived from the rise of global digital networks of communication as the fundamental symbol-processing system of our time."³⁷

It is this ability to find instant, yet often incomplete information, 'fake' news which leaves many with the feelings of anxiety expressed by Ezra. This

---

36. See plastic taste's comment in Ezra, "George Ezra - Don't Matter Now."
37. Castells, *Communication Power*, 4.

is also an aspect of Ulrich Beck's *Risk Society*.[38] Here, Beck argues that the absence of a metanarrative, which society historically used corporately to work towards and to help make sense of life when things do not go to plan, is countered as seeking to avoid significant risks that may cause ontological insecurity.[39] These risks may include issues relating to human rights, reactions to global markets, migration and the local interpenetration of world religions.[40]

Again, feelings of risk and fear are a central theme in Lily Allen's song 'The Fear' (2009; Fig. 6). She sings of consumerism interpolating her actions alongside her need to commodify herself. The level of dissonance is such that she sings of her inner fear in not knowing how she should truly feel anymore, again a lyric which speaks of the need for authenticity.

Figure 6. Lily Allen, 'The Fear'

A recurrent theme of the video shows her walking towards the foreground, emphasizing the ongoing speed of societal change. Yet, there is never a sense of her arriving at a destination. Rather, at the end of the video the camera pans out, moving into the clouds, providing a feeling of her being ultimately left behind in her fear. Alongside reflecting on the fluid nature of society, Allen's comment reflects the evolution of a society away from a communal telos to that of an individualistic society. This articulates aspects of both Bauman and Beck's reflections on dis-ease, risk and fear.

38. Beck, *Risk Society*, 5.
39. Beck and Levey, "Cosmopolitanized Nations," 10.
40. Beck and Levey, "Cosmopolitanized Nations," 12.

This is echoed by Allen's fans who, for example comment, "It's 2018 . . . 10 years later this song feels more relatable than ever . . . what a shame."[41] Also, "It's scary how art imitates life, and then life imitates art even more so than before."[42]

3. How Popular Music Expresses a Need for Belonging

A further, more poignant example of restlessness and the need for belonging can be seen in Avicii's song 'Wake Me Up' (2014), where the video includes a brief but valuable dialogue that is not included in the song's lyrics, focusing on the issue of feeling 'out of place' and of dissonance requiring resolution. This is a song about wanting to make sense of one's otherness in relation to those they live with. The lyrics tell the story of two sisters not fitting in with social expectations and of wanting to find a place where they feel they belong with an amount of urgency.[43] In turn, the video frames this on issues of identity and restlessness. The two sisters are seen waking in a town that is set in 1950s 'dustbowl' America, walking down the high-street being watched with suspicion by other residents (Fig. 7), although there is one teenager who looks at the sisters in a manner of both curiosity and of wanting to mirror them. The video cuts to the older sister romantically horse riding out of the town into the bright lights of a modern city where she discovers others very much like her.

Figure 7. Avicii, 'Wake Me Up'

41. See itssandytime's comment in Allen, "Lily Allen | The Fear."
42. See Anal Del Gay 666's comment in Allen, "Lily Allen | The Fear."
43. "Avicii Premieres."

As an aside, the horse-riding motif is also found in both the 'Fast Car' video and within 'Restless.' It is used in each video as a romantic image of protagonists striving for freedom, of escaping a restrictive situation. Starr argues that we draw a kinetic energy from watching an image that contains movement, becoming entrained towards the symbol and what it stands for.[44] Here, the image of a moving horse holds metaphoric value to help individuals connect with the idea of escape, where the kinetic energy may even encourage escape from a situation where someone does feel trapped.

Within 'Wake Me Up,' restlessness finds symbolic resolution through a tattoo that the sisters see on the arms on the young people they encounter in the city, which is the symbol that Avicii uses as a trademark. The older sister returns to collect her sibling to escape where they are living for the city, to be with other likeminded people.

The added dialogue included in the video is a short conversation between the two sisters where the younger one asks why the inhabitants of the down do not like them. The older sister replies that she does not know, although it is clear from the video that it is because they act and dress so differently from the townsfolk. A further dialogue between the sisters is heard where the older tells the younger to pack her thing. The younger sibling asks where they are going to which her sister replies to where they belong. The video frames the lyric around the issue of cognitive dissonance, of difference and of the need to "fit in."

Comments left on differing social media platforms emphasize the issue of difference and belonging. For example, one YouTuber simply comments that the "song is about everyone being different."[45] Another also notes the issues of difference, concluding "I know I'm different and I don't care it makes me different from everyone else and I just wanna be me!"[46] One commentator, Kenya Ravine Walsh goes as far as noting "It means that everyone has a place in life."[47]

What the video and the comments highlight is the need for interdependence with likeminded individuals in seeking to make sense of life within liquid modernity. Bauman picks up on this theme in his analysis of the need to live as ethically, and therefore, relationally as possible. Reflecting Emmanuel Levinas' influence,[48] Bauman suggests that: "Ontologically, we are at best with each other. Side by side may even be physically close, literally

---

44. Starr, *Feeling Beauty*, 81, 88.
45. See Syr's comment in Avicii, "Wake Me Up."
46. See onlysavvygurl's comment in "Wake Me Up! lyrics."
47. See Kenya Ravine Walsh's comment in "What Is the Meaning?"
48. Smith, *Zygmunt Bauman*, 32.

rubbing each other's shoulders and yet infinitely remote: two separate and self-enclosed beings, Leibnizian monads of sorts, each existing through guarding its *ipseite*, its identity-with-itself, its boundary, its space."[49]

Whereas postmodernism is caricatured by individualization and ethical freedom, Bauman's liquid modernity, with its understanding of our need to rub shoulders with those around us, provides space for both the fluid nature of postmodern thinking while retaining the need for ethical relationships which frame the discourses that shape our subjective understanding of ontological security.

> Jean-Paul Sartre suggested that ego is born of self-knowledge, but that this self-knowledge is triggered by the gaze of the Other: a scrutinizing gaze, evaluating gaze, 'objectifying' gaze." . . . Not so, says Levinas. The self may be born only out of union. It is through stretching myself towards the Other that I have become the unique, the only, the irreplaceable self that I am.[50]

The Other, as Bauman helpfully concludes, "is not a force, but a face."[51] With this in mind one can say that it is within our discursive conversations that we seek to explore the Otherness in each other through which interdependence and ontological security begins to manifest.

Exploring Otherness is a re-occurring theme within popular music. It can find expression in commenting on both the otherness seen in people as well as commenting on the Otherness of the divine. Bauman would want to emphasize the need to show how relating to the other helps to articulate our own sense of self. By expressing either acceptance or rejection of otherness we are becoming drawn towards a like-minded community or seeking to move away from one.

Selena Gomez' song 'Who Says' (2011) seeks to reinforce a listener's strength of character against a perceived continued bombardment of being told by others about your short-comings, yet being drawn towards a community of likeminded people.

In writing about the song, Gomez notes how she composed it for her fans to build up their self-esteem in the face of negative comments posted on social media.[52] Her fan base becomes a community where issues of self-esteem can help draw people together, a fact noted by a fan who affirms: "This song is not to push others around. Not to bully people. No one is

---

49. Bauman, *Postmodern Ethics*, 70.
50. Bauman, *Postmodern Ethics*, 77.
51. Bauman, *Postmodern Ethics*, 79.
52. "Who Says."

perfect. Everyone has their own beauty inside. It teaches you to say who says that you are perfect. Everybody is pretty. Do not make fun of people."[53]

Likewise, 'Born This Way' (2011), sung by Lady Gaga, is a song that celebrates the difference in others compared with God's omniscience. It is a song about religious acceptance as much as the hope for religions to be accepting of different sexual orientations. While this is a transgressive song for those holding to a traditional Christian understanding of sexual relationships, the need to accept difference is reflected regularly in comments on social media, such as: "It's all about equality. Yes, it's for that gay boy. Yes, it's for that Asian girl. Yes, it's for that person with red hair and freckles. Yes, it's for that girl who was born with a physical/mental disability. It's for anyone who has ever been judged for something they can't help or judged for being who they are. You were born the way you are for a reason."[54]

These last two songs function in the manner of drawing like-minded individuals together. In contrast, the Radiohead video 'Burn the Witch' (2016), written some thirteen years before its release, draws on the theme of fear caused by the difference seen in others. The video is a stop-motion animation based on the 1960 children's television programme Trumpton which portrays an episode that is based on the 1973 film *The Wickerman*.[55] It tells the story of an unnamed official who inspects the village, being shown different scenes of village life which show both Pagan imagery and a glimpse of a darker side to village life: a woman sitting on a witch's ducking stool; a woman tied to a tree while men with deer masks dance around her in a ritualistic manner; a gallows decorated with flowers; a wickerman (Fig. 8) in which the official becomes imprisoned. The wickerman is set on fire and the song draws to a close, the fate of the official unknown. However, the video continues and the official is seen having escaped his incarceration.

---

53. See mysterious2000's comment in "Selena Gomez – Who Says."
54. See blanketmonster's comment in "Lady GaGa – Born This Way."
55. Tume, "Radiohead."

Figure 8. Radiohead, 'Burn the Witch'

Lyrically, the song speaks of a frightened society where individuals become singled out, where small talk can become misconstrued and where eye contact in the wrong social setting can bring serious consequences. It tells of the need to blend in with society, where differences in the other becomes seen as a threat, while it concludes with the sentiment of killing those who are seen as a threat. This song has been interpreted as a political comment on current western governments with their pursuit of nativism,[56] while others have viewed it as a comment on the migrant crisis facing the West.[57] Certainly, it appears to draw to the surface some of the tensions experienced in society. The group, though, remain silent as to its meaning. However interpreted, this and the afore mentioned songs make comments both about the need to belong and of making sense of otherness.

4. How Popular Music Expresses a Fear of Belonging

While there is a need to draw together with likeminded people, there is still a fear about belonging to particular cultural groups and of wanting to maintain independence. The video for Sia's 'Cheap Thrills' (2016) focuses on the theme that many are fearful of commitment, of holding a particular identity. Bauman

56. Hogan, "Decoding the Politics."
57. Kaufman, "Radiohead."

stresses the ongoing need for community and ethical relationships. He notes how community (*Gemeinschaft*) is a word that has a "feel" to it, something that is longed for, yet which is a form of "paradise lost—but one to which we dearly hope to return, and so we feverishly seek the roads that may bring us there."[58] That 'community' may have a certain 'feel' to it is to bring an aesthetic quality to the pursuit of de facto identity and ontological security: a *feeling* of security. Yet, for Bauman, the loss of community is the compromise for pursuing autonomy: "Missing community means missing security; gaining community, if it happens, would soon mean missing freedom. Security and freedom are two equally precious and coveted values which could be better or worse balanced, but hardly ever fully reconciled and without friction."[59]

It is this paradoxical process of wanting security and yet wanting the freedom to experience happiness which will also challenge a secure identity and which can lead to restless feelings. One never feels entirely safe. Following Bauman's thinking—also Lash and Friedman[60]—as soon as an individual feels that their sense of security has resulted in a lack of autonomal freedom, so the desire to break free becomes stronger. The pursuit of a de facto identity must continue afresh. Bauman does note that ontological questioning may happen at different levels of our sense of self and that where a person feels 'out of place' or 'sticking out', it will cause some degree of cognitive dissonance which ultimately will need to be resolved.[61]

Figure 9. Sia, 'Cheap Thrills'

58. Bauman, *Community*, 3.
59. Bauman, *Community*, 4.
60. Lash and Friedman, "Introduction," 9.
61. Bauman, *Identity*, 12.

Shot in black and white and showing a pastiche of a 1950s American dance-show (Fig. 9), the video highlights the hope of *Gemeinschaft* by again focusing on the nostalgia of a former age. Yet, the video also emphasizes the need for autonomy. The dance-show presenter is seen walking through couples dancing, marking their ability to interpret the music as he goes. Two central dancers, who are identifiable in black and white wigs while their faces have been blacked-out, express their autonomy over the other performers by performing dance moves that are both nostalgic and contemporary, marking them out from the crowd. The couple win the "dance-off" before leading all the dancers through some of their moves with the presenter unsuccessfully attempting to join in. This is the story of two people seeking freedom yet it is contrasted with the nostalgic image of a simpler, past time where a stronger sense of community was enjoyed.

5. How Popular Music Expresses a Need for Differing Cultural Symbols: The Cultural Omnivore

If such symbolism can be understood to represent something of how we feel living in liquid modernity, then one must expect to see a fluid and ever expanding supply of symbols to draw from. This is created not just through the forces of consumerism, but through the effects of the cultural omnivore theory. There are three aspects to this that require comment. (1) An understanding of the theory will provide further insight into the fluid nature of society and how we are making sense of the symbols we hear and see around us. While the omnivore theory focuses on the distinction between 'high' forms of musical culture and popular culture, we will see (2) how the proliferation of musical signs is also affecting the boundaries that once firmly made clear distinction between differing popular music genres. (3) This will help us understand a third aspect which will be considered under the next subheading, that of the pursuit of cosmopolitanism.

(1) One's cultural preferences were once seen as representing one's social standing.[62]

For example, those who listened exclusively to intellectualized music forms, such as to opera, saw themselves with a higher social standing than those who listened solely to mass cultural products. Now, in liquid modernity, there is far greater freedom to cross cultural lines of distinction. The term

---

62. E.g., Bourdieu, *The Logic of Practice*.

'cultural omnivore'[63] has been used to describe those who appreciate many forms of music, such that Richard Peterson and Roger Kern note this development "may suggest the formulation of new rules governing symbolic boundaries."[64] It is the elasticity of these socio-cultural boundaries which provides the wider pool of symbols from which we poach or 'saw up' in our search for ontological security.

However, the breadth of omnivorism has been the subject of ongoing debate.[65] Alan Ward, David, Modesto Gayo-Cal are critical of Peterson's work to the extent of noting they are "very suspicious of the notion of the omnivore as a characterization or ideal type of cultural actor" and that social boundaries still remain.[66] However, education has been acknowledged as a significant factor in encouraging cultural omnivorism,[67] and that omnivores tend to be older, middle/upper class individuals[68] rather than younger people. Motti Regev does make the point that while some will not crossover into classical styled music, omnivorism does still occur with individuals moving across genres of popular music.[69] However, as we will see, the effects of education and technology are trickling down to a younger generation enabling them, too, to further benefit from the effects of the omnivore theory.

The crossover, or deconstruction of the perceived division between high culture and popular culture[70] can be seen clearly in popular music that is played by orchestral instrumentation. The Pete Tong Heritage Orchestra represents the fluidity of the cultural omnivore theory, expressing how individuals who would not normally utilize such diverse sonic symbolism are now more than happy to do so. Here, the genre of house music has been set to classical instrumentation by the DJ producer Pete Tong, being performed at the BBC Proms in 2016, long seen as a bastion of 'high' culture.[71] Its popularity is such that the one off concert has been replicated through a national tour together with an album entitled 'Classic House.' A further example of the success of this musical genre is that of the award winning Manchester Camerata who, with their Hacienda Classical gigs, have classicized music

---

63. Peterson, "Understanding Audience Segmentation."
64. Peterson and Kern, "Changing Highbrow Taste," 904.
65. E.g., Rimmer, "Beyond Omnivores and Univores," 300.
66. Ward et al., "Understanding Cultural Omnivorousness," 160.
67. Ward et al., "Understanding Cultural Omnivorousness," 309; Ward and Gayo-Calb, "The Anatomy of Cultural Omnivorousness," 142.
68. Hanquinet et al., "Eyes of the Beholder," 112.
69. Regev, *Pop-Rock Music*, 128.
70. See Partridge, *The Lyre of Orpheus*, 21–31.
71. Tong, "Classic House."

first made popular in the Mancunian Hacienda Club.[72] Here, the cultural distinction of the classical concert hall merges with the electronic dance music scene. The Omnivore, though, can be seen as a two-way street with popular music influencing the writing of classical music, such as seen in the work of Max Richter, with his work such as 'Sleep,' an eight-and-a-half hour composition for piano, Cello, two Violas, two Violins, Organ, Soprano vocals, Synthesizers and Electronics (2015).

(2) While accepting that the omnivore theory provides a lens through which to see that our musical consumption has become more fluid, we need to see evidence that such omnivorism is affecting the popular music choices of younger people.

While popular music does hold distinction between genres, there is evidence that the algorithms used by music streaming services is making the boundaries between genres more fuzzy. The use of genre does enable the music industry to organize itself from helping musicians to find the right producers and venues, while genres can help fans to locate the music they are looking for.[73] Daniel Silver, Monica Lee and Clayton Childress have noted how genre expectations are weakening, for example, through the effects of social media and streaming and that technology allows musical products to affect music production in new ways. One aspect which continues to reinforce the fuzzy boundaries is the algorithm used by streaming services. Here, search engines are finding new ways to sort music into more flexible classifications which are sensitive to consumer preferences to the point that "genres thus fade in consumer salience."[74]

That said, they have also noted that some genres have become "hard subgenres," such as Death Metal which are more strident in their differentiation.[75] Yet, their analytical work analyzing the user profiles of MySpace users shows how the once ridged lines of demarcation have become fluid in nature. Their dendrogram (Fig. 10) shows three main "music worlds" which then hold sixteen further genre communities where they see much greater freedom in crossing genre boundaries.[76] Here, we can see how technology is helping to breakdown cultural barriers.

72. Youngs, "The Orchestra That Won."
73. Silver et al., "Genre Complexes in Popular Music," 1.
74. Silver et al., "Genre Complexes in Popular Music," 1.
75. Silver et al., "Genre Complexes in Popular Music," 3.
76. Silver et al., "Genre Complexes in Popular Music," 12.

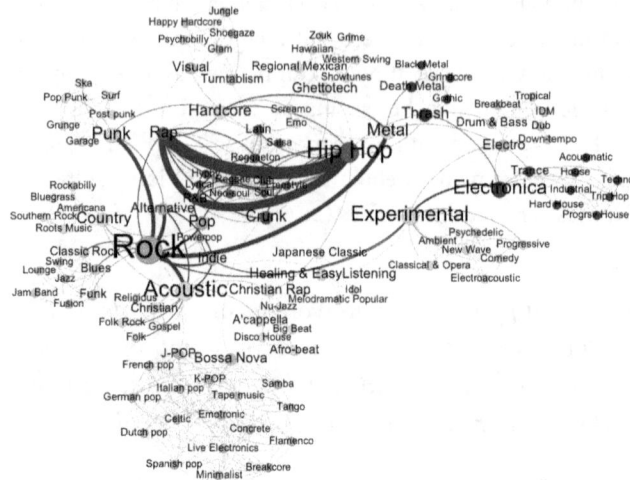

Figure 10. Silver et al., Dendrogram of 'Music Worlds'[77]

Streaming can be seen as "the industry's latest white knight but after decades of grappling with pirates, new technologies and evaporating sales, music executives know there will be twists to come."[78] It becomes part of the cultural milieu from which, to follow Michel De Certeau and Bauman, we draw on in our search for a secure identity.[79] In a qualitative survey of thirteen to thirty-two year olds, the research organization YPULSE (2015) noted that 76 percent of respondents noted that they listen to music multiple times a day, and 80 percent say music is an important part of their lives. Of particular note is that 79 percent responded that they do not have a specific genre that they followed. Just 11 percent said that they only listened to one genre of music.[80] This wider engagement with popular music is also seen in the growth of festivals, where bands of different genre share the same stage. As Peter Robinson records in an interview with the V Festival organizer Bob Angus "It's absolutely conscious. Music tastes have broadened massively and we absolutely want to celebrate that."[81] The cultural omnivore theory helps to set the scene for understanding how popular music both expresses and facilitates cosmopolitanism.

77. Silver et al., "Genre Complexes in Popular Music," 12.
78. Nicolaou, "How Streaming Saved Industry."
79. See also Mulcock, "Creativity and Politics," 169.
80. "Millennials & Teens Sound Off."
81. Robinson, "Pop, Rock, Rap, Whatever."

6. How Popular Music Expresses a Frustrated Pursuit of Cosmopolitanism

The omnivore approach reflects also the growth of world music.[82] For example, Peter Gabriel, who established both WOMAD and the Real World label, is a British musician who is known for his incorporation of ethnic sounds, such as in his song 'In Your Eyes' (1986) in which the Senegalese musician Youssou N'Dour sings in his native Wolof.[83] N'Dour has collaborated with other Western musicians such as Neneh Cherry, Paul Simon, Bruce Springsteen, Tracy Chapman and Lou Reed. From the opposite perspective, the Japanese hip-hop group Home Made Kazoku utilize a western genre through which they reflect aspects of Japanese culture (e.g., 'Tsubaki,' 2008). Similar examples will be found in most cultures. The fusion between traditional instrumentalists and Western musical forms takes many forms, from Western songwriters incorporating traditional instrumentation to ethnic musicians engaging with Western genres.

Philip Bohlman notes the powerful influence of music on the formation of Empire, indeed, in the shaping of nationhood through imbalances of political power.[84] Yet, now, reflecting Certeau, Bohlman notes how technology means that we appropriate music which is "both local and global, individual and collective, personal and political."[85] The effects of appropriation of Western music's symbolism is such that "Musical westernization has been central to state-sponsored modernization projects." In this way, musical appropriation can be politically motivated.[86] Equally, in poaching differing symbolism individuals are beginning to express constructions of the sacred,[87] that is, those values which hold an authority over one's life.

Such a fluid approach to music consumption enables different cultural groups to engage with other cultural signs, which, in turn provides the cultural elasticity required to pursue cosmopolitanism. Regev notes that "when individuals, as members of one national or ethnic culture, have a taste for cultural products or artworks that unequivocally 'belong' to a nation or ethnicity other than their own, they display aesthetic cosmopolitanism."[88]

82. See Bohlman, "Introduction," 606–33.
83. Qureshi, "Sufism," 600.
84. Bohlman, "Introduction," 4.
85. Bohlman, "Introduction," 8.
86. Shepherd, "Global Exoticism and Modernity," 610. See also Blankenship and Renard, "Pop Songs on Political Platforms," 33.
87. Partridge, "Religion and Popular Culture," 559; Riis and Woodhead, *Sociology of Religious Emotion*, 180.
88. Regev, *Pop-Rock Music*, 8.

Regev notes how it is Western forms of popular music that are transcending cultural and national boundaries.[89] Such popular culture becomes a way of showing political longing, which concerns the pursuit of a more secure future. Cosmopolitanism becomes, to use Certeau's urbanistic discourse, a Hobbesian city of utopia.[90] A collective narrative identity has formed around Western music, around the success of its auteurs which is widely promoted by globalization and networked consumerism that has influenced many. Its pursuit has become a secularized telos, yet restlessness remains.

David Hesmondhalgh, in particular, draws the conclusion that, for some, the pursuit of cosmopolitanism is a reaction to the failure of modernity to bring security.[91] Fueled by the rise of globalization over that of past understandings of the importance of the nation-state, he notes how the term has become detached from its ethical meaning of equating the moral standing to all peoples.[92]

While many pursue such a lifestyle, Bauman provides a bitter-sweet end-note in that he feels cosmopolitanism is only something which the financially elite may aspire to:

> The "cosmopolitan" lifestyle of the new secessionists is not meant for mass imitation, and the "cosmopolitans" are not the apostles of a new and better life model and not an avant-garde of an advancing army. What their lifestyle celebrates is the irrelevance of place, a condition most conspicuously beyond the reach of ordinary folks, of the "natives" tied fast to the ground and (in case they try to disregard the shackles) likely to meet in the 'big wide world out there' sullen and unfriendly immigration officers rather than invitingly smiling hotel receptionists. The message of the "cosmopolitan" way of being is simple and blunt: it does not matter where we are, what matters is that we are there.[93]

In its purest form, this is what Bauman calls a "community free" zone, where only successful business and culture-industry people may reside, and where security is perceived to be found.[94] So, while many pursue cosmopolitanism, it is with the knowledge that it will never be fully attainable: "The idols accomplish a small miracle: they make the inconceivable happen; they

---

89. Regev, *Pop-Rock Music*, 6.
90. Certeau, *Practice of Everyday Life*, 94.
91. Hesmondhalgh, *Why Music Matters*, 130.
92. Hesmondhalgh, *Why Music Matters*, 152.
93. Bauman, *Community*, 56.
94. Bauman, *Community*, 67.

conjure up the 'experience of community' without real community, the joy of belonging without the discomfort of being bound."[95] The community free zone, which provides ontological security wherever you are globally, is fully immanent, that is, where an individual can resource their spiritual needs from within their sense of self, without reference to the divine. Yet it is unattainable except to a select few. For Bauman, this is to reinforce the restlessness and dis-ease of liquid modernity within which we are situated.

Beck and Levy hold a view different to Bauman's view on cosmopolitanism. If Bauman sees cosmopolitanism as something which only a few hyper-mobile entrepreneurs can achieve,[96] their view is that "cosmopolitanization is the mechanism through which nationhood is reimagined."[97] Their interpretation of cosmopolitanism is an outcome of Beck's *Risk Society*, where they note "In the absence of a dominant narrative about the future, global risk frames structure how national experiences are informed by global expectations and how global experiences are shaping national expectations. Perceiving the future through the prism of risk perceptions reveals how representations of catastrophes of various kinds (e.g., ecological, human rights) are challenging the ontological security once provided by the temporal narratives of nation-states."[98]

In their view, cosmopolitanism does not prevent nationalism,[99] rather there becomes a greater fluidity for the symbols of nationhood to reside underneath the more universal values of cosmopolitanism.[100] Here, cosmopolitanism becomes a discourse that limits the risk that has resulted from the cessation of meta-narratives, in particular the lack of ontological security once offered through religious narratives becomes replaced by the values of cosmopolitanism which, they argue, are transmitted through media content within which are embedded social, cultural, historical, and economic values.[101] Risk, here, can come in the form of issues raised through human rights, global market imperatives, migration and the local interpenetration of world religions.[102]

To this extent, Bauman's views on the exclusivity of cosmopolitanism are over-realized. More widely, there are those who reside outside of Europe

---

95. Bauman, *Community*, 69.
96. Bauman, *Community*, 56.
97. Beck and Levy, "Cosmopolitanized Nations," 6.
98. Beck and Levy, "Cosmopolitanized Nations," 9.
99. Beck and Levy, "Cosmopolitanized Nations," 8.
100. Beck and Levy, "Cosmopolitanized Nations," 9.
101. Beck and Levy, "Cosmopolitanized Nations," 22.
102. Beck and Levy, "Cosmopolitanized Nations," 12.

and North America who long for the privileges of Western society and their musical consumption reflects their hope. Even within the West there is a never-ending supply of individuals who seek their five minutes of fame precisely to resource both their financial stability as well as their sense of self, evidenced in the ever-growing market for reality television participants and social media influencers. This is not to suggest that such desire for fame within cosmopolitan society is flippant or shallow. Rather, it reinforces the steps that individuals will take in their pursuit for ontological security.[103]

What this reinforces is that the effects of the Cultural Omnivore theory and cosmopolitanism mean that liquid moderns are becoming very adept at Certeau's *bricolent,* redistributing and claiming aspects of "everyday art" from the music's symbolic and emotional content for their own purposes.[104]

7. How Popular Culture Expresses the Happy Narrative and the Narcissist

In the absence of a communal telos from which to find the resolution of cognitive dissonance, many now seek to live life 'in the moment' pursing happiness as the ultimate goal.[105] However, most experiences of happiness are fleeting, leaving deeper feelings of restlessness unresolved. The theme of happiness, and that of the relentless, yet unfilled search of the narcissist, is a significant theme that influences many people's pursuit for ontological security.

Bauman remarks how solid modernity "fixated" on its need for ongoing social progress, whereas liquid modernity is governed by the need to find your own level of security.[106] Liquid moderns do still see value in the solid modern hope of emancipatory progress, yet, in being faced with the fate of finding a secure identity with which to negotiate life, its final objectives and hopes are no longer known. Within such fluid uncertainty, Bauman notes that the language of rights, especially the right to happiness, has come to the fore as a way of attaining security: "Modem society announced the right to happiness: it was not just the improvement in living standards, but the degree of happiness of the men and women involved that was to justify (or to condemn, in the event that that degree refused to climb to ever greater heights) society and all its works."[107]

---

103. See also, for example, Ward, *Celebrity Worship.*

104. Certeau, *Practice of Everyday Life,* 66.

105. I.e., Tay and Diener, "Needs and Subjective Well-Being," 354; Bauman, *Culture,* 41; Layard, *Happiness.*

106. Bauman, *Culture,* 74.

107. Bauman, *Community,* 83.

Happiness has become not only a 'right' but, for many, "the supreme purpose of life, and the promise made in the name of society and its powers to secure conditions permitting a continuous and consistent growth." However, where the pursuit of happiness becomes focused on issues of income and when material living standards see no improvement, so restlessness will increase.[108]

Richard Layard's work on the pursuit of happiness is of interest as he draws attention not only to aspects of the philosophy that shaped the ideology of the Enlightenment, such as the pursuit of Jeremy Bentham's 'Great Happiness.'[109] He also notes that, despite cognitive therapies and positive psychology to help individuals pursue positive thinking and happiness,[110] the decline of orthodox Christianity has created a "moral vacuum." This loss undermines progress towards a corporate telos and a recognition of value in the relational aspect of communal life.[111] Despite a significant increase in individual wealth, he notes that happiness has not been the result.[112]

The pursuit of happiness as a late modern telos is noted by many besides Bauman,[113] and is considered to be a key feature in the pursuit of both good mental health[114] as well as economic policy.[115] However prominent the theme of happiness in popular music culture, it needs to be remembered that, unless Maslow's first level of universal needs is met, feelings of happiness will be ungrounded and restlessness will remain.

Happiness may be experienced episodically, that is, as being in a good mood, in high spirits.[116] It can be seen as a life-goal, to be pursued as an "emotional condition,"[117] or be seen in someone as a personality trait. Yet, Jason Raibley notes that such experiences of happiness will be inconsistent: "Engagement is a high-activation emotional state; calmness and tranquility are low-activation mental states commonly classed alongside stillness,

---

108. Bauman, *Community*, 78.
109. Layard, *Happiness*, 112.
110. Layard, *Happiness*, 9.
111. Layard, *Happiness*, 92.
112. Layard, *Happiness*, 30.
113. I.e., Csikszentmihalyi, *Flow*; Tay and Diener, "Needs and Subjective Well-Being," 354.
114. E.g., Boniwell, "What Is Eudaimonia?"
115. E.g., Stratton, "David Cameron Aims Happiness"; Layard, *Happiness*, 133.
116. Raibley, "Happiness," 1107.
117. Layard, *Happiness*, 1109.

idleness, and passivity. These states could be present only in alternation or cycle."[118]

In other words, the pursuit of happiness does not equate to an ongoing deep sense of inner peace and will never run smoothly, nor necessarily, be permanently attained. Riis and Woodhead note that when such overemphasis is placed on this feeling "that anything other than happiness is a problem that requires some form of treatment."[119] Layard, for example, suggests that through positive thinking *and* cognitive therapy society could move towards its goal of happiness, yet there is no evidence to show his theory working in practice. Indeed, by his own arguing, despite an increase in affluence we are less happy now than we once were.[120]

Likewise, Mihaly Csikszentmihalyi developed his concept of "flow," arguing that: "Happiness, in fact, is a condition that must be prepared for, cultivated, and defended privately by each person. People who learn to control inner experience will be able to determine the quality of their lives, which is as close as any of us can come to being happy."[121] He argues that this may be achieved through "achieving control over the contents of our consciousness."[122] Through developing the skills to focus on nothing else other than the activity at hand, he suggests that a state of happiness may be found.

This is a very cognitive approach which requires discipline to attain[123] which, he notes, not all will be able to access due to social limitations such as "slavery, oppression, exploitation, and the destruction of cultural values is the elimination of enjoyment."[124] Yet, to draw on Bauman's understanding of the implausible nature of a secure identity, so Csikszentmihalyi and Layard's arguments are weakened as one's sense of self *does* feel oppressed by the forces of liquid society—that is the whole problem of restlessness. A more fundamental, organic approach to self-actualization and fulfilment is required.

Yet, for many, where the 'here and now' is all that is recognized, the pursuit of happiness becomes akin to a secularized telos. Pharrell Williams captures the pursuit of happiness in his song 'Happy' which was the bestselling single in the United Kingdom in 2014 selling 1.5 million copies. Williams sings of happiness as a form of truth and of wanting to be happy in all situations in life, even when you are in a roofless room. In other words, even

---

118. Layard, *Happiness*, 1110.
119. Riis and Woodhead, *Sociology of Religious Emotion*, 185.
120. Layard, *Happiness*, 3, 194.
121. Csikszentmihalyi, *Flow*, 2.
122. Csikszentmihalyi, *Flow*, 2.
123. Csikszentmihalyi, *Flow*, 35.
124. Csikszentmihalyi, *Flow*, 85.

when you cannot protect yourself from the storms of everyday existence. Interestingly, the video portrays a gospel choir singing the repeated refrain expounding happiness which, at one point, the accompanying soundtrack becomes diegetic in nature, that is the sound becomes 'live' on set, rather than remaining as the soundtrack,[125] implying a sense of real time.[126]

This has the effect of drawing the listener to that particular narrative in a fresh way. Here, it focuses attention on the gospel choir and its religious symbolism (Fig. 11). A common perception is that black gospel music holds a particular vibe of happiness, although that cannot really be separated from the discourse that supports that—that of robust Christian belief, setting an interesting contrast between two distinct narratives.

Figure 11. Pharrell Williams, 'Happy'

Happy's positivistic rationale does feature in comments on social media, as seen in a comment placed on the official YouTube page of the music video: "Happiness is a decision. You are as happy as you decide to be. Place an imaginary gate on your brain. Consciously close it every time negativity requests or as often is . . . demands a visit. That helps me tremendously . . . and I hope it will help you too "[127]

For some, happiness is not found through such a positivistic framework, rather, through the purposeful transgression of some of society's social norms. This can be expressed as the comparison between Apollonian

125. I.e., Gorbman, *Unheard Melodies*, 15.
126. Chion, *Audio-Vision*, 17.
127. See Catewade's comment in iamOTHER, "Pharrell Williams – Happy."

and Dionysian views of culture. The Apollonian need to keep the *pure sacred*, here, keeping to a society's expectations of behavior, can be contrasted with the Dionysian need to transgressively cross that boundary, pursuing the *impure sacred*.[128] Musically, this can be seen in the Punk movement with songs such as The Sex Pistols' album *Never Mind the Bollocks, Here's the Sex Pistols* (1977) which musically and socially encouraged transgressing many of the social norms of the late 1970s. Here we can see how popular music can help challenge, even breakdown those Christian based narratives that had become sedimented into Western culture, transgressing the *pure sacred* of its historic past.

Such Dionysian behavior can be seen in many musical cultures, such as Electronic Dance Music.[129] Here, the Dionysian behavior is as much about finding happiness in a manner that transgresses social norms, leaving Chris Gibson and John Connell to note how EDM helps to "enhance the feelings of distance from suburban life."[130] A cursory look at EDM videos reflecting, for example, the scene in Ibiza reinforces Michel Maffesoli's view of a lack of impulse control in the dancer's pursuit for happiness.

However, when the pursuit of happiness becomes so unresolved, narcissistic feelings may arise. Both Richard Sennett[131] and Christopher Lasch's[132] observations on dissonance have focused on narcissistic feelings. They have separately argued that the fluid nature of society is causing individuals to evolve, becoming more narcissistic in nature. Here, a person discovers that at the moment of gratification the object they have craved is not able to provide fulfilment and so restlessness remains.

For Lasch, this has been caused by the erosion of the family as the conduit for passing on traditional cultural values and has caused "long-term shifts in the structure of cultural authority." Such narcissistic, or hedonistic, behavior is expressed through the absence of impulse control requiring "spectacle" in order to gain satisfaction.[133] This is the result of what Lasch views as a cultural devaluation of past ways of looking at society where individuals have "suffered from a feeling of inauthenticity and inner emptiness."[134] This helps to evidence why understanding the reasons behind restlessness are such major issues to consider. The narcissistic approach

---

128. Partridge, *The Lyre of Orpheus*, 68.
129. I.e., John, *Tecnomad*, 19.
130. Gibson and Connell, *Sound Tracks*, 207.
131. Sennett, *Fall of Public Man*.
132. Lasch, *The Culture of Narcissism*.
133. Lasch, *The Culture of Narcissism*, 238.
134. Lasch, *The Culture of Narcissism*, 239.

becomes a very negative interpretation of our life experience such that: "The narcissist has no interest in the future, in part, he has so little interest in the past. He finds it difficult to internalize happy associations or to create a store of loving memories with which to face the latter part of life, which under the best of conditions always brings sadness and pain."[135]

Nicholas Abercrombie and Brian Longhurst comment that "The notion of a narcissistic society embodies the idea people act as if they are being looked at, as if they are at the center of the attention of a real or imaginary audience."[136] The strain of being the center of attention can be seen in videos such as Beyoncé's 'Video Phone' and in Robbie Williams' 'I Love My Life.' Whether society is viewed as being narcissistic, or where society's telos is seen as the pursuit of happiness, so feelings of restlessness are ultimately set to remain.

The symbolism contained in the official video for Robbie Williams' 'I Love My Life' (Fig. 12) captures something of the unresolved nature of Lasch's understanding of narcissism. Here, Williams sings of both his success and *joie de vivre*, concluding that he was content with his life. In the lyric he both recognizes mistakes that he has made and that life's troubles are still likely to come his way. However, the video, which is essentially Williams singing to camera, is filmed on a windswept beach and depicts him surrounded constantly by women who are all similarly dressed in black while holding video cameras to film him.

Figure 12. Robbie Williams, 'I Love My Life'

135. Lasch, *The Culture of Narcissism*, xvii.
136. Abercrombie and Longhurst, *Audiences*, 88.

The manner of the women's "filming" is similar to Beyoncé's 'Videophone,' where two men dressed as video cameras voyeuristically film both Beyoncé and Lady Gaga. There is an incongruity between Williams' lyrical sentiments and the video's imagery. Certainly, the video seeks to showcase Williams as an auteur who has reached the pinnacle of his career, reflecting Goodwin's feelings towards ideology and auteurship in popular music[137] as well as Bauman's thinking about cosmopolitanism. Yet, the bleakness of the video would suggest a darker side to William's sense of ontological security, more akin to his reported struggle with anxiety and depression.[138]

What we see with these examples, some which some can be seen as binary opposites (i.e., the need to belong, yet the fear of belonging), are feelings being expressed by the artist and 'owned' by their fans which express feelings of powerless in achieving ontological security. This is the discourse schema with which fans engage. In the face of such restlessness, one can also see that there is a tactical pursuit for something more than simply this expression of restlessness and which the hegemony of liberal pluralism cannot provide. This is a tactical expression that there should be more to life than the unfulfilled pursuit of happiness, or more to life than simply what you experience in the 'here and now.' From a Christian perspective, this would reflect the differences between that which is seen and that which would be considered as unseen. Take, for example, Colossians 1:16: For in him all things were created: things in heaven and on earth, visible and invisible, whether thrones or powers or rulers or authorities; all things have been created through him and for him.

In commenting on this verse Tom Wright notes what "all things" refers to everything being viewed as a "single whole," be they visible or invisible.[139] The visible order represents our lifeworld and that which lies beyond the horizon of the lifeworld can be captured by invisible. Indeed, from a Christian perspective, even that which is not now 'of Christ' owes its existence to Christ. While rulers and authorities can be demythologized to represent civil authorities within our lifeworld Wright is keen to point out that this should not rule out an understanding of the demonic and supernatural powers.[140] Again, this is an aspect that lies beyond the horizon of Western society's lifeworld.

As we will see in the next chapter, secularization *and* subjectivization have moved Western society away from such a traditional narrative

---

137. Goodwin, *Dancing in the Distraction Factory*, 5.
138. E.g., Freeth, "I Felt More and More Isolated."
139. Wright, *The Epistles of Paul*, 71.
140. Wright, *The Epistles of Paul*, 72.

of Christianity. Yet, the pursuit of that which is lies beyond the horizon of an individual's lifeworld in order to bring a fuller understanding to the complexities of life is still widely prevalent. Needless to say, unless specifically stated, this tactical expression should be understood not simply as a representation of the Christian narrative. Rather, it is true of all forms of subjective discourse that seek to express that 'which is hidden.'

8. How Popular Culture Wants to Explore Beyond the Lifeworld

We will see in the next chapter how Christianity has lost its place as the traditional Western provider of ontological security. Yet, rather than being replaced by a positivistic discourse, we have witnessed the process of subjectivization—the turn to the self.[141] Rather, our journey into liquid modernity and Bauman's fate of identity sees cultural expressions that reflect a search for that which may lie beyond the horizon of our lifeworld. As Partridge describes it: "There is a popular feeling, not far from the surface, that reality may not be quite as stable as we have been led to believe and that enchanted discourses may contain more than a nugget of truth."[142]

The subjectivization of belief alongside the commodification of religious narratives provides space for all forms of what Partridge terms "spiritual lifeworlds" to prosper. As he observes, "that they do thrive indicates that the processes of disenchantment are unlikely to lead to an absolutely secular condition." Building on his understanding of Deriddian hauntology, he asserts that: "New religious belief— like all religious belief— relies on the persistence of "unknowing," on intimations of a "beyond," on the unfalsifiable nature of the nonsecular. On the basis of such unfalsifiable ideas, new believers deconstruct the dominant readings of "reality," thereby confirming suspicions that . . . we would do well not to count on the density and solidity of the living present."[143]

This understanding provides a further framework within which to interpret popular music videos such as New Order's 'Restless' which provides an articulation of such inner thought. This can be seen in the juxtaposition between the scenes set in the present and those which are constructed around popular legends. The video provides a good example of how popular culture expresses "the ordinary enchantment of the everyday and those

141. E.g., Partridge, "Occulture and Everyday Enchantment," 318; Houtman and Aupers, "The Spiritual Turn," 315.

142. Partridge, "Occulture and Everyday Enchantment," 316.

143. Partridge, "Occulture and Everyday Enchantment," 316.

processes by which particular nonsecular meanings emerge, are disseminated, and become influential in societies and individual lifeworlds."[144]

Such hiddenness is the tension that Partridge seeks to express in his understanding of occulture[145] and is different to what Bruce terms as latent religiosity.[146] The songs cited thus far are examples of individual songwriters and, indirectly video directors, seeking to make more sense of what is 'lying not far from the surface' and, as such, bringing into the public sphere ideas which then help others to construct meaning. The numerous websites that are dedicated to people blogging their own interpretation of popular songs further contributes to this understanding.

As the authority of 'religion' decreases, so the capital of the 'spiritual,' 'well-being' and 'occulture' increases.[147] As Partridge asserts: "Our mental furniture may have been rearranged by the Enlightenment, but the shadows of premodernity haunt it: They explain the unexplained, give meaning to anomalous experiences, and, as such, have the power to subvert the rational and to undermine the dominant discourses of modernity. Much new religious belief is rooted in this transgression of the secular, this suspicion of scientific thought and technical mastery of the world."[148]

We will subsequently consider songs which reflect popular music's questioning pursuit of the Christian discourse through songs such as Mel C's 'Dear Life' (2016) and Florence and the Machine's 'Big God' (2018), yet popular music shows a wide gambit of spiritual worldviews. Popular music is used to express what we feel is of importance to us and, in that way, alternative spiritual identities become expressed.[149] For example, Robyn Sylvan notes that some EDM experiences are centered on chakras drawn from Indian yogic and tantric traditions,[150] while Fritz views EDM as a ritual, sacred space where individual dancers are "connected by a mystical, universal energy."[151] Sylvan is also keen to argue the influence of West African possession religion on contemporary American popular culture and, in that way, point to a worldview beyond our lifeworld.[152] He asserts that "We appear to be entering a time when these hidden religious dimensions are no longer

---

144. Partridge, "Occulture and Everyday Enchantment," 320.
145. See also Lynch, *Sacred in the Modern World*, 4.
146. Bruce, *God Is Dead*, 203.
147. Partridge, "Occulture and Everyday Enchantment," 319.
148. Partridge, "Occulture and Everyday Enchantment," 320.
149. E.g., Marsh and Roberts, "Listening as Religious Practice (Part One)," 126.
150. Sylvan, *Trance Formation*, 82.
151. Fritz, *Rave Culture*, 43.
152. Sylvan, *Traces of the Spirit*, 45.

hidden but brought consciously into full view, acknowledged and celebrated for their spiritual power."[153] That said, Gordon Lynch is critical of Sylvan's "disciplinary imperialism" by inferring too much in his observations.[154]

9. Concluding Comment

We have highlighted eight overlapping themes that are expressed in varying degrees within popular music which explore risk or fear, happiness, a need to belong yet a fear of commitment, the pursuit of cosmopolitanism yet, also, the eclectic search for any narrative or symbol that may provide hope. These are issues that must help frame the telling the Christian story today, primarily though speaking into these issues. The examples from popular music thus given reinforce the argument that within liquid modernity many individuals are 'making do' from the symbolism they come across to express feelings of resistance towards those structures that induce restlessness, while 'poaching' symbols in order to construct a discourse around them that aids security. We will also look at secular popular music songs that purposefully pursue the Christian discourse over the following chapters.

Bauman would be keen to draw attention to the unfulfilled struggle of locating an identity that can offer a liquid modern ontological security robust enough to deal with these often conflicting themes. To hold this alongside Maslow's thinking that the base level of one's individual needs require "some sort of satisfactorily coherent, meaningful whole"[155] on which subsequent levels of attainment must be built, is to suggest that unless issues surrounding the need for a secure "meaningful whole" are first addressed, which 'poaching,' 'sawing up,' 'making fit' or 'making do' do not encourage, then this sense of restlessness can only develop further. Now, having described more fully where and how restless feelings are being expressed within popular culture, we can turn to how that traditional source of security lost its cultural hold. This will provide further pointers to how the Christian discourse may be effectively told within liquid modernity.

---

153. Sylvan, *Traces of the Spirit*, 13.
154. Lynch, "Role of Popular Music," 482.
155. Maslow, *Theory of Human Motivation*, 16.

3

Christian Belief and Secularization

ZYGMUNT BAUMAN EXPRESSED FEELINGS of freedom in being released from the religious discourses that had structured the post-Enlightenment West.[1] However, towards the end of his life he began to view religious language in the public sphere as enriching, albeit aware that by using the language of God, a higher authority becomes evoked which cannot be objectively critiqued.[2] He also recognized that there is ontologically more to the world around us than he could account for sociologically. In this chapter we will explore how Christianity lost its cultural authority and wider society 'won' its freedom. That said, many today still, like Bauman, seek to make sense of that which lies beyond the horizon of the lifeworld albeit that it cannot be epistemologically proven. This chapter will reflect aspects of Bauman's thinking. It will also emphasize the differing ideological forces which the Church needs to tactically overcome in order for its discourse to be more clearly listened to today.

Until greater recognition is given by the institutional church towards the ideological factors which prevent the Christian discourse from being listened to within wider society it will continue to struggle to promulgate its core discourses. By understanding how the Church lost its hegemonic influence we can begin to see how its discourses may be best told in a liquid modern context. Again, the significance of our examination of popular music is that it can highlight the mood of wider society, here concerning the religious.

1. Bauman, *Culture*, 24; Bauman, *Community*, 3.
2. Bauman and Obirek, *Of God and Man*, 44–56.

By understanding more about our use of popular music we can glean tactical pointers that can help the Church to tell its discourses more effectively. For example, the way we may use music to help regulate our sense of self (see chapter 5) or by the way the lyrical content expresses a point of view that we hold dear (see chapter 4) can help us to understand what we feel is sacred, of ultimate concern to us. Within the fluidity of liquid modernity this can help us to understand where people are coming from, what their needs are that the Christian discourse can to speak into. However, we also need to understand what social forces have caused the decline of the Christian story, again to gain insight into how feelings of restlessness are being framed.

To explore the decline of Christian hegemony we will consider: (1) the secularization and subjectivization of belief, reflecting on how this has affected our pursuit of ontological security. We will see how (2) the secularization argument has itself needed to evolve in order to take into account the robust nature of religious narratives in the West alongside the ongoing need to make sense of what cannot be epistemologically proven. The outworking of this can be seen (3) through Jürgen Habermas' understanding of postsecularism and Woodhead's work around the 'rise of the nones.'

While arguments supporting the growth in secularization are prominent, our use of symbolism and narratives within popular culture show that there is still a deep need to express that which 'lay hidden,' such imagery often being drawn from the Christian tradition. This is surprising, given the pervasive nature of the secularization argument. Musical examples will, again, be given to highlight specific points. Firstly, and more theoretically, we must turn to the roots of the subjective turn. Not simply from a historical point of view, but to make the point that the effects of the Enlightenment Project still affect how we interpret religious and spiritual discourses within liquid modernity.

1. From Corporate Religious Belief to the Enlightenment

For Bauman, the Enlightenment Project became the basic tool behind the building of the nation-state.[3] As an emerging philosophical movement, the project covered a wide range of ideas that emphasized the need for fresh discovery and reason following on from eighty years of European wars. Ulrich Beck and Daniel Levy note that while Christianity consolidated its power for almost one millennium, the rising sixteenth century political

3. Bauman, *Liquid Modernity*, 8.

scene challenged both religious and traditional conceptions of time.[4] In Colin Greene's view, the Peace of Westphalia in 1648 not only ended years of religious war, but sowed the seeds of the Enlightenment.[5] Following such lengthy conflict, a different way of thinking about the world needed discovery, of which a key strand would be the developing secularization argument, that is, the process of making religion more worldly and of seeing the social increase in the irrelevance of religion.[6]

Bauman viewed the Enlightenment project as an intellectual creation for "cultivating the people."[7] In Alasdair Macintyre's view key thinkers sought to critique and, in places, disassemble the social and moral history of their predecessors, so encouraging the subjective 'turn to the self.' The project could never meet its potential due to "internal incoherence" between its key thinkers: "I want to argue that any project of this form was bound to fail, because of an ineradicable discrepancy between their shared conception of moral rules and precepts on the one hand and what was shared—despite much larger divergences—in their conception of human nature on the other. Both conceptions have a history and their relationship can only be made intelligible in the light of that history."[8]

However much some Enlightenment thinkers hoped to witness a new social freedom and a secularized society, with such diverse strands of thought (e.g., Auguste Comte's positivism, Jeremy Bentham's 'Great Happiness', and Adam Smith's moral sentiments), there was an absence of a coherent metanarrative undergirding the project. This can be held in contrast to Abraham Maslow's concern for life to hold "some sort of satisfactorily coherent, meaningful whole" in order for higher levels in his hierarchy of needs to be achieved.[9] This absence of internal coherence highlights feelings of existential instability which will only be further exacerbated by the fluid nature of liquid modernity.

Early Enlightenment proponents, such as René Descartes, Georg Hegel and Immanuel Kant, included religious belief in their thinking.[10] Hence, in effect, they renewed a tradition of progressive religious thought. However, other key thinkers argued against belief in the divine (i.e., John Locke, Denis Diderot, Voltaire), so heralding a tradition of secularization. Culturally,

---

4. Beck and Levy, "Cosmopolitanized Nations," 8.
5. Greene, *Christology in Cultural Perspective*, 280.
6. Ostwalt, *Secular Steeples*, 8.
7. Bauman, *Liquid Modernity*, 51.
8. Macintyre, *After Virtue*, 51–52.
9. Maslow, *Theory of Human Motivation*, 16.
10. I.e., Stone, *Value of Popular Music*, 37; Brown, *Tradition and Imagination*, 13.

this was boosted by encouraging the disenchantment of the Bible, reducing it to a benign cultural object, *Bildungskultur*, rather than a book connecting individuals with the divine. As Jonathan Sheehan notes: "But the Enlightenment was precisely the moment when the authority of the Bible was reconstituted as a piece of the heritage of the West. The reconstruction was first conjured up by a host of scholars and literati who together forged a model of biblical authority that could endure in a post-theological era."[11]

Further cultural differentiation occurred as Hegel and Kant incorporated religious content into their respective aesthetical theories. Both made a distinction between what they viewed as fine art, from that which was otherwise to be considered as an everyday cultural expression, such as popular entertainment or common art of their day. For Hegel, such aesthetical distinction required art to hold religious or serious metaphysical content and to be visibly concrete in content, as well as being presented in an appropriate form. Hegel's aesthetic appreciations would not include popular content because, as he viewed it, it was only able to provide momentary pleasure.[12] Kant, likewise, made room to comment on religious belief and was equally unappreciative of related emotional connections. The creation of such dualism not only helped create a false distinction between what some still view as high and low culture, but has helped reinforce a strong sacred or secular divide, through the search for what may be considered as sublime.

Musically, Philip Bohlman traces the progress of secularization through the development of musical form. For example, musical signifiers which were, in pre-enlightenment times seen as sacred, such as the chorale, become used in public spaces, such as within opera. A further example is the romanticism and sacralization of folk songs. Bohlman carries his argument, too, to the growing public use of what was seen as private, religious space. As he asserts, "Public religion is the space of the private that is opened through music, coming from outside-in."[13]

The Enlightenment's side-lining of emotion also reinforced a strongly dualistic rationale as it helped to distinguish rationality from what was thought to be irrational/imaginative.[14] Ole Riis and Linda Woodhead sum up the fundamentals of this issue in noting that the: "stark opposition between reason and emotion that goes back to the beginning of the modern era and has played an important role in structuring Western thought ever

---

11. Sheehan, *The Enlightenment Bible*, xi.
12. Stone, *Value of Popular Music*, 37.
13. Bohlman, "Music Inside Out," 209–12.
14. E.g., Frei, *Eclipse of Biblical Narrative*, 141; Damasio, *Feeling of What Happens*, 39.

since. For Enlightenment thinkers reason held the key to progress, and unreason was the enemy."[15] Ironically, Edmund Rolls' humanistic approach to emotions and decision-making helps to redress that balance.

We cannot fully appreciate the lived-experience or the agency created by the differing social forces that were played out as the Enlightenment took hold, especially around understandings of religious belief. In following Wilfred Smith's rationale, Diana Bass notes how it was only from the seventeenth century that Christian writers began to use the term 'religion' to signify a system of beliefs about God which, over time, would become more fixed, so defining what the subject of belief could or could not be.[16] Prior to this, belief was viewed as more experiential over cognitive—God was simply 'there'. This also reflects what Charles Taylor describes as the shift from the "porous self," where cosmic forces such as spirits, relics, sacraments and the like were believed to affect an individual, to that of the "buffered self," where the individual's sense of self is removed from an enchanted world.[17]

In the face of such strong, emergent thinking, the seventeenth and eighteenth century Church sought to retain its political and cultural power through the strengthening of its Evangelical discourse, the establishment of the Oxford Movement, and the emergence of liberalism. Callum Brown makes the link between the rise of Evangelicalism and the Enlightenment precisely for its rational understanding of faith.[18]

The Church also strove to maintain its intellectual and cultural power against the forces of industrialization. Daniele Hervieu-Léger observes how industrialization enabled many to move away from the village priest's control as they moved from village to city. Influenced by the French tradition of anticlericalism, her reasoning provides further evidence for why the Church became unable to keep its religious "chain of memory" going.[19] While writing from a particular French perspective, her understanding reflects the historical situation in the United Kingdom as well. But while this all heralds the advent of moral and social freedom, this is not the same as a rejection of the divine. It simply means that traditional understandings have evolved.[20] It also demonstrates that the forces which the Church faced are more complex and subtle than simply arguing that the West has become secularized. The point here is that, while secularists such as Bruce would see the journey into

---

15. Riis and Woodhead, *Sociology of Religious Emotion*, 14.
16. Bass, *Christianity after Religion*, 97.
17. Taylor, *A Secular Age*, 37.
18. Brown, *Death of Christian Britain*, 32.
19. Hervieu-Léger, *Chain of Memory*, 18.
20. See also Brown, *Death of Christian Britain*, 169.

modernity and the rise of secularism as a *fait accompli*, such reasoning is too simplistic. We can see this complexity in how the secularization theory has, itself, needed to evolve.

2. From 'Hard' to 'Soft' Secularization

Steve Bruce sought to show how societal change has resulted in a 'hard' form of secularization.[21] This centers around the veracity of religious discourses: as modernization progresses, so religious discourses become less cogent and, therefore, decreasingly significant in the lives of individuals and of society as a whole:

> In brief, I see secularization as a social condition manifest in (a) the declining importance of religion for the operation of non-religious roles and institutions such as those of the state and the economy; (b) a decline in the social standing of religious roles and institutions; and (c) a decline in the extent to which people engage in religious practices display beliefs of a religious kind, and conduct other aspects of their lives in a manner informed by such beliefs.[22]

He notes that there will still be those in society who will seek to be religious, and that the outcome of his secularization paradigm is not that of atheism per se.[23] Neither is this decline due to individuals becoming convinced of the falseness of the Christian narrative, nor specifically through the rise of scientific thinking.[24] Rather Christianity "simply ceased to be of any great importance to them."[25]

Drawing on what Bruce views as the Puritanical work ethic of generations subsequent to the Reformation, society formed a secularized and capital accumulating attitude towards belief, work and economy, such that the virtues of capitalism are now "obvious."[26] For example, he views the rise of the Evangelical movement, especially that of Methodism, as the Church's attempt to reunite those who had moved from country parishes to big towns with the Christian story.[27] Yet he notes that in as much as some individuals

21. Bruce, *God Is Dead*.
22. Bruce, *God Is Dead*, 3.
23. Bruce, *God Is Dead*, 41.
24. Bruce, *God Is Dead*, 27.
25. Bruce, *God Is Dead*, 3.
26. Bruce, *God Is Dead*, 5–6.
27. Bruce, *God Is Dead*, 25.

were drawn back under the authority of the church, many were not. These developments have resulted in an ongoing low level of socialization into religious belief.[28]

It is evident that since World War II church attendance within the United Kingdom has declined. We have already noted aspects of Brown's thinking concerning the relaxation of social morals. In exploring this, he, in particular, notes how the 1960s was a time when womankind found a new voice in society. If, in the 1950s, to be feminine was to be homely and a return to pre-war values, then the 1960s was to see the social gains that women found during the war reimagined with a new zest. This was helped along by new technologies which enabled the mass distribution of fresh narratives and symbolism from which women could 'make do' and 'poach.' Brown specifically draws on the increase in popular magazine sales of *Boyfriend* and *Jackie* to make this point, providing evidence of how engaging with the popular culture of the day changed society's expectations. He views the changing role of womanhood as a significant factor in the decline in church attendance as the 1950s female moral figurehead became influenced by the more socially relaxed values of the 1960s.[29]

Of particular note is the role that popular music played in the recalibration of society's values. Again, Brown notes how the whole process of buying, listening and dancing was socially significant. As he notes, pop music's impact, in particular upon girls, was reinforced by such media as *Jackie* magazine, which he views as paramount in this process of social change. This is *ut pictura poesis* in action. By the mid-1960s, the domestic ideology of the 1950s, which included a high moral piety, had been weakened to the extent that is affected western Christianity as a whole.[30]

Here we see what Middleton notes are moments of "cross-connotation," where two or more different sociological elements coalesce, symbolize and denote one another.[31] In this way, differing musical movements are able to pick up on social moments. Such examples are the 1970s relationship between punk music and social isolation which can be contrasted with 1980/90s hedonism and the rise of syncopated dance music. The point here is that while not being systematic in nature, popular music is very adept at giving expression to society's angsts and inner workings.

In the last decade within the Anglican Church in England there has been little change in average weekly attendance, which suggests, at the very

---

28. Bruce, *God Is Dead*, 13.
29. Brown, *Death of Christian Britain*, 176–77.
30. Brown, *Death of Christian Britain*, 179.
31. Middleton, *Studying Popular Music*, 9.

least, a robustness in the handling of traditional understandings of religious discourse and, again, challenges hard versions of secularization. That said, when one looks more closely at the age profiles of those attending worship it is clear that this position will change significantly as those now aged sixty-plus are not being replaced in anything like equal numbers in younger generations. In 2019, 20 percent of regular worshippers were aged under twenty, whilst 33 percent were aged seventy or over."[32]

Yet, following Habermas, religion can still be seen to shape Western political, social and economic thinking, which further calls; into doubt hard understandings of secularization theory. This all allows Robert Warner to conclude, "What is clear is that subjectivized religion is capable of enduring, even in the relatively secularized culture of Western Europe, at the very least as a minority interest."[33] This situation is clearly evolving, as we will see below in looking at Woodhead's 'the rise of the nones.'[34]

The assumption has been that modernization is the driving factor behind religious decline. However, it is not clear whether modernization is simply the result of economic growth, to be viewed primarily as social differentiation, or as a form of social rationalization.[35] As Grace Davie, Linda Woodhead and Rebecca Catto assert, "The essential point is that a wide variety of ideas are embedded within the single concept of secularization, not all of which are compatible with each other," their point reinforcing the original disjointed nature of the Enlightenment project.[36]

There has also been a growing acceptance that the boundary between tradition and modernity is far more translucent than first envisaged so providing the space for a resurgence of religious practice within modern societies, such that Christopher Partridge observes "There has been a confluence of disenchantment and enchantment."[37] This is the confluence where individuals continue to yearn for what lies beyond the horizon of the secular. Again, this is very evident within popular music culture, where many differing expressions of our need for spirituality are expressed. In what Partridge terms as the "sacralization of popular culture," he notes that for many, popular culture "is increasingly the only space where existentially meaningful commitments can take shape."[38]

32. Church of England, *Statistics for Mission*, 3–13.
33. Warner, *Secularisation and Its Discontents*, 60.
34. Woodhead, "Rise of 'No Religion,'" 252.
35. Pollack, "Varieties of Secularization Theories," 61.
36. Davie et al., "Secularism and Secularization," 604.
37. Partridge, "Occulture and Everyday Enchantment," 327.
38. Partridge, *Morality and Music*, 139–41.

We will consider how aspects of popular music culture enable liquid moderns to express spiritual longing in the following chapter, but for now we can note examples such as the level of immanent spiritual resourcing gained from a fan's devotion to a group—not that such devotion should be confused with religious observance,[39] or in the feelings experienced within the EDM scene when a rave "goes off,"[40] providing a group transcendent-like experience. The pursuit of such experiences of effervescence and communitas, often described in the scene as connectedness, has left some to raise the question as to whether EDM should be considered as a new religious movement.[41]

To return to the secularization theory, Brown, Davie and Warner,[42] amongst others, have drawn attention to its evolving nature with, for example, Karel Dobbelaere providing a more nuanced secularization model with three particular foci. Dobbelaere firstly notes that the measurement of decline in church attendance simply charts individual involvement in religious organizations and not in how either a society understands its relation to the religious or how a religious organization seeks to evolve in response to how society itself has changed.[43] Next, he notes how functional differentiation, that is the growing professionalization of differing roles within society such as medicine and academia, have helped individuals to inadvertently move away from the influence of the Church, the historic provider of these services. Alongside that, he notes that there are those societies which maintain clear policies which seek to limit the power of religious discourse, such as countries living under communism, where such narratives retain their robustness. We are also arguing, here, that liquid modern ideology prevents many from pursuing what may lie beyond the horizon of the lifeworld.

Of particular note is Dobbelaere's argument that this affects what Peter Berger has described as 'the sacred canopy,' which helped to hold social norms and boundaries firmly in place.[44] These changes reflect what Dobbelaere terms a societal level of secularization. Thirdly, there is what he identifies as organizational secularization reflecting how an organization such as the Church absorbs secular values in response to its changing

---

39. Partridge, *Morality and Music*, 140. See also McCloud, "Popular Culture Fandoms," 188.

40. Fritz, *Rave Culture*, 179.

41. E.g., Olaveson, "Connectedness and Rave experience," 85; Gauthier, "Rapturous Ruptures," 65.

42. Brown, *Death of Christian Britain*; Davie et al., "Secularism and Secularization"; Warner, *Secularisation and Its Discontents*.

43. Dobbelaere, *Secularization*, 18.

44. Dobbelaere, *Secularization*, 20; Berger, *The Sacred Canopy*.

situation.[45] What Dobbelaere is seeking to emphasize is that secularization is not a deterministic venture, but, following Berger, rather one that becomes contextualized by the relationship between secularization at individual, societal and organizational levels.

Bruce recognizes that his paradigm places him at odds with other commentators[46] and while he empathizes with those who seek to study the evolvement of religious narratives, even latent religiosity, he is concerned that such views "inflate the numbers of the unconventionally religious."[47] Bruce views his paradigm as having taken into account issues such as those highlighted by Dobbelaere: the failure of New Age narratives to replace the Christian narrative,[48] or the increase in the attendance of charismatic style churches. For Bruce, such differentiation is still a result of secularization and the end result will be ambivalence.[49]

Bruce's views are informed by his observations of capitalism[50] and his definition of religion, along with negative views towards institutionalism.[51] Yet, if we consider Bauman's reflections on the fluid nature of society we can note that individuals in general are not committing themselves to the authority of any institutional structure for fear that the institution's narratives will not provide a sense of long-term happiness[52] or that they may restrict a feeling of autonomy.[53] Thus, Bauman's thinking emphasizes that it is not just the societal bond of religious narratives that have become fluid in nature, but all forms of institution that have historically provided a sense of societal bond have become fluid, so helping to underline that a more flexible approach to secularization, such as Dobbelaere's, is needed to explain its effects.

The point here is that there are many social forces at work which facilitate the progress of secularism, while the need to express religious belief within liquid modernity is still very present. To begin to see how the complexities of the secularization debate are reflected in popular music we can, at this point, introduce the Black Eyed Peas' song 'Where Is the Love?' (co-written with Justin Timberlake), which was written in 2003 and subsequently re-released in 2016. To follow Brian Longhurst and Danojela

---

45. Dobbelaere, *Secularization*, 26.
46. Bruce, *God Is Dead*, 186.
47. Bruce, *God Is Dead*, 203.
48. Bruce, *God Is Dead*, 137.
49. Bruce, *God Is Dead*, 176.
50. Bruce, *God Is Dead*.
51. Bruce, *God Is Dead*, 2.
52. Bauman, *The Individualized Society*, 153.
53. Bauman, *Community*, 4.

Bogdanovic's comments on the need for the musicological study of popular music to be updated, we will again consider the semiology of the music video alongside content analysis of the lyrics.[54] Such a song can be considered as Rupert Till's "the sacred popular,"[55] or, in a more nuanced manner, what Steven Thomsen, Quint Randle, and Matthew Lewis term as "secular hymns." The latter provide "a form of self-reflection, healing, redemption, deliverance, and temporal salvation. The meanings of these songs become a highly individualistic and nuanced experience that is less dependent on cognitive content than on the combined aesthetic effects of personal need, setting, context, aural quality, and emotion."[56]

Therefore, as a social commentary,[57] listeners connect with the song as it resonates with their own feelings. Tia DeNora notes how "The song is you."[58] Likewise, Ulrik Volgsten argues:

> Music, when it functions socially, acts as a mediator of social relations. The listener becomes a "friend" (or "enemy") with the music and, by extension, with others. The ideological dimension appears when we consider the specific contents of the discourses that are affectively articulated through musical sound. The contents of these discourses are either accepted or rejected by the listeners' belief systems, and so they logically sanction certain kinds of action at the expense of others.[59]

The 2003 version of 'Where Is the Love?' was written as a response to the events of 9/11 which all but calls for a withdrawal of the United States army from Iraq. It also comments on what the group saw as American government hypocrisy, gang crime and racial intolerance. In the context of 9/11 and against the background of secularization, 'Where Is the Love?' could be interpreted as a song critical of religious belief. Yet Will.i.am, the lead singer, commented that following the attack on America, "My grandma said a prayer, and said that we shouldn't stay at home afraid when you're being called on to do as much healing as you can with the gift that was given to us."[60]

54. Longhurst and Bogdanovic, *Popular Music and Society*, 159. Also Tagg, "Analyzing Popular Music," 74; Middleton, "Popular Music Analysis," 104; Machin, *Analyzing Popular Music*.
55. Till, *Pop Cult*, 172.
56. Thomsen at al., "Pop Music," 147.
57. E.g., Machin, *Analyzing Popular Music*, 78.
58. DeNora, *Music in Everyday Life*, 56.
59. Volgsten, "Between Ideology and Identity," 76.
60. "Where Is the Love?"

CHRISTIAN BELIEF AND SECULARIZATION   99

This does not give the song a primarily religious meaning. Yet, by acknowledging his grandmother's comment within the context of his songwriting song Will-i-am points to the lyrical content as holding spiritual capital, indeed, as argued by Clive Marsh and Vaughan Roberts expressing something of people's ritual needs.[61] While many view the West as being predominantly secularized,[62] in the prevalent discourse schema that society holds to, religious sentiment is not simply abandoned.[63] The lyric begins with the invocation of God as Father, of the person invoking God's name seeking divine help in answering the question as to why such act of terror could be completed.

The video draws attention to this plea through the band 'tagging' many surfaces with a stylized '?' as they journey through east Los Angeles, rhetorically asking "Where Is the Love?" (Fig. 13). While this does not represent an overly positive view on religion it is not employing a mocking use of language. Rather, it is asking the question 'why are you not acting, God?' which is to raise a different theological issue: that of a lack of a cogent theodicy rather than of the song expressing a secularized disbelief in God.

Figure 13. Black Eyed Peas, 'Where Is the Love?'

The lyrical content of the song represents more than simply sentiment, suggesting that popular culture still holds a voice about religious discourses which is more than Bruce's ambivalence: it is seeking to challenge religious

61. Marsh and Roberts, *Personal Jesus*, 9.
62. E.g., Bruce, *God Is Dead*; Brown, *The Death of Christian Britain*.
63. E.g., Bossius et al., "Introduction," 7.

views, that there may well be something of the Divine that we need to be accountable to, yet, more than that, the song calls for such narratives to be more thoughtful and refined. While one could argue that the diminishment of religious narrative is the result of secularization, it can also be argued that this is popular culture asking for religious thinking to develop rather than to be secularized. We will return below to the 2016 re-release of this song, to see how its developed lyric further reflects how views on spirituality and religion are evolving.

3. From the Postsecular to the 'Rise of the Nones'

As Habermas points out, while traditional church attendance has shown a marked decline in Europe (as well as Australia and Canada), attitudes towards religious behavior have not markedly changed. In recognizing the controversial nature of his term 'postsecular,' Habermas asserts the following:

> My impression is that the data collected globally still provides surprisingly robust support for the defenders of the secularization thesis. In my view the weakness of the theory of secularization is due rather to rash inferences that betray an imprecise use of the concepts of "secularization" and "modernization." What is true is that in the course of the differentiation of functional social systems, churches and religious communities increasingly confined themselves to their core function of pastoral care and had to renounce their competencies in other areas of society. At the same time, the practice of faith also withdrew into more a personal or subjective domain. There is a correlation between the functional specification of the religious system and the individualization of religious practice.[64]

It's been argued that church attendance is maintained by those simply holding to the tradition, as part of a Western 'habitus.' Such a conclusion is aired by Warner who, like Bruce, asserts that without socialization into a religious discourse, religion in its present form will fade within a generation or two.[65] However, Habermas' rationale is that postsecular countries are pursuing a *sonderweg*, in that, globally, he sees a "resurgence of religion" evidenced through missionary expansion and fundamentalist radicalization.[66] This is not to suggest that Habermas is wishing to promote religion.

64. Habermas, "Secularism's Crisis of Faith," 19.
65. Warner, *Secularisation and Its Discontents*, 51.
66. Habermas, "Secularism's Crisis of Faith," 18. See also Abraham, "Postsecular

What is it about the predominantly European situation that is so different to the wider world? For Davie, the roots of the European *sonderweg* may be found within the schema of Christendom. She asserts that "these shared legacies go back as far as Constantine," and, as such, "they are deeply embedded in the psyche."[67] Bruce specifically critiques Davie's view.[68] However, where there were once feelings of control and authoritarian abuse, Davie describes a sense of detachment from the structures of the Church that enables individuals to "believe without belonging" (2002, 10).

As the hegemony of Christendom waned, so capitalism could abound. If liberal pluralism ideologically leads individuals to a point of ambivalence towards religious narratives, then it is plausible that individuals will remain receptive to a point where the hegemonic boundary of ambivalence sets in. Indeed, Davie concludes that individuals are not less religious, but rather that they are less able to believe. Her assessment suggests that there has been a long, ongoing sedimentation of feelings *against* Christendom's legacy. It is fair to say that as an abandoned hegemony, the discourse that once maintained the Church's political and cultural power will be viewed less than positively. History is written from the point of view of the victor.

Yet, against this *sonderweg* and deepening subjectivization, Woodhead's research into the rise of the none religious shows that many individuals still see themselves as being spiritual, albeit that this is not necessarily the same as holding a traditional understanding of transcendent religion. In analyzing the increasing numbers of those who complete questionnaires as holding "no religion" rather than describing themselves as Christian (Fig. 14), she notes, too, that to identify one's self as a 'none' is not to necessarily identify as being secular.[69] Atheists hold an older age profile than that of the emerging 'nones,' while atheism has not increased to the same degree as the increase of the 'nones.' From this she deduces that, overall, "a typical none is younger, white, British-born, liberal about personal life and morals, varied in political commitment but cosmopolitan in outlook, suspicious of organized religion but not necessarily atheist, and unwilling to be labelled as religious or to identify with a religious group."[70]

Punk," 95.

67. Davie, *Europe*, 2.
68. Bruce, *God Is Dead*, 71.
69. See also Lynch, "Role of Popular Music," 481.
70. Woodhead, "Rise of 'No Religion,'" 250–52.

Table 2. 'No religion' and religion by age.

Age cohort	'No religion' (%)	Christian (%)	Other religion (including those who prefer not to state their religion) (%)	'No religion' as per cent of the population (excluding Other religion) (%)
18–24	60	27	13	69
25–39	55	32	13	63
Under-40s aggregated	56	31	13	65
40–59	45	46	7	49
60+	34	60	5	36
Over-40s aggregated	40	54	6	43
TOTAL	46	44	10	51

Source: Linda Woodhead/YouGov December 2015

Figure 14. Woodhead, 'No Religion' and Religion by Age[71]

This, again, reflects Bauman's arguments that individuals are fearful of committing to a particular identity out of fear that it may not provide the hoped for security. Indeed, the 'rise of the nones' epitomizes liquid modernity, as reflected in Bauman's later views that, "agnosticism (the kind that I . . . adhere to) is not the antithesis of religion or even of the Church. It is the antithesis of monotheism and a closed Church."[72] An outcome of this is that the 'rise of the nones' again undermines "simplistic accounts of secularization that imagined all countries propelled to the same secular destination point by the irresistible forces of modernization." That said, Woodhead does include a health warning, that in her view, "the current fashion for dismissing such theories is overdone; the best of them can still shed light if not on universal trends at least on particular cases, like the rise of 'no religion' in Britain."[73]

By drawing on Berger's recent thinking she notes how pluralistic cultures make it more common for religious belief to be questioned, so making it harder for belief to be passed on to the next generation. However, she does affirm that "This does not necessarily lead to religious decline, but it places new pressures on religious institutions, which can no longer depend upon affiliation by default or religious identity by ascription rather than choice."[74] The lack of socialization is understandable if one accepts that the ideology of liberal pluralism together with distrust in religious institutions interpolates individuals away from the Christian discourse. We have noted Brown's work, which indicates that popular musical cultures had a significant impact on Christian hegemony and, therefore, the erosion of Christendom. Yet, as

---

71. Woodhead, "Rise of No Religion," 246.
72. Bauman and Obirek, *Of God and Man*, 2.
73. Woodhead, "Rise of 'No Religion,'" 254.
74. Woodhead, "Rise of 'No Religion,'" 254.

already mentioned, popular music also gives expression to alternative spiritual identities,[75] such as expressed in 'Nirvana' by The Icicle Works (1982).

We can also see a developing need to express liberal values by considering some of the values held within the EDM scene. Within its short history the scene sought to encourage the development of a counterculture based on the values of peace, love, unity and respect, described by the early scene's use of the acronym PLUR.[76] Perhaps more significantly, the scene is recognized as playing a central role in breaking down barriers affecting gender, ethnicity and sexuality within wider society, reinforcing significant values which liquid moderns value today.[77] Our cultural consumption gives insight to what we hold as sacred.

Woodhead is keen to emphasize the point that increases in human rights legislation and equality legislation has meant that "pluralism de facto has been reinforced by pluralism de jure."[78] The right to pluralism has become legally enshrined. This is of interest as it reinforces pluralization as a key value to be ascribed to. Indeed, she sees the pursuit of political liberalism as being particularly marked in Britain: "there is actually a massive moral consensus about the importance of individual freedom of choice, with the overwhelming majority of British people (about 90 percent), both religious and non-religious, affirming ethical liberalism."[79]

This has become a key ideological value of our day within which the subjectivized self can comfortably reside. Yet Woodhead concludes that, whereas society is typically liberal the institution of the Church has sought to reinforce anti-liberal values.[80] Indeed the Church has sought to strengthen its process of legitimation, as evidenced by its debates over women in leadership and sexual ethics. In other words, it still hankers for the Christendom past, when it held political and cultural power, while it struggles to make sense of how the story may be told within liquid modernity.

Woodhead's conclusions have become accentuated in subsequent research, such that the 2016 British Social Attitudes survey notes that 53 percent of British people say they hold no religion—an increase of 5 percent in just a year. This is most marked in the views of young people when, in 2016, seven out of ten respondents (71 percent) aged between eighteen and

---

75. Lynch, "Role of Popular Music," 482.

76. E.g., Fritz, *Rave Culture*, 3; Sylvan, *Trance Formation*, 26; John, *Tecnomad*, 169.

77. E.g., John, "Electronic Dance Music," 279; John, "The Difference Engine," 21; Till, *Pop Cult*, 57.

78. Woodhead, "Rise of 'No Religion,'" 255.

79. Woodhead, "Rise of 'No Religion,'" 256.

80. Woodhead, "Rise of 'No Religion,'" 257.

twenty-four responded that they followed no religion, significantly up from 62 percent in 2015.[81]

The Church may hold a level of success in reaching out to those individuals who hold a late modern worldview, appreciative of dualistic understandings of the world, primarily through charismatic styled churches. Yet, unless it can recognize how best to communicate its discourse to those of a liquid modern disposition who appreciate broader ontological expressions of belief, it will struggle to see much improvement in the number of people socialized into Christian belief. This is not to decry those approaches, rather to make the point that a broader approach to the issues raised by liquid modernity and the 'rise of the nones' needs to be taken.

Pete Ward notes the tension between these two approaches by noting that since the 1950s a reduced Christian discourse focusing on doctrines of creation, the fall (i.e., the effects of sin), the need for repentance and the soteriological outcome of heaven and hell has become prominent.[82] Ward notes that "such developments are not deliberate or intended, but they have come about because of the fluid movement of culture and the lived culture,"[83] that is, the result of the post-Enlightenment church's ongoing struggle to be heard. Significantly, this reduced discourse favors epistemological over ontological outcomes, which are promulgated effectively through courses such as Alpha and Christianity Explored. James Smith is suspicious of such a pedagogical system which "belie an understanding of Christian faith that is dualistic and thus reductionistic: It reduces Christian faith primarily to a set of ideas, principles, claims, and propositions that are known and believed. The goal of all this is 'correct thinking.'"[84]

The outworking of this for Smith is that belief becomes "a matter of getting the right ideas and doctrines and beliefs into your head in order to guarantee proper behavior" over that of "being the kind of person who loves rightly—who loves God and neighbor and is oriented to the world by the primacy of that love."[85] This becomes that stark difference between being governed by an epistemologically governed discourse and one which is primarily about encountering ontological reality. Smith poetically contends that it is not possible to routinely swing from one approach to another: "Instead, we adopt the pedagogies of rational modernity and drop Christian

---

81. "British Social Attitudes."
82. E.g., Ward, *Liquid Ecclesiology*, 66.
83. Ward, *Liquid Ecclesiology*, 66.
84. Smith, *Desiring the Kingdom*, 32.
85. Smith, *Desiring the Kingdom*, 32.

ideas into the machine. But that's a bit like taking a pizza crust, putting kidney and mushy peas on top and then describing it as British cuisine."[86]

The Church overly favors epistemological forms of communication and learning meaning, partly because there is some success in drawing people towards Charismatic and Evangelical strands of belief. Yet, those who are searching for more ontologically driven answers, such as expressed in Bauman's later feelings towards religious language[87] or those voiced within popular culture, are using a different language to express their needs.

James Landau captures the essence of this in noting how music which triggers an ecstatic response, such as found in EDM, highlights "a transgressive relationship to binary thought. . . . For in dissolving the mind's organizational dualisms, including, most profoundly, that of the self/Other dichotomy, ecstatic raving is an 'experience' discursively dominated by recurring motifs of unity, holism and interconnectedness. In the crucible of the rave, barriers are said to disintegrate as once disparate entities overlap and intermingle."[88]

Here, we can note a contrast between those needing knowledge, episteme, in response to their existential angsts and those who need, literally, to feel an answer to their quest for understanding. Kutter Callaway draws on this in noting the effect of film music on individuals, in particular its emotional quotient in causing transcendent feelings, while theological reflection is focused on "the tidiness of abstract theological conceptualizations."[89]

Generally speaking, the Church is not responding to this difference for fear that its discourse would be seen to become weakened. The perceived need for the institution to keep continuity with how it dealt with its Enlightenment battles is simply too great. Yet, as modernity is increasingly left behind, the Church finds itself still seeking to make sense of how it engaged with its enlightenment past, neglecting how it may help society make sense of the future. These two fundamentally different 'languages' will affect outcomes of how individuals become socialized into the Church's discourses. Hence, if this thesis is right, it is sadly a limited strategic plan to focus so strongly on epistemological methods of evangelism.

As Woodhead has shown, liquid modernity is witnessing the 'rise of the nones,' meaning that increasingly, individuals are being drawn away from hard and fast understandings of religious belief, albeit that they still

---

86. Smith, *Desiring the Kingdom*, 33.
87. E.g., Bauman and Obirek, *Of God and Man*, 2.
88. Landau, "The Flesh of Raving," 107.
89. Callaway, *Scoring Transcendence*, 4.

hold a desire to resource the spiritual self.[90] A significant question, which frames what follows, is how can the Christian story be best told in an environment that is suspicious of epistemologically driven evangelism? We can begin to find some answers to this question in looking at how religious narratives and images are being portrayed within popular music.

4. Religious Narratives and Imagery in Popular Music

Some utilization of religious symbolism in popular culture will simply be because it has been there for a long time, it has become sedimented and no religious connection will be made. Yet, the majority of usage will reflect a religious connotation, positive and negative and of wanting to make more sense of that which may lie 'beneath the surface.' This can be viewed as Certeau's tactical expression of resistance to a society that struggles to speak openly about its hopes and fears for religious and spiritual belief, yet seeks, still, to make sense of that which cannot be seen or epistemologically proved. We will look at three popular music songs that are not dismissive of Christian belief, rather they reflect our developing religious and spiritual scene, offering a fair critique of institutionalized belief while still being open to encounters with the divine.

One can see the evolvement of subjectivized belief in the 2016 re-release of the Black Eyed Peas' 'Where Is the Love?' The song was re-released following a series of terrorist attacks in Europe and in America, alongside tensions in race relations specifically in America with the title of '#WhereIsTheLove' to help differentiate it from the earlier version. In commenting on what Will.i.am viewed as public fatigue over these issues,[91] he recounts how the song was re-released by popular demand.[92] In other words the song resonated with popular sentiment expressed lyrically and semiotically,[93] rather than being listened to by just fans of the Black Eyed Peas.

Again, in being sung by a variety of leading American vocalists the song has wider social ownership. As much as America is understood to hold a differing religiosity to that of Europe, Woodhead's recent research suggests the United States is beginning to reflect European understandings of belief,[94] meaning that, while this song was primarily released in America, the outcomes of this song will reflect Western Europe as well. Indeed, even

90. Woodhead, "Rise of 'No Religion,'" 250.
91. "Black Eyed Peas Remake."
92. "Where Is the Love?"
93. Machin, *Analyzing Popular Music*, 77, 98.
94. Woodhead, "Rise of 'No Religion,'" 253.

the years after its re-release, the YouTube page continues to act as a center for expressing hopes and fears following further terrorist attacks, including the New Zealand attack of 2019.

The lyrical evolution in the 2016 version interestingly reflects the development in the subjectivization of belief since the song was first released, as well as echoing the nature of traditional forms of religious belief. The song focuses on the indiscriminate violence on children caught up in war zones and the video makes evocative use of imagery to convey its message. The video begins by using the '?' sign seen in the first video. The same question is again raised, that of why it is so challenging for one's actions echoing one's behavior, especially around religious themes of love. In the re-released video the image of a vicar is seen. Later in the video, as the words are reprised, an image of Muslims at prayer is shown. In both cases it is inferred that religion is a less than positive influence. These images, when placed against the way the accompanying lyric is sung, suggests a wider frustration with the institution of religion.

To again follow Philip Tagg's methodology, the discourse schema could, therefore, be viewed as humanistic, with its recurrent anti-discriminatory theme with lyrics which express how the pursuit of self-interest alone was unhelpful. Yet, there is also frustration expressed with a humanistic worldview alone, too, as the song asks why humanity is not more tolerant and loving towards one another. As the song and video inter-objectively develop so the acceptance of differing religious and spiritual viewpoints becomes aired positively.[95] In the video accompanying the song, images of a Jewish man, an Islamic woman and a black American serviceman are also viewed against the opening invocation for divine help.

Together, this semiotically expresses a positive need for religious and non-religious outlooks to be tolerant towards one another.[96] Pluralism is recognized as positive. Indeed, the recurring invocation for divine assistance, with, at one point in the video, the singer raising his eyes upward towards the heavens helps to express a wish that both immanent and transcendent approaches to spirituality and belief can be expressed (Fig. 15).

---

95. Tagg, *Analyzing Popular Music*, 10.
96. See Machin, *Analyzing Popular Music*, 99; Tagg, *Analyzing Popular Music*, 7.

Figure 15. Black Eyed Peas, '#WhereIsTheLove'

Towards the end of the song a rap celebrating the value of love is heard. While this could be viewed as a humanistic cry to love, the earlier lyrics show that the religious viewpoint still holds capital, indeed, a positive direct connection is made between love and God. Criticism is also expressed about consumerism and misuse of the media, challenging the hegemony of liberal pluralism with its pervading ambivalence towards religious discourse.

There is a long history of anti-war protest songs, yet the Black Eyed Peas song is more than that. Rather, the song reflects a number of subjectivized and postsecular viewpoints. It expresses what Slavoj Žižek has termed "symbolic reality."[97] The song acts as resistance to the hegemony of consumerism, yet also express a variety of spiritual and religious beliefs.

While an older song, The Verve's 'Bittersweet Symphony' (1998; Fig. 16) provides a useful example of a musical commentary on engagement with religious practice *and* the power of consumerism. While the song expresses a restlessness towards life, it also expresses our inability to escape consumerism's influence. The song makes reference to religious practice as a forlorn hope using the imagery of prayer which the singer feels is a futile act, but such is his desperation for resolution to his restlessness that he is still wanting to be prayerful. This is the language of wanting freedom from consumerism's ideological hold but not knowing how that may be attained. The Verve's prayer remained unanswered, yet, that the language of intercession is utilized at all gives rise to the opportunity that prayer could be of use.

97. Žižek, *Looking Awry*, 32.

Figure 16. The Verve, 'Bittersweet Symphony'

The song is a tactical expression of resistance to the strategy of consumerism. The Verve's song certainly reflects Bruce's sentiments around the values of advanced capitalism. Yet, that religious praxis is referenced at all does mean that within liquid modernity it must hold some level of cultural capital. The language of the lyric does not mock prayer, rather it conveys desperation and of wanting to draw from traditional schemas, such as hope in a transcendent divine encounter, to find respite from a problem. If the language regarding prayerful praxis held no cultural relevance it would not be used. In other words, these are song lyrics expressing an honest wrestling with issues that, for many, remain hidden.

A third song worth mentioning here is Hozier's 'Take Me to Church' (2014), in that it speaks into the complexity of institutions. He describes his song in terms of a comment on the institutional response to sex: "But an organization like the church, say, through its doctrine, would undermine humanity by successfully teaching shame about sexual orientation—that it is sinful, or that it offends God."[98]

However, he states his song is not anti-faith, but rather that it is a reflection on the power of the institution to hail an ideological response. Here, rather than being an issue of ambivalence, religious belief is viewed as acceptable. His concern over the negative influence of powerful institutions in

98. Shepherd, "Q&A."

general becomes further reinforced in that the video to the song focuses not on religion, as the song title might suggest, rather, it focuses, instead, on the institutional abuse of homophobia in Russia. Hozier's lyric may be using the language of church metaphorically to explore institutional abuse, yet, he is clear that this should not be seen as being critical of religious belief.

5. Concluding Comment

As Bauman has noted, the traditional Western source for resourcing ontological security may have become side-lined. Yet, as an act of resistance against feelings of restlessness, narratives and images relating to the Christian tradition are clearly still used within popular culture, again echoing his later developed thinking. Indeed, rather than seeing great antipathy towards the use of religious symbolism, one sees that their use is not mocking. It may be critical, but it can also be respectful and connects with those who listen to such music. It can ask profound questions about belief, such as those asked by The Black Eyed Peas, to raising concerns about institutional abuses while still remaining open to the possibility of belief, such as seen in Hozier's 'Take Me to Church.'

This, perhaps, captures the zeitgeist: in the face of restless society, deep spiritual searching to counter such internal disquiet is much needed. This is a pursuit for ontological reality, more critically looking at what is considered to reflect reality. Again, such cultural expression is reflecting something of Woodhead's 'the rise of the nones,' which does not favor secularization, rather a society which is liberal and pluralistic: subjectivized rather than simply secularized. As she observes, pluralism de jure is firmly our cultural soil and we should expect to see more of such imagery and narrative be expressed in popular musical form.

Four significant conclusions can, therefore, be noted thus far. (1) That popular music can be utilized as a theological resource, a barometer to look as aspects of our society, especially in how it views spirituality and religion. (2) In particular, our consumption of popular music highlights Bauman's observations that ontological dissonance is part of living within liquid modernity. (3) That there is a divergence between the Church's preferred evangelistic stance, which is epistemologically driven, and the need expressed within popular culture to express concerns more generally and in a manner which is more ontological in nature. Individuals do not simply want facts, they need a sense of emotional connection. This is the difference between understanding more of what it means to be human, in this case, in relation to the divine than simply accepting epistemologically governed dogma about how that relationship should function. (4) Despite being viewed as a liberal pluralistic culture, our sociological engagement shows how key Enlightenment values around dualism and making sense of our emotions still affect how many view the Church. This is significant as it is also a barrier that the institution of the Church must tactically respond to if its discourses are to be more widely appreciated.

To help see how the Church may tactically respond to this challenge we will first look at the functional attributes of a song: its lyric, how it is discussed and how we may then act as a result. We will then reflect this into our story telling of the Christian discourse to see how popular music can inform our telling of the Christian story today.

4

Lyrical Content, Transcendence, and Shalom

IN ORDER FOR US to communicate effectively with one another there does need to be similarity in what Zygmunt Bauman and Rein Raud describe as our respective "interiorities." In conversation with Bauman, Raud describes interiority as "not an 'inner self'—it might rather be conceived as the space within which 'self' happens, as a process."[1] The self, they assert, is formed through our interiority rubbing alongside other peoples' worlds.[2] This will involve both our verbal and physical engagement with one another and what we draw from such activity.

Carl Barat and Pete Doherty of The Libertines express the rubbing alongside of their respective worlds in the song 'Can't stand me now' (2003). This biographical song expresses the relationship between band members which eventually led to the group's breakup. Barat initially expresses how he felt that Doherty was responsible for the group's breakup. In response, Doherty tells of how the group's behavior towards him led to his much reported use of heroin. Yet, what they could agree on and sing about publicly in this display of the group's 'inner life' was it was very challenging to be together!

Such a description of interiority will also inform our understanding and use of affective space, which we will subsequently see, can be a central aspect to communicating the Christian story today (see next chapter). Barat

---

1. Bauman and Raud, *Practices of Selfhood*, 36.
2. Bauman and Raud, *Practices of Selfhood*, 39–40.

and Doherty's clashing would have been felt by both of them, in some way re-lived each time the song was sung. It would have affected them. In speaking of affective states, Jonathan Baylin and Daniel Hughes define *affect* as "the bodily expression of our emotional state."[3] What we feel has something to say about our understanding of events. It is felt knowledge.

In noting the geographical and artistic attributes of affective space, Derek McCormack observes how different people can make use of the same space and draw different experiences from it. He cites an example of three adjacent rooms which face onto a corridor. When the occupants find their way to their rooms they can make use of their own space. However, the corridor is not only a shared space, but the experience of passing through it, the atmosphere of it, alongside whatever is encountered there, will affect what the three occupants eventually take into their rooms.[4]

McCormack's corridor is an analogy for affective space. Fans still watch the official YouTube video of 'Can't stand me now,' leaving positive comments such as reliving their youth. As they watch, they form an affective space which allows them to recall positive feelings. The viewing experience, perhaps rekindling images of fashion, of going to concerts, buying merchandise all cause emotional affects, all influence how these fans are shaping their lives now.[5] This chapter focuses on what we may draw from our use of popular music and 'bring' into our affective space to order aspects to our lives or bring meaning to them.

We can, for example, draw from our understanding of a song's lyric (i.e., content analysis) or any semiology connected with a musical piece, such as contained in a video. We may appreciate why we purchase merchandise related to a song or consider the salience of why a group's iconography works.[6] It could be we consider how a song helps us to express key life moments such as loss and bereavement.[7] In this way, we can also say that how we use popular music can express something of our ritual needs.[8] Philip Tagg also notes how popular music can be "used for crosschecking analytical hypotheses and for putting the whole analysis in its sociological and

---

3. Baylin and Hughes, *Neurobiology of Attachment-Focused Therapy*, 118.

4. McCormack, *Refrains for Moving Bodies*, 22.

5. See also Shuker, *Understanding Popular Music Culture*, 8; Longhurst and Bogdanovic, *Popular Music and Society*, 9; Tagg, *Analyzing Popular Music*, 6.

6. Machin, *Analyzing Popular Music*, 48.

7. E.g., Partridge, *Mortality & Music*; Marsh and Roberts, *Personal Jesus*, 92.

8. Marsh and Roberts, *Personal Jesus*, 9; see also Regev, *Pop-Rock Music*, 124.

psychological perspectives."⁹ This is the process that Callum Brown undertook in his work (See chapter 3).¹⁰

Our musical consumption can also help reveal what we feel to be sacred. Here, sacred does not refer to what is normally seen as religious or supernatural, rather it concerns that which individuals "'set apart' from everyday life in some absolute sense."¹¹ Indeed, Gordon Lynch draws a helpful differentiation between a "sociology of religion" and a "sociology of the sacred,"¹² showing how our understanding of the sacred ought to be contextualized.¹³ While Lynch does express reservations about traditional understandings of ontology, which "transcends signification," he argues that "the crucial distinction here is between the claim that there is an actual ontological referent for sacred forms, and the idea that sacred forms constitute *what people take* to be absolute realities that have claims over their lives."¹⁴ Therefore, within one's personal *lifeworld*, the popular music we connect with holds the potential to say something about what we say holds absolute reality. As he asserts, "the sacred is a communicative structure focused on absolute realities around which the meanings of social life are constituted and that exert normative claims on the conduct of social life."¹⁵

With this as our backdrop, the first part of the chapter will (1) consider how our discursive engagement with a song further shows how liquid moderns are making sense of their need for ontological security. We will look in particular at how some popular music songwriters and fans are exploring feelings of transcendence as a way of expressing connection with the divine (to be explored below). The second part of the chapter will (2) provide a theological response as to how this may help us to tell the Christian story today, for which we will draw on the work of Paul Tillich. The final section of the chapter will (3) ask the question whether these functional attributes of popular music can help (re)enchant someone into religious belief, concluding with five practical points that will be of assistance in helping us to tell the Christian story within liquid modernity.

---

9. Tagg, *Analyzing Popular Music*, 6.
10. Brown, *Death of Christian Britain*.
11. Partridge, *The Lyre of Orpheus*, 4; see also Lynch, *Sacred in the Modern World*.
12. Lynch, *Sacred in the Modern World*, 5.
13. Lynch, *Sacred in the Modern World*, 15.
14. Lynch, *Sacred in the Modern World*, 15.
15. Lynch, *Sacred in the Modern World*, 133.

1. Security and Ultimate Concern in Song

Stuart Hoover comments that religion and media, which will include popular music, "occupy the same spaces, serve many of the same purposes and invigorate the same practices in late modernity."[16] This is to capture both the way we may heuristically engage with popular music to overtly express our sentiments towards spiritually and religion, as well as how our use of non-religious music can help fulfil some of the social functions that religious activity once performed in the past. As William Dyrness notes, "While [society] may have given up the formal institution of religion, none have given up the satisfactions that religion has traditionally supplied: all of them have found activities that they enjoy and that give them a sense of fulfilment. Furthermore, their regular practices have given a kind of ritual structure to their lives that gives them strength and offers them meaning."[17]

Similarly, Clive Marsh and Vaughan Roberts' research into our use of popular music has concluded that "while music use cannot be referred to as religious, a religion or a form of spirituality in any direct or simplistic sense, there is evidence of the seriousness and intensity with which listeners make use of their listening practices in the activity of meaning-making."[18]

This could, as mentioned, include 'religiously' buying merchandise related to an artist, or devotedly searching for information on social media. It could be that a particular lyric, such as found in Peter Gabriel's protest song 'Biko,' draws together a group of people for a reason that extends beyond simply enjoying the song. In a similar fashion, Ian Peddie notes how the presence of heavy metal music in the Middle East and North Africa "attest to the deep sense of discontent that pervades the Zeitgeist of youth in the Middle East, they also indicated the lengths to which people will go to in order to express protest."[19] Here, individuals are expressing ultimate concern by engaging with music that profanely crosses a cultural sacred divide.

Such performances can also cause a sense of collective effervescence between those listening to the performance, drawing the group together in a way that particularly reinforces the bond between them. A further example could be the ritual activity that a singer or DJ leads the audience in may mimic the interaction between a vicar leading a congregation in certain liturgical actions, such as crossing one's self at particular points of a service.

---

16. Hoover, *Religion in Media Age*, 9.
17. Dyrness, *Poetic Theology*, 4.
18. Marsh and Roberts, "Listening as Religious Practice (Part Two)," 291.
19. Peddie, "Music," 36.

It can also lead to liminal experiences with music, which we will consider in the following chapter.

We can specifically consider how the lyrical content of a song helps someone to engage with society. We could do this from several angles. We may consider a lyric for what it may say about a particular group or performer, such as views held or particular practices enacted (e.g., Madonna and her use of Kabbalah). We could also think of the discursive conversation that occurs verbally or virtually between likeminded fans which will say something about how a song, a group or artist has helped them to function socially. Such conversation enabled participants of the early EDM scene, with its overt political leanings, to sonically and aesthetically challenge hegemony through what Graham St John termed as "secret sonic societies."[20] Conversations could, though, be more mundane in nature, as seen in comments placed on websites and social media as fans discuss how particular songs make them feel.

A song need not hold overt religious language to express ontological longings. Rather it can simply help us to function in a religious-like manner through which we may gain feelings of security that would once have been found through religious practice. Here, music can help us to express our ongoing need for spirituality, either as an immanent resourcing of the self or felt as transcendent encounter. This opens up opportunity for non-religious popular music to act as a looking-glass into society's ongoing religious and spiritual expectations.[21]

For example, by drawing on how both religious and non-religious individuals make use of popular music, Marsh and Roberts' have mapped four axis along which we use popular music, framing this with theological language to help highlight how we may draw meaning from our musical engagement. For example, a song such as Robbie Williams' cover of 'Angels' (2005) can, as it builds be uplifting, maybe even offing a listener a sense of transcendence as the song builds, whereas Christina Aguilera's ballad 'Twice' (2018) with its opening lyric expressing her wonder about the purpose of life itself, is more relaxing in nature, restoring the immanent self. Music which may be joyful or provoke sadness can likewise elicit emotions which are religiousesque where one may use language such as ecstasy and reflectiveness. This enables Marsh and Roberts to speak of a "spirituality of

---

20. John, *Tecnomad*, 79. See also John *Global Tribe*, 26; John, "The Difference Engine," 22.

21. I.e., Marsh and Roberts, *Personal Jesus*, 4.

music," albeit they conclude "such a 'spirituality of music' falls considerably short of any structured belief system or 'theology.'"[22]

Similar comments have been made concerning the ritual activity we may complete when attending a cinema[23] or a sporting event.[24] Bauman has even drawn similar connections concerning our "pious and devout" use of the internet.[25] In the context of film Robert Johnston has argued that through the films we watch "non-Christian artists are the unconscious inheritors of Christian tradition."[26] However, the same reasoning should not be suggested when listening to popular music, although the argument here is that there will be many an instance when a moment of divine connection can still be experienced.

This, again, helps to highlight why popular music should be considered as a very practical theological resource. The very way we engage with it can shine light on our personhood and understandings of the world around us, including what we hold to be sacred, even of ultimate reality. We are using popular music, therefore, to help order our experience of the world around us, both that which is seen in the world as well as that which we may feel lies beyond the horizon of our personal lifeworld which is expressed through both our discursive engagement and inner self-talk.

In observing that we all belong to differing interpretative communities, Partridge notes how we become "shaped by various presuppositions that influence our expectations as to what meanings we might discover in a text." He also observes how "Constructions of the sacred (and the profane), those sacred forms around which people everyday lives are oriented, are organically woven into the process of reading."[27] In other words, the differing interpretative communities to which we belong help us to express the numerous religious and spiritual beliefs we carry.

As Raymond MacDonald, Dorothy Miell and Graeme Wilson conclude, "In talking about music, people are both signaling their membership of and also contributing to a 'community of reasoners'—a community of likeminded others."[28] We draw on the wider narratives which become attached to the music's transmission alongside its emotional effect (we will explore this in the next chapter). In this sense, to become involved in a musical

---

22. Marsh and Roberts, "Listening as Religious Practice (Part Two)," 305.
23. I.e., Lyden, *Film as Religion*; Ostwalt, *Secular Steeples*.
24. Hervieu-Léger, *Religion as a Chain of Memory*.
25. Bauman and Raud, *Practices of Selfhood*, 76.
26. Johnston, *Reel Spirituality*, 92.
27. Partridge, *Lyre of Orpheus*, 42.
28. MacDonald et al., "How Do People Communicate," 322.

community of whatever genre, be that as a listener or ardent fan, is to share something of your worldview with those around you.

Readymade interpretive communities that comment on songs and their lyrics are abundant on the internet. In what follows we will look at how fans have commented and interpreted the official videos of a selection of songs posted on the interpretive community called YouTube. This will help us to see how these fans are utilizing the song and video to help them make sense of the world around them.

(a) Understanding Transcendence

We will look at four songs which explore elements of a traditional understanding of us transcendently encountering the divine. As the differing functional components that have been highlighted begin to coalesce, we can find ourselves reacting to the music we listen to in deeper ways. From time to time we all experience uplifting feelings which make us feel as though we have transcended our sense of self (we will look specifically at the process of this in the following chapter), even encountering a sense of something far greater than who we feel we are. This can be both an individual experience as we listen to music alone, as well as corporate in nature, too.

We should also note a discussion around the ontology of music. Popular music can be both performed live as well as disseminated in differing formats. Theodore Gracyk notes the tradition of seeing a difference between a work/song and its performance, which can be heard in differing contexts in numerous ways. This can affect how a song's ontological nature is understood, producing what can be interpreted as "thicker" and "thinner" interpretations of a song.[29] Here, we are arguing that popular music that causes transcendent experience must be considered by the listener as a 'thicker,' authentic experience which holds agency.

A significant question to ask must be what such transcendent experiences mean? For some this will be interpreted as encountering the divine. Bauman notes that while every culture looks for a sense of transcendence there is an "astounding inventiveness" in those cultures whose

> 'main business' is to supply ever new, as yet untried and undiscredited variants of transcendence strategies and resuscitate ever anew the trust in the ongoing search despite the way explorers stumble from one disappointment to another frustration. The trade in life meanings is the most competitive of markets, but with the 'marginal utility' of the commodities on offer unlikely

29. Gracyk, "Aesthetics of Popular Music."

ever to shrink, the demand prompting competitive supply is unlikely to dry up.[30]

Within popular music, streaming services and the cultural omnivore theory can be seen to help supply a wide variety of new symbols encouraging possible transcendent experiences. To recall Rolls' work, such feelings of transcendence could simply be viewed as our emotional senses becoming over stimulated.[31] For Frank Burch Brown, whose focus is that of exploring religion and art, feelings of transcendence can be viewed in three ways. Firstly, that of radical transcendence, which "conveys, instead, a sense of God as the Holy Other and infinitely distant one whom we cannot approach, though that Other can approach us and paradoxically can accommodate our incapacity."[32]

Secondly, he views proximate transcendence, which "is sacramental, generating a sense of divine mystery and grace within and among and beyond things earthly and tangible."[33] This, he views, is the experience that may be felt in appreciating the mixture of beauty and mystery of a stained glass window. It is worth noting here that this is not a metaphysical appreciation of mystery, rather, that mystery is put in place by the watcher who fills out any narrative gaps that may be present. In other words, such feelings of transcendence become governed by whatever narrative is being appreciated by the listener at that point. Brown's third understanding of transcendence is that of an immanent transcendence, where "the sacred is altogether immersed in the ordinary."[34]

Charles Taylor is keen to plot a midway path between these understandings, noting that "The great invention of the West was that of an immanent order in Nature, whose working could be systematically understood and explained on its own terms, leaving open the question whether this whole order had a deeper significance, and whether, if it did, we should infer a transcendent Creator beyond it."[35] Yet, he also wants to affirm how such experiences can allow for both human-flourishing and opportunity for humanity to self-transcend towards the divine.[36]

Taylor's view is that while some who hold Christian belief would "think that the whole move to secular humanism was just a mistake, which

30. Bauman, *The Individualized Society*, 4.
31. Rolls, *Emotion and Decision-Making*, 540.
32. Brown, *Religious Aesthetics*, 120.
33. Brown, *Religious Aesthetics*, 120.
34. Brown, *Religious Aesthetics*, 120.
35. Taylor, *A Secular Age*, 15.
36. Taylor, *A Secular Age*, 44.

needs to be undone," he himself values aspects of how the Enlightenment focused on the primacy of human life. He rightly notes how "this gain was in fact unlikely to come about without some breach with established religion," yet, he does assert that "the metaphysical primacy of life espoused by exclusive humanism is wrong, stifling, and that its continued dominance puts in danger the practical primacy."[37]

Clearly, we cannot return to past understandings of the porous self, yet, there is something in Taylor's midway thinking which we should affirm. Such experiences may help us to flourish as individuals, while other experiences may allow us to be open to encountering the divine. Either way, such experiences help us to make sense of who we are as humans and should be recognized as a Kairos moment, a particularly significant moment in time which holds the potential to help us to understand our sense of self.[38] A moment loaded with learning potential.

Aware of Taylor's thinking, Marsh and Roberts conclude that "Whatever transcendence may be, it is vital that we recognize the importance of the emotional, aesthetic, ethical, and cognitive work that occurs in the affective spaces inhabited by contemporary Western citizens when listening to and experiencing popular music, and acknowledge what is being termed transcendence within that space. Where the activities and experiences described do seem to require the use of that term, we suggest, then we need to recognize, too, that the sense of being taken beyond oneself is an essential element in developing a full appreciation of what it means to be human."[39] In other words, such experiences are fed by other factors such as our aesthetical appreciation of both the song and the place where it is performed alongside how we cognitively make sense of these moments alongside others.

As Marsh and Roberts further note, "The tingle factor puts us in touch with that which we cannot quite identify, but which is vitally important for human life, and which is very much the subject of theology."[40] To recall Anne Blood and Robert Zatorre's work around the chills and 'shivers-down-the-spine,' such feelings can and should be linked to our need for safety and our understandings of ontological security.[41] In other words, transcendent experiences, however interpreted, should be considered ontological in nature, helping us to identify more of what it means to be human and to feel ontologically secure.

37. Taylor, *A Secular Age*, 637.
38. See, for example, Marcuse, *The Aesthetic Dimension*, 145.
39. Marsh and Roberts, *Personal Jesus*, 85.
40. Marsh and Roberts, *Personal Jesus*, 89.
41. Blood and Zatorre, "Intensely Pleasurable Responses."

What becomes the defining issue is the respondent's own understanding of the discourse which interprets such experiences—the interpretative community they are part of at that time.[42] For example, we can see the issue of interpretation in action in a piece of research completed by Gordon Lynch and Emily Badger. Their ethnographic research of thirty-seven Mainstream Clubbers considered whether such transcendent experiences encountered on the dancefloor could be considered as a religious experience. Only one person made overt connections between Mainstream EDMC and spirituality. Importantly, the lady concerned already held a Christian worldview.[43] This reflects Lynch's thinking about the sacred holding "*what people take* to be absolute realities that have claims over their lives."[44] A key thing to draw from this is the learning opportunity about our sense of self that can be drawn from such moments.

(b) Singing about Transcendence

We can see elements of these differing views on transcendence in the following four songs. Again, we will draw on David Machin's understanding of *discourse schema*.[45]

(i) 'Dear Life'

Mel C, in her song 'Dear Life' (2016), wonders about the existence of God or weather life events are steered by fate. The song overtly asks questions which reflect Mel C's agnostic feelings towards God. The accompanying video rather subverts the lyric. It relates to a story of a young couple who are in love. However, through the video's framing the song becomes a story reflecting the girl's insecurity as to whether the boy's love for her will continue. The dissonance of the song's lyric and its video reflects a level of challenge to Mel C expressing her views. YouTube comments reflect this dissonance. For example, one fan comments: "Why? This song is amazing and the video is so poor. Nothing special, nothing relevant. If this is a talk about her life, it should be times better if they use footages of her career and life."[46]

---

42. E.g., Lynch, *Sacred in the Modern World*, 5, 15.
43. Lynch and Badger, "Mainstream Post-Rave Club Scene," 33.
44. Lynch, *Sacred in the Modern World*, 15.
45. Machin, *Analyzing Popular Music*, 73.
46. See Hukk's comment in Melanie C, "Dear Life."

Yet, the lyric is affirmed by her fan base. A different fan commented: "I don't know if you will ever get a chance to read this. But honestly, you nailed how I'm feeling about my life right now."[47] To follow Richard Middleton's observations concerning musical code, Mel C's lyric holds *popular competence*: it is understandable at a wide, popular level as a song concerning the divine. There is no sense that aspects of the song's lyric are 'undercoded,' that is not understood.[48]

Yet the chorus speaks of her being aware of an intermittent feeling of divine presence. There is awareness of something greater than her which supports her in life, yet there is also the recognition that such feelings are not always present. Despite the video, the lyrics are quite clear—this is a song asking what may lie beyond the horizon of our lifeworld. It expresses a hope for transcendent encounter. In the second verse, Mel C sings of whether she should keep her belief private or not, to simply conform to hegemony. The bridge section of the song expresses her ultimate hope despite the finitude of life, there was more to life than can be seen. The song picks up on the hegemonic forces that curtail a search for what is hidden. Yet it also expresses something of Mel C's ultimate concern and her need for ontological security. This song suggests that there is more to life than what is concretely experienced within the lifeworld. Mel C is not 'known' for her theologizing, enabling the song to hold a transgressive element as her song crosses new boundaries. Yet, it is also a song which expresses hope for transcendent encounter.

Keith Kahn-Harris and Marcus Moberg make a constructive point concerning the similarity between feelings of transcendence and transgressive behavior. They view transcendence as experiential, "a dynamic along which people may desire to travel in order to attempt to experience a kind of 'weightlessness', a sense that everyday reality no longer applies, a sense that there is something greater than oneself and one's immediate environment." Hence, they note that transgressive behavior "breaks the boundaries of the everyday."

However, transgression "also implies a much stronger, often antagonistic relation to everyday life." The suggestion here is that such non-religious popular music is able to help some listeners to view the world around them in a more transgressive and life-enhancing manner which will begin to change who they are as they respond to the song.[49] Lynch terms such

---

47. Seen Jason Pankey's comment in Melanie C., "Melanie C—Dear Life."
48. Middleton, *Studying Popular Music*, 175.
49. Kahn-Harris and Moberg, "Religious Popular Music," 90–104.

life-enhancing motion as the "impure sacred."[50] The transgressive nature of a non-religious popular song such as Mel C's suggests the potential added agency. It is a challenge, a type of speech-act. It engenders activity and new ways of thinking about a situation.

This is an example of how such a song can provide a tactical opportunity for the Church to tell its discourses in more imaginative ways. In this way, Christians who enjoy popular music can seize the opportunity to help listeners to construct what Paul Ricoeur would call a "conflict of narrative programs,"[51] where a new discourse can begin to be explored. As Ricoeur notes, "In effect, what is to be interpreted in a text is a proposed world, a world I might inhabit and wherein I might project my own most possibilities."[52] For him, this possibility arises through the opportunity of religious texts to be considered as "kinds of poetic texts" which metaphorically "offer modes of life."[53] Or, to use Richard Niebuhr's Christ and culture typology, this is to suggest that such songs represent his "Christ of culture" category, where Christ is revealed *within* culture.[54] To view popular music in this metaphorical fashion reinforces the opportunity for songs which hold transgressive opportunity to function as a theological resource, helping others to see as clearly as possible the new world that is being described for them.

(ii) 'Mr Skeng' and 'Blinded By Your Grace'

We can further see in genres such as hip-hop and grime content that contains overt transcendent expressions of spirituality, often residing alongside political discourses that resource the imminent self. Lyrics that are violent in nature often stand alongside content which express Christian or Muslim spirituality. Some artists speak of themselves as holding divine characteristics in a way to highlight their influence on their scene. Certain contrasts may express disappointment with the expressed spirituality not providing the hope or justice it historically promised, or that such hope still stands but remains to be fulfilled.[55] As Diane Railton and Paul Watson have noted about black representation within music videos, "This impels us towards a more complex understanding of the relationship between reality and the

50. Lynch, *Sacred in the Modern World*, 20.
51. Ricoeur, *Figuring the Sacred*, 239.
52. Ricoeur, *Figuring the Sacred*, 43.
53. Ricoeur, *Figuring the Sacred*, 43.
54. Niebuhr, *Christ and Culture*, 83; Also, Partridge, *Lyre of Orpheus*, 199.
55. Winters, "Rap and Hip Hop," 312–15.

way that reality is manifested in representations."[56] Such aesthetic creation creates a feedback loop between what listeners seek to be and how others perceive the authenticity of who they claim to be.

Kanye West and Jay-Z are referenced as examples of songwriters drawing on the dissonance between the sacred and profane;[57] for example, Kanye West's 'Jesus Walks' (2004) or Jay-Z's 'Empire State of Mind' (2006). Here, though, we will view the contrast in two songs by the grime artist, Stormzy. Grime is a British genre that draws on hip-hop. As one of its commercially successful artists Stormzy crosses the divide between the sacred and profane, not with irony, but with a clear statement of hope in his transcendent belief. Yet, cultural ambiguity can be seen in comparing the lyrics of his song 'Mr Skeng' (2017) with 'Blinded By Your Grace, Part 2' (2017).

There is no official video posted for this song on YouTube, only bootleg videos taken at concerts. 'Mr Skeng' is taken by the majority who have commented as being representative of Grime. Its lyrical content would be offensive to some, yet, culturally, it resonates with those who value the genre; the language finding a new sense of power and reappropriation. The comments posted in relation to 'Blinded by Your Grace' are, primarily very positive towards the song as well. Yet, there is a counter-tension by some who view Stormzy as selling out from the original values of grime, such as "Don't get the hype. Only made it because white lefty students wank over him. Far better grime artists out there who don't get the recognition."[58] However, aware of such a tension, the song clearly expresses lyrical content that holds a traditional understanding of transcendence and God. Reminiscent of the hymn Amazing Grace, Stormzy speaks of how he understands his relationship with God to be using the theological concept of grace and salvation. Far from expressing the ironic messaging that some would draw from Mr Skeng, this song shows that Stormzy feels that ontological security can be attained by encountering that which he sees as God.

The juxtaposition between religious belief and secular life, often characterised by violence, reflects a key Old Testament theme: that of the nation of Israel wrestling with God, and of needing to make sense of the Divine (e.g., Gen 32:28). Yet, despite the positive comments made above about 'Blinded By Your Grace,' that both hip-hop and grime, generally speaking, holds onto their violent roots suggests that ontological security has not for the majority been found. There is a sense, to again reference Niebuhr's modelling, of viewing the genre as *Christ and culture in paradox* where there is a

---

56. Railton and Watson, *Music*, 28.
57. E.g., Bailey, "Existentialist Transvaluation," 38.
58. See Wall yoof's comment in Stormzy, "Blinded by Your Grace."

dualist approach of recognizing the reality of the spiritual realm, but, here, of *not* fully wanting to enter into its discourses.[59] Rather it is a genre that still expresses its ontological insecurity.

Yet, there is a transgressive element to Stormzy's song which enables it to demonstrate the potential for popular music to help individuals playfully consider socialization into a religious worldview. That "Wall yoof" (see n58) reacted negatively shows the potential for individuals to also react positively to it (his comment does say something of the greater need for political representation for those who feel dis-empowered by society). The power of play, to heuristically engage with the lyrics, gives permission for someone to try out fresh views on life, as mentioned earlier. To draw on the imagery used by St. Paul in Galatians 3:27, it is about giving playful permission to become clothed in Christ. We will return to the value of play when considering the notion of affective space in the following chapters.

(iii) 'Ghost'

Having considered two songs which express aspects of traditional transcendent belief we come to a third song, 'Ghost' by Ella Henderson (2016). What is of interest with this song is how her fans engage with both the song and the symbolism contained in the video. Here, the use of sacralized narrative and imagery holds more ambiguous outcomes. The imagery, to use Middleton's term, is 'undercoded.'[60] Listeners are more free to find their own understanding of the symbolism used within the song, joining up missing parts of the code for themselves. The song, reportedly written by Henderson in twenty minutes,[61] tells of her need to go, as it were, to the river to pray. She expresses a need for something that can wash her sense of dissonance away, yet how the memory of past events keeps her from finding the peace she seeks. Within the lyric there are symbolic transcendent references to the soul, spirit, evil, hell, the Devil and sin.

The video, constructed over a far lengthier period of time and after greater reflection, still draws on these religious themes. The video becomes the story of Henderson's murder where the troubles she sings of ultimately become the demons held by both the individual wrongly convicted of her murder, as well as the murderer himself. The closing scene of the actual murderer's arrest focuses on a red wall with a large, highly aestheticized crucifix, highlighting the gravity of his anguish and guilt (Fig. 17).

59. Niebuhr, *Christ and Culture*, 149.
60. Middleton, *Studying Popular Music*, 173.
61. Carlin, "New Music to Know."

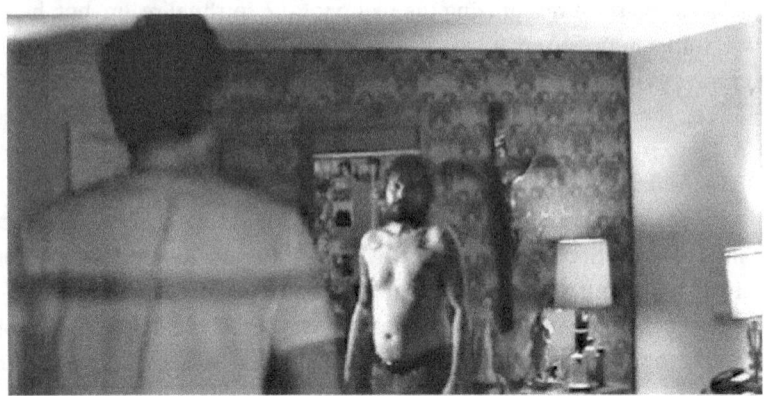

Figure 17. Henderson, 'Ghost'

Considering the speed this song was written and the measure of religious connotation in both lyric and video, it is difficult to avoid the conclusion that the aim is to provide insight into Henderson's inner life and ultimate concern. Or perhaps Henderson is simply using language that came to her in the writing process? Norman Fairclough notes that our use of language, which can also include signification and communication through visual imagery, expresses something of our social practices.[62] In other words, what is spoken must reflect our social practices in order for our language to make sense, meaning that Henderson's song holds a level of social significance for those who engage with it.

We could, at this point, consider Peter Berger's and Thomas Luckman's sedimentation theory where they posit that not all human experiences are retained consciously. Rather, aspects of our communication form a sign system which becomes sedimented over time, so enabling such symbolism to travel across generations.[63] Is Henderson's song-writing simply a sedimented experience of religious symbolism? Possibly. Should the West be considered as heavily secularized, such language should have lost the capital given to it through its social practices and, therefore, its ability to connect with those who listen to it.

Yet, the song became the sixth best-selling song of 2014 in the United Kingdom, selling 750,000 copies, suggesting that something of the language and imagery resonated with people deeply. We can again draw conclusion from Machin's discourse schema.[64] That the language and symbols we use

---

62. Fairclough, *Analyzing Discourse*, 24.
63. Berger and Luckman, *Social Construction of Reality*, 85.
64. Machin, *Analyzing Popular Music*, 80.

reflect something of our social practice and that a younger song-writer felt confident to use such imagery, feeling it would resonate with her fan base, must raise the question as to what social practice this focuses on. A curiosity to look for what lies beyond the horizon of the *lifeworld* is clearly there, with a hope, too, for transcendent encounter.

In a separate video interview describing the song's meaning Henderson speaks of her frustration at the song-writing process and that the chorus of 'Ghost' acts as a metaphor expressing this aggravation which "has a hold over you." In speaking of this dissonance she gives permission for her fans to use the metaphor to express their own feelings of frustration as it "can relate to so many people in so many different ways."[65] Giving her fans permission to 'join the dots' as they feel fit provides them with an opportunity for spiritual resourcing as they heuristically explore the imagery for themselves.

Comments from Henderson's fan base focus largely on the story of the video where there are several interpretations of the song's narratology. Some fans have interpreted her song as autobiographical, that she survived an abusive relationship,[66] so reflecting an immanent approach to the song. An anonymous respondent on Lyricinterpretations.com notes how "it depends what the River is. Either she was drowning her pain in alcohol or seeking guidance from 'the Source' on getting over an abusive boyfriend."[67] Another anonymous contributor thought that "the song is solely about letting someone go. It goes back to Christianity. Ella goes to a river to pray (the river where people were baptized). We always revert to religion when things are messed up. We try sleeping the pain away."[68] This reflects a bricolage project, incorporating, differing understandings of spirituality and transcendence which are seen as being expressed through the imagery of the video.

This is far more representative of Woodhead's outcomes around the 'rise of the nones,' of being open to spirituality but not constrained by institutional belief. It is a statement that reflects a belief that there is more to life than can be seen. While not purposefully written with that in mind, this provides a 'bottom-up' example of the opportunities of popular music to be utilized as a prosthetic technology.

---

65. Hutchinson, "Ella Henderson."
66. Hutchinson, "Ella Henderson."
67. "Ella Henderson: Ghost Meaning."
68. "Ella Henderson: Ghost Meaning."

(iv) 'God's Plan'

We can see further how fans engage with transcendent sentiment by looking at Drake's 'God's Plan' (2018). Again, it is useful to consider the comments found on the official video's YouTube page. Here, Drake tells the story of how he views his time in the music industry as being part of God's plan for him, despite those who have stood in his way. The video shows Drake giving away lots of money to people he meets (Fig. 18).

Figure 18. Scenes from Drake's 'God's Plan'

The video holds an altruistic, messianic quality about it, which reinforces the narrative of Drake's story of divine influence. There is a short, yet poignant discussion on the YouTube page which highlight the perceived strength of the song and artist, alongside a critique of the video. One fan writes: "Wow. I love how this music video actually means something instead of being stupid and meaningless. I love how he helped people and everyone's reactions. I will never see him the same way again."[69] In response, one fan responds: "It means that Drake pulled off a sublime public relations marketing campaign for only one million dollar that will give him many more in revenue. Haha. Real heroes don't seek for the approval of their good actions, just for the good of it, seriously guys that lesson is in every super hero movie.[70]

What is of interest here is that, again, the criticism is not aimed at the belief in divine intervention. Rather cynicism is expressed about Drake's marketing strategy. The religious sentiment simply raises no adverse reaction. Far from being a distant voice, religious sentiment that focuses on transcendent experiences can be expressed vocally and visually loud and clear, with criticism, here, aimed at the marketing of the video. To follow Michel De Certeau's thinking, this bottom-up tactical expression can be viewed as a further challenge to Habermas' belief that it is not plausible to look for what may lie beyond the horizon of our consumerist lifeworld.

69. See CeCe's comment in Drake, "God's Plan."
70. See Daemn27's commen in Drake, "God's Plan."

We can also view something of the relationship between fan and celebrity to see further examples of functional, para-religious behavior at work. Stars provide something that we long for which we may emulate and be inspired by.[71] To recall Bauman's understanding, cosmopolitanism is unattainable except to an elite few in for culture-industry.[72] He also notes that many who follow celebrities recognize the non-reality of such life-styles.[73] The notion of celebrity allows those who can never attain a cosmopolitan lifestyle to aspire, yet ultimately lampoon the person concerned. Pete Ward also captures this paradox by noting that some may give their favored celebrities divine characteristics suggesting "celebrity worship is a kind of religion or it is related in some way to religion,"[74] while at the same time asserting that "Celebrity culture is fundamentally different from religion because no one takes celebrity culture seriously."[75]

However, there is a different direction that our understanding of celebrity can take us, that of an artist helping a fan to shine light on that which is ultimately real to them. A further comment from a fan simply is: "Yo Drake, you rock. Loved what you do for humanity."[76] While we may enjoy following our favorite celebrities, even relishing when they do get something wrong, their viewpoints can also help us make sense of what we feel to be important, even that which holds ultimate reality for us. To recall the comment made in response to New Order's 'Restless,' one fan notes the group's ability of "Tapping into forgotten recesses of the human psyche, recognizing and identifying the important aspects of one's life that appear meaningless and mundane on the outside and giving all those inexplicable, repressed feelings a voice, a sound."[77]

Again, we could recall Giles Deleuze's comment of how film, here music video, can reveal something of the depth of our spiritual needs.[78] In other words, these examples show people articulating what they may not feel able to articulate themselves concerning their deeper ontological needs. In Drake's case, Cece's comment (see n69), "I love how this music video actually means something instead of being stupid and meaningless" reflects

---

71. E.g., Till, *Pop Cult*, 53.
72. Bauman, *Community*, 67.
73. Bauman, *Liquid Modernity*, 87.
74. Ward, *Gods Behaving Badly*, 19.
75. Ward, *Gods Behaving Badly*, 85.
76. See Jennifer Corcho's comment in Drake, "God's Plan."
77. See Amanda Laggan's comment in Neworder, "New Order – Restless."
78. Toubiana, "The Brain Is the Screen."

a positive expression both of her own need to see a world where justice and fairness is seen, but a world where meaning is also found.[79]

This is to suggest that who we may follow and positively react with will reflect something of our own needs for ontological security. It, again, demonstrates that our musical engagement reflects something of how we function in the world. To draw on Roll's notion that our emotional responses are linked to both our decision making and our pursuit for safety over punishment, we 'follow' the celebrities that make us feel good about ourselves because they represent something significant to us in our hunt for ontological meaning and security. The functional nature of the music we listen helps to express our need for ontological security.

2. Tillich and Ultimate Concern

We need to ground such revelatory experiences within a theological framework and will do so by drawing on the work of Paul Tillich. Tillich suggests that our engagement with culture can reveal knowledge about what he terms ultimate reality of the world around us[80] and about our ultimate concern.[81] This, as John Hick's articulates, is the "distinction between the Ultimate as it is in itself and that same ultimate reality as it impinges upon us and is conceived by our little human minds."[82] Tillich's thinking is born of personal experience when during a period of leave from the horrors of the First World War he viewed Botticelli's Madonna with Singing Angels in Berlin. He recounted, "As I stood there, bathed in the beauty its painter had envisioned so long ago, something of the divine source of all things came through to me. I turned away shaken."[83]

While, for Tillich, the experience was driven by art, there are few differences in the effects of our engagement with different forms of artistic expression, be it aural or visual. This is to return again to the Renaissance notion of *ut pictura poesis*, of the similarity in emotional and heuristic affects between the visual, aural and poetic based arts.[84] While this notion was a mainstay of Renaissance aesthetics the phrase fell out of favor due to the term being seen as holding an idealism towards the rhetoric of poetry over other art forms, being overtaken by Kant and the Romantic pursuit

---

79. YouTuber11, YouTube, "Drake—God's Plan."
80. Tillich, *Systematic Theology*, 1:102.
81. Tillich, *Systematic Theology*, 1:14.
82. Hick, "Religious Pluralism," 14.
83. Tillich, *Systematic Theology*, 1:235.
84. Braider, *The Paradoxical Sisterhood*, 168.

of the sublime.[85] However, the phrase is useful. The term reminds us of the link between the various art forms we engage with—they each hold the potential to move us emotionally and, therefore, to become a resource in our pursuit of ontological security.

Tillich's work can help us theologize what we feel as we listen to popular music, so that such experiences may be considered as more than simply the result of the over-stimulation of the amygdala. What is of particular interest is how profoundly a "strong experience with music" (SEM), to use Alf Gabrielsson's term,[86] can affect us, with some interpreting such experiences in a similar way to Tillich's response to art. We will consider the effects of SEM in the following chapter. For now, Marsh and Roberts affirm a similar stance by asserting that popular music is a medium through which the divine may be encountered in ways that are "genuine and wholly consistent with what happens in baptism and Holy Communion."[87] We can also recall Till's understanding of such musical encounters as the "sacred popular."[88]

While themes from Tillich's work are often drawn on by present day scholars in their reflections on the relationship between popular culture and religion,[89] Kelton Cobb has pointed out that Tillich held "a strong aversion to popular culture."[90] This is perhaps unsurprising bearing in mind Tillich's friendship with Theodor Adorno.[91] However, Tillich developed a theology of culture which is "the attempt to analyze the theology behind all cultural expressions, to discover the ultimate concern in the ground of a philosophy, a political system, an artistic style, a set of ethical or social principles."[92]

A key aspect of his theology is the acknowledgment of the relationship between human finitude and humanity's awareness of the infinite of which he or she is excluded, a theme that is often reflected on by secular thinkers, such as Karl Jaspers. Tillich views the "threefold form of cognitive, artistic and communal participation" as a way of seeking "reunion" between the finite and infinite.[93] This places him as looking for an "ontological concept of life," aware of the existential questions this raises, which leaves him

85. Braider, *The Paradoxical Sisterhood*, 170–75.
86. Gabrielsson, *Strong Experiences*, 2.
87. Marsh and Roberts, *Personal Jesus*, 176.
88. Till, *Pop Cult*, iv.
89. E.g., Brant, "Music and How We Became Human"; Cobb, *Theology and Popular Culture*; Lynch, *Theology and Popular Culture*.
90. Cobb, *Theology and Popular Culture*, 99.
91. See Cobb, *Theology and Popular Culture*, 99. Adorno's views were explored in chapter 1.
92. Tillich, *Systematic Theology*, 1:39.
93. Tillich *On Art and Architecture*, 17.

asking the question "can we analyze the existential ambiguities of all life processes correctly and express the quest for unambiguous or eternal life adequately?"[94] Such thinking clearly places him at odds with the humanist approaches of Jaspers and Habermas, yet his view reflects the sentiments contained in Mel C's song, 'Dear Life,' Stormzy's 'Blinded By Your Grace, Part 2' and even Drake's 'God's Plan.'

Tillich argued that we gain insight into ultimate concern through the artistic form we engage with, especially when that form reflects something of the cultural zeitgeist. For him, this was Expressionist art.[95] The liquid modern zeitgeist should be viewed as our ability to appropriate popular culture and to express ourselves through that. Herbert Marcuse has also commented on the relationship between artistic form and revelation, noting there is an "aesthetic power of silence" that viewers may encounter, enabling a "break with the familiar" where a moment of social rather than divine revelation may occur.[96] Like Tillich's moment of epiphany, such occurrences should be viewed as opportunities for self-learning.

Tillich asserted that "every artistic expression is religious in the larger sense of religion. No artistic expression can escape the fact that it expresses qualities of ultimate reality in the forms it shows."[97] Or, as he also describes, "Religion is the substance of culture and culture is the form of religion."[98] Therefore, what he sees as authentic art is able, through aesthetic deduction, to reveal something of the artist's own pursuit for ontological truth, while, as Joseph Price suggests, it also encourages the viewer to encounter ultimate reality.[99]

Tillich's hope, therefore, is that such revelatory encounter will enable moments of "real union of and with the world."[100] Such art holds agency as "it expresses, it transforms, it anticipates,"[101] albeit that there can be no "pure revelation."[102] It reveals. As Price notes, "[Tillich] has liberated us from the notion that the content or subject matter of a work of art is the determinative factor in judging its religious significance. He has charted our shift of

---

94. Tillich *Systematic Theology*, 3:12.

95. Tillich, *On Art and Architecture*, 4; see also Price, "Expressionism and Ultimate Reality," 492.

96. Marcuse, *The Aesthetic Dimension*, 117.

97. Tillich, *On Art and Architecture*, 33.

98. Church, "Aspects of a Religious Analysis," 103.

99. Price, "Expressionism and Ultimate Reality," 492.

100. Tillich, *On Art and Architecture*, 64.

101. Tillich, *On Art and Architecture*; Tillich, *Theology of Culture*, 7.

102. Tillich, "Theology and Symbolism," 5.

focus from that of content to that of style."[103] Jonathan Brant captures an important aspect of Tillich's understanding of revelation, particularly concerning the Christian tradition: "This is not to suggest that human experience is a locus for fresh revelation (a new script), that will counter or contradict the script provided by Scripture, doctrine and tradition. It is however to recognize that the questions that we ask of Scripture and theological traditions always emerge from some context."[104]

This means that revelatory experience is primarily about gaining new perspectives on life's situations which may affect our sense of ontological security, such, as we will see in the next chapter, as those echoed in the accounts given by recipients of SEMs.[105] For Tillich there is no "pure revelation."[106] It is about discovering more of what it means to be human, be that in relation to the divine or not. This means that Mel C's transgressive ruminations around God's existence should be viewed as a legitimate theological expression, which some within the Church will, wrongly, view as banal.

While Tillich's work predominantly reflects his post-World War I setting, there is sharpness to his writing which reflects aspects of liquid modernity. For him, the world had become secularized, yet the function of symbolic thinking enables us to connect and express issues that hold for us ultimate concern.[107] The opportunity to similarly use the symbolic to express ultimate reality within liquid modernity is clearly there. Tillich also voices similar frustrations with the Church that I have expressed, as being "contradictory," wanting to hold onto its doctrinal and traditional self, yet wanting to use symbols of "the industrial spirit against which they were fighting."[108]

Tillich is not alone in seeing the possibility of encountering the divine in a more open fashion, be it within the wider tradition of Liberal theological interpretation seen in Fredrich Schleiermacher's 'God-consciousness'[109] or Rudolf Otto's encounters with holiness, in what he describes as *mysterium tremendum et fascinosum*.[110] Alongside the possibility of divine revelation occurring far beyond the boundaries of the Church, Tillich wanted

---

103. Price, "Expressionism and Ultimate Reality," 492.
104. Brant, "Music and How We Became Human," 127.
105. Gabrielsson, *Strong Experiences*.
106. Tillich, "Theology and Symbolism," 5, 8.
107. Tillich, *Systematic Theology*, 1:38.
108. Tillich, *Theology of Culture*, 45.
109. Schleiermacher, *Christian Faith in Outline*, 17.
110. Otto, *Idea of the Holy*, 12; see also Lynch, *Sacred in the Modern World*, 10.

"eternal truth" to be drawn out from "temporal expressions of this truth" which he felt reflected the fundamental approaches of biblical theology that he especially encountered in America. As he views it, "When fundamentalism is combined with an antitheological bias, as it is, for instance, in its biblicistic-evangelical form, the theological truth of yesterday is defended as an unchangeable message against the theological truth of today and tomorrow. Fundamentalism fails to make contact with the present situation, not because it speaks from beyond every situation, but because it speaks from a situation of the past."[111]

However, he notes a three-way tension between what he identifies as kerygmatic theology, which he notes must be "the only real theology" as it speaks into eternal truth, with that of fundamental approaches to theology, which speaks little into particular contextual situations, and the social and psychological advances found in new situational contexts.[112] This sets the poles of his correlative method of theology, which he validates through noting how theologians throughout time have always built on the work of preceding generations ("Even the Reformers were dependent on the Roman tradition against which they protested").[113] His wider understanding of religion "opens up the depth of man's spiritual life which is usually covered by the dust of our daily life and the noise of our secular work. It gives us the experience of the Holy, of something which is untouchable, awe-inspiring, an ultimate meaning, the source of ultimate courage."[114]

As Jeremy Begbie notes, "Fundamental to his entire project is the desire to view religion as a dimension of the whole of existence rather than a special zone in which specifically religious things are said and done."[115] In this way, Tillich's approach is utilitarian where the purpose of all art is to communicate aspects of our ultimate concern.[116]

Building on that, a further key term for Tillich is "spirit," seen here as an "inner awareness" which "actualizes within itself, another dimension, that of the personal-communal or the 'spirit.'" It is the "power of life,"[117] which is to recall Laing's understanding of psyche. Tillich also speaks of "spiritual presence"—a universal presence which he notes becomes designated in differing cultures through language, so that the "Logos" becomes

---

111. Tillich, *Systematic Theology*, 1:3.
112. Tillich, *Systematic Theology*, 1:7.
113. Tillich, *Systematic Theology*, 1:36.
114. Tillich, *Theology of Culture*, 9.
115. Begbie, *Voicing Creation's Praise*, 19.
116. Price, "Expressionism and Ultimate Reality," 491.
117. Tillich, *Systematic Theology*, 3:21.

the "criterion of every particular logos."[118] As Brant observes, "it is necessary to understand 'spirit' as the distinctively human dimension of life which is manifest in the spheres of morality, culture, and religion."[119]

To facilitate the correlative conversation between theology and philosophy, Tillich grounds revelatory experiences in the language of technical and ontological reason, where he sees the former as needing to reside within the latter.[120] Brant comments "Ontological reason points beyond itself and even beyond the structures of reality that it engages."[121] What Tillich terms theonomy thus enables the Spiritual Presence to bring revelation into differing situations concerning "truth and expressiveness," "purpose and humanity" and "power and justice."[122]

Again, similar forms of revelation, be it expressed through technical or ontological reason, are expressed in the thick narratives provided by Gabrielsson's research into SEM.[123] When such revelation occurs it will act with a sense of "breakthrough," providing a sense of "creative ecstasy" and enabling a sense of "belief-ful realism."[124] Brant observes Tillich's hope that belief-ful realism could unite "a reference to the transcendent eternal source of meaning and being with the sober-eyed depiction of the scientist or realist artist of things as they are."[125] The comments made by Henderson's fans in relation to 'Ghost' exhibit their understanding of belief-ful realism.

Yet, perhaps surprisingly, given the experiential nature of revelation, Tillich speaks out strongly against being emotional over revelatory experiences. "Emotion is powerless against intellectualism and aestheticism, against legalism and conventionalism, if it remains mere emotion. But, although powerless over reason, it can have great power of destruction over the mind, personally and socially. Emotion without rational structure (in the sense, of course, of ontological reason) becomes irrationalism."[126] Or, as he notes elsewhere, "'Ecstasy' must be rescued from its distorted connotations and restored to a sober theological function," although he makes the point that this is more to such experiences as one's experience of reason

---

118. Tillich, *Systematic Theology*, 3:254; emphasis mine.
119. Brant, "Music and How We Became Human," 65.
120. Tillich, *Systematic Theology*, 1:73.
121. Brant, "Music and How We Became Human," 64.
122. Tillich, *Systematic Theology*, 3:252–62.
123. Gabrielsson, *Strong Experiences*, ch. 5.
124. Tillich, *On Art and Architecture*, 4.
125. Brant, "Music and How We Became Human," 55; see also Begbie, *Voicing Creation's Praise*, 25.
126. Tillich, *Systematic Theology*, 1:93.

becoming overloaded.[127] Therefore, revelation maybe ecstatic, yet it should also be a logical experience.

A final point to make about Tillich's theology at this juncture, and akin to his thought about revelation, concerns the value of searching for Godly wisdom, for which he sees the highest form of revelation as that of Jesus Christ.[128] As he notes, "Wisdom, *sapientia*, is the knowledge of the principles, of truth itself."[129] He further asserts that: "Wisdom can be distinguished from objectifying knowledge (*sapientia* from *Scientia*) by its ability to manifest itself beyond the cleavage of subject and object. The biblical imagery describing Wisdom and Logos as being "with" God and "with" men makes this point quite obvious. Theonomous knowledge is Spirit-determined Wisdom."[130] We will see in chapter 6 that the pursuit of Godly wisdom over simply responding to a reduced form of Christian belief may help with wider socialization into Christian belief.

Tillich's work is helpful in four ways. Firstly, he argues that cultural objects can help us to express our longing for ultimate reality. Secondly, there is a fluidity and breadth to Tillich's approach that resonates with both Bauman's 'liquid modernity' and Woodhead's pluralism de jure.[131] Thirdly, having argued that aspects of the present day church are held captive by its recent past, Tillich helps to progress the Church's institutional discourse away from its Enlightenment encounters. Lastly, he sees the opportunity of ontological reflections as a way to draw people towards God. However, that is not to say his work is without its critics.

For example, Tillich's metaphysical framework, whereby God is viewed as an impersonal spirit, runs contrary to the traditional Christian view of God as relational and approachable, seen primarily in the incarnation of Jesus Christ.[132] Stanley Grenz has also criticized Tillich's correlative method for not being Christo-centrically governed, suggesting that a stronger form of Christian/cultural reflection would be obtained by engaging with conversational partners of scripture, reason, tradition and experience alone, in other words, keeping such reflection as intratextual rather than that of an extratextual conversation between religion and philosophy.[133] Likewise, Begbie asks whether Tillich, "despite his intentions was adequately shaped

---

127. Tillich, *Systematic Theology*, 1:111.
128. Tillich, *Systematic Theology*, 1:137.
129. Tillich, *Theology of Culture*, 14.
130. Tillich, *Systematic Theology*, 3:256.
131. Woodhead, "Rise of 'No Religion,'" 255.
132. Schwobel, "Paul Tillich," 641; Grenz, *Theology Community of God*, 103.
133. Grenz, *Theology Community of God*, 19.

by the saving economy of God in Christ, and thus distinctively Christian insights."[134] Begbie is also concerned that Tillich's interpretation of artistic symbolism lies beyond the traditional use of artistic symbolism, which have held particular traditional and structural meanings,[135] while Tillich then further extends their interpretation to provide divine revelation.[136]

While that is true, we have seen how popular music demonstrates that we do now 'poach' and 'make do' with the symbols we see in a far more fluid manner than our past, in a manner that does resonate with Tillich's wider use of symbolism, especially concerning authenticity and revelation. It is clear that we draw on the signs and symbols that we engage with and use them to help construct a narrative around ourselves that can either help us express our frustration or resistance to hegemony, or can express feelings that reflect our sense of ontological security. Yet, how can the Church draw on this knowledge in a manner that is deeper than a vicar simply playing her favorite music from the pulpit in the hope that the congregation enjoy themselves?

3. Can Popular Music Re-enchant?

While Bauman may want to hold a wider understanding of the ontological opportunities in the world around him, it is unlikely that he would go as far as to suggest that popular culture can draw you into religious belief. Yet, the argument here has been that through our authentic appropriation of popular culture we can become attuned to revelation concerning the divine. We have established that symbols hold agency,[137] that the visual can express something of our spiritual needs[138] and as we utilize such symbolism we begin to take on board the discourse that surrounds it. We have also noted that transgressive music can help someone to see a differing worldview than the one they inhabit. Yet is it plausible to suggest that a song can (re)enchant Christian belief?

Gavin Hopps sees the opportunity for the "re-enchantment of contemporary culture" and "a paradoxical openness to the possibility of the impossible."[139] However, he also sees a weakening of religious discourse in general in order to lessen the potency of religious fundamentalism. Bauman viewed that liquid society' need for certainty is a breeding ground

134. Begbie, *Voicing Creation's Praise*, 256.
135. E.g., Hall, *Dictionary*.
136. Begbie, *Voicing Creation's Praise*, 51.
137. I.e., Riis and Woodhead, *Sociology of Religious Emotion*, 8.
138. E.g., Toubiana, "The Brain Is the Screen."
139. Hopps, "Theology," 91–92.

for fundamental views.¹⁴⁰ Hopps' point, though, is significant as it helps pinpoint the threshold where religious belief is seen to be a threat to the present hegemony. Candi Staton's 'You've Got the Love' (1986 and 1991) is recognized as a song speaking about our need for God, yet its lyric is not overtly Christo-centric, meaning that the threshold of overt belief is not crossed and wider public ownership of this lyric is accepted. Yet, the conundrum which hegemony cannot solve remains: how to limit discussion around worldviews, when so many feel the tension and restlessness of needing to look beyond the lifeworld.

However, Hopps also notes what he terms as a "metaphysical shuddering," where music may cause transcendent like feelings to occur, which "may even turn out to be an ally of the religious."¹⁴¹ We will see in the next chapter more of how this may be the case. Hopps also highlights the tension that postmetaphysical individuals are likely to be sceptic of such experiences noting that "its envisioning of the beyond tends to be characterised either by an anonymous 'excess' or an 'ontological abundance.'" As he notes, "These 'porous' or 'enchanted' spaces— which renounce a secular construal of reality without adopting an exclusively religious stance—are the hallmark of a post-secular outlook."¹⁴² This is helpful as it, again, highlights the opportunity of affective space as a place to consider issues of ontological reality such as the Christian story. This is notably similar to the conclusions drawn by Woodhead and her interpretation of a 'typical none.' In a rather complex manner, Hopps notes "The point of importance to take from this is that affects are (not uncontroversially) supposed to liberate a space that is distended with potentiality and a pluralized openness within the smudged becoming of subjectivity, prior to the refinements of conscious perception. And whilst they are only fugitive moments on the way to awareness, these fecund interstices in conscious experience permit a different, less conceptualized encounter with things, which is radically hospitable to a diversity of possibilities."¹⁴³

He views this postmetaphysical era as holding a "radical ontological hospitality."¹⁴⁴ However, a key aspect that Hopps does not focus on so greatly is the defining nature of our emotional state in the formation of transcendent-like experiences and the overwhelming need to find ontological security within liquid modernity. It is through the emotion that we open

---

140. Bauman and Obirek, *Of God and Man*, 30; see also Bauman, *Identity*, 85.
141. Hopps, "Theology," 91–93.
142. Hopps, "Byron and Post-Secular," 96.
143. Hopps, "Byron and Post-Secular," 98.
144. Hopps, "Byron and Post-Secular," 98.

ourselves up to the opportunity of radical ontological hospitality. Where I would agree is the understanding that within such a paradigm: "which takes for granted a framework of 'closed immanence' and refuses a priori the legitimacy of alternative perspectives—has been 'normalized' by years of institutional acceptance and so appears, to many, as a form of neutrality. And yet it is as dogmatically prejudicial as its religious counterparts and has, I suggest, resulted in a serious impoverishment of Romantic art."[145]

Hopps notes how such ontological hospitality gives space for epiphanic experience, that is a revelatory "expansion of vision" akin to that of Tillich's.[146] He uses the term "transivity" to express how one may become drawn into the dramatized events of a song, and therefore, drawn into a space where epiphanic moments may occur.[147] That is, rather than musically describing such an experience, the music draws you into the experience.

We will see in the next chapter, though, that music does not so much draw you in, rather that it holds the ability to induce emotion within you with which we then react. For Hopps, music by groups such as Fleet Foxes or Mount Eerie draw him into such a space.[148] Here we see the subjective nature of music in action. Hopps' choice holds no such effect on me, rather, progressive trance, a genre within EDM holds such ability. Not that such experiences should be equated with religious experience, rather that this simply demonstrates the tools through which a religious experience may take place and the creation of an affective space where radical ontological hospitality may occur. We will see in the next chapter that the opportunity for such musically generated transcendent experience is far wider than that suggested by Hopps.

Jeff Keuss has also commented on the opportunity for popular music to reenchant belief. His observations on the relationship between popular music and specifically Christian belief begin with his own experiences of a transcendent, while listening to music. For him, music provides "a connection with other people who thought in terms of melodies and lyrics more than doctrines and platitudes,"[149] representing Ward's thinking on the subjective operant theology that is active as much in America as within the United Kingdom.

He suggests that the expression of one's true feelings through popular music culture, as opposed to Contemporary Christin Music (CCM), is akin

145. Hopps, "Byron and Post-Secular," 106.
146. Hopps, "Theology," 87.
147. Hopps, "Theology," 84–87.
148. Hopps, "Theology," 84.
149. Keuss, *Your Neighbor's Hymnal*, 2.

to the "mystical experience that is deep in the Christian tradition." Whether one agrees with his approach, there are clear similarities here between Tillich and his wish to express themes of ultimate concern. For Keuss, "Many people listen to pop songs not as a distraction but with a deep hunger for something spiritual and transcendent," which this work, thus far, demonstrates.[150]

As an aside, while CCM is a sub-genre in its own right, operating akin to country and western music around a commercial center of Nashville,[151] there are differing views as to the veracity of the genre.[152] While some view CCM primarily as a mode for evangelism,[153] there are also artists who view themselves as musicians-who-happen-to-be Christian,[154] such as the group Sixpence None the Richer.[155] Yet, for Heather Hendershot, "Christian music seems to lag about ten years behind country music in terms of budget, and perhaps even farther behind in terms of gaining mainstream respectability."[156] In other words, while the genre often appeals to those who already embody an evangelical belief, the genre is not, generally speaking, viewed as transgressive enough to help spiritual seekers find belief. Hendershot additionally notes that "Christian music has changed to compete in the mainstream, and the result is not so much a secularization of the music as a smashing of the literalism that dominated early CCM, a literalism that persists in the work of artists without crossover aspirations."[157] In other words, the genre itself has lessened its transgressive content, ironically reinforcing Keuss' observations around our use of popular music and our need for mystical experiences. Again, this reinforces our use of popular music as a theological resource.

Keuss also notes how socialization into belief must equip people for "mobility and depth" rather than "fixity and certainty," to counter "the destabilizing nature of identity formation" and to be engaged "with the aesthetic nature of culture, which allows for fluidity in self in convert with divine action."[158] This is the difference between fixed epistemological approaches to belief and that of arguing that religious belief enables a person to feel more aware of what it means to be human. Of particular note for Keuss is

---

150. Keuss, *Your Neighbor's Hymnal*, 8–10.
151. Hendershot, *Shaking the World for Jesus*, 53.
152. E.g., Romanowski, "Evangelicals and Popular Music," 105.
153. Hendershot, *Shaking the World for Jesus*, 82.
154. Hendershot, *Shaking the World for Jesus*, 64.
155. See also Howard and Streck, "Splintered Art World."
156. Hendershot, *Shaking the World for Jesus*, 54.
157. Hendershot, *Shaking the World for Jesus*, 84.
158. Keuss, *Blur*, 36.

that teaching requires "a renewed emphasis upon the *form* of being in relating to the *content* of being."

Yet, he also asserts that "One of the most important things to install in young people is the very basic premise: faith is not certainty."[159] What we see in both Hopps and Keuss' observations are the importance of expressing subjective feelings within a Christian setting which can express our ontological, very human longings for security. The argument of this section has also been that music and video can help prompt individuals to consider changes to their personal lifeworld when existential restlessness requires resolution.

With all that has been noted concerning the struggle for a distinctive Christian voice to be heard within the cacophony of differing ideological forces at work within liquid modernity, the Church is reticent to give expression to feelings of the subjective self for fear that it will further erode its authority. Yet the need to express subjective feelings must be seen as a significant aspect of our self-expression of belief especially within liquid modernity. In other words, our own socialization into belief needs an understanding about how and why belief makes us feel rather than simply learning key epistemologically driven facts about belief.

For example, by focusing on 'proof texts' from the bible which act as statements of epistemological certainty of belief, the Church is losing its ability to share and draw others into those stories which help give expression to the subjective self. There are many examples within the bible where feelings are clearly expressed, such as found within in the book of Lamentations and in many of the psalms, with the ability to express sorrow, or within the book of Song of Songs, which expresses feelings of erotic love, yet little teaching time is given to engage with bible passages which express such subjectivity. Similarly, the learning opportunity provided when a subjective experience such as when we feel 'the chills' as we worship needs to be taken seriously. By taking such experiences more seriously we are opening ourselves up to a "break with the familiar" where a moment of revelation, a moment of learning about belief may occur.[160]

4. Lyrics and Theology

Our engagement with the functional aspects of a song is cognitive, discursive and emotive. Lyrics may act symbolically, leading to a deeper search for ultimate reality, such as Henderson's video using religious symbolism to

---

159. Keuss, *Blur*, 65.
160. Marcuse, *The Aesthetic Dimension*, 117.

expresses themes of judgement and justice. It can also help frame a wider discursive conversation that gives wider understanding to life beyond our lifeworld, such as expressed within Mel C's 'Dear Life.' In this way greater credit ought to be given to lyricists and video directors of popular music songs for the opportunities they may afford us. To suggest that such lyrics as the ones we have been considering are of lesser poetic value simply because they are from the genre of popular music is simply to be excessively influenced by Adorno's legacy, drawing attention, again, to the structural forces at work from previous generations.

At this point our functional engagement with popular music can identify five particular points that will help shape how we best tell the Christian discourse within liquid modernity.

(1) Within liquid modernity the ideological preference for postmetaphysical, rationally driven argument does place the Church on the backfoot. This informs why the Church predominantly pursues discourses which emphasize logical explanations of belief in response, such as seen in courses such as Alpha. Yet, popular music's representation of spiritual issues shows that individuals are keener to explore ontological human/divine relationships as a way to deepen their understanding of what it means to be human.

Perhaps, to slightly subvert a biblical reference, this is to discover more deeply what it means to 'live life in all its fullness' (John 10:10). John Sloboda draws on Diana Raffman's work in commenting on the "ineffability" that allows music to show the difference between "knowing" what is understood within the world and that which we are able to "say" about the world.[161] While Raffman's approach is cognitively focused rather than favoring that emotions in music are induced, her understanding of the ineffability of music, that it holds knowledge which is felt or, to use her term, nuanced, yet which cannot be expressed in words is helpful.[162] It opens up a conversation concerning the ontological nature of music as well as its metaphorical nature, which our exploration of popular music draws on. This echoes Bauman's reflection that "We are led from a world of "being" to a world of "becoming." In other words: for most practical intents and purposes, the condition of 'uncertainty' has been shifted from the realm of epistemology (the study of cognition) to that of ontology (the study of being)."[163]

Popular culture would suggest that many individuals want to connect with God, not from the starting point of doctrine—that can always be subsequently understood—rather, simply to *know* that reality and to be sure of

---

161. Sloboda, "Music and Worship," 116.
162. Raffman, *Language*, 2.
163. Bauman and Raud, *Practices of Selfhood*, ix.

that first through an emotional connection. Savage Garden's 'Affirmation' (1999) expresses such an ontological yearning. Its creedal style lyric bombards the listener with differing statements, such as the need for forgiveness and the ironic statement that God does not approve of American style TV evangelists. Yet it is the feel of the song which ultimately communicates the essence of what the group feels it is to be human.

While Lynch would argue that ontological thinking should be viewed through a cultural-sociological lens, focusing on what is considered to be sacred in a particular context,[164] the notion of musical ineffability and the way popular music makes us feel needs to be given greater credence, certainly from a theological viewpoint. For example, when someone new to a worship environment is brought to tears through the positive content of a service, it should be recognized as a moment of encountering the divine. This reflects Tillich's thinking of the relationship between culture and religion and its ability to shine light on our innermost needs.

(2) More importantly, it shows that liquid moderns are prepared to wrestle with the divine, reflecting an aspect of Woodhead's 'rise of the nones' which shows young people as being open to spiritual encounter, yet not wanting to be constrained by the institution of the Church.[165] The pursuit of what may lie beyond the horizon of our lifeworld clearly is still a route that many will take despite the ideology of postmetaphysicalism. The significant truth of Habermas' reticence to look beyond the Lifeworld is that the failure to do so is as much an act of faith that there is nothing beyond the lifeworld as it does to believe there is. The problem is that by focusing on epistemological arguments for belief the Church has lost its confidence to allow for such simple ontological appreciation. Yet, such Kairos moments need to be viewed as a learning opportunity and individuals encouraged to talk about a divine encounter. Moments of transcendent connection, however nebulous that may seem to someone holding an epistemologically focused outlook, must be seen as an opportunity for theological learning.

There are two significant and related reasons for such reticence. With the Evangelical voice still in its ascendency within church circles, as seen with the growing divergence between the Church's values and those held by wider society,[166] so epistemological models of evangelism will continue to be favored over discourses that simply allow for transcendent feelings to be expressed as an encounter with the divine. Related to this is also the

---

164. Lynch, *Sacred in the Modern World*, 15.
165. See Woodhead, "Rise of 'No Religion,'" 252.
166. See Woodhead, "Rise of 'No Religion,'" 258.

Church's lack of understanding of the fluid nature of the society within which it seeks to tell its story.

(3) The Church's lack of understanding of the social forces at play, including, for example, the voices exerted by subaltern counter republics, hinder its theological reflection and understanding of the missiological opportunities still open to it. How can a Church focus on one overriding discourse of belief (i.e., Evangelical) when one looks at the various fluid sociological forces at play? Rather, the institution of the Church acts as though the effects of the last two hundred years have not affected it. This is where ontological appreciation should be viewed as something that can unite: a common ground that feelings of divine encounter are real.

This is not to suggest a revisionist agenda to the Church's traditional doctrines, rather to say that different understandings of Christian belief must be listened to and respected by the wider Church. To return to Lynch's sociology of the sacred and his views on ontology,[167] the heated discussion between differing theological viewpoints could be viewed through such a hermeneutic, where the ontological nature of the Jesus story can be owned by all tribes, while the remaining differences could be viewed as a particular tribe's cultural-sacred. A broad theology and generous spirit is required.

Within our present liberal-pluralistic schema, discourses which are regarded as fundamental in nature will be resisted. This does not mean that such views cannot be held, rather a wider appreciation of *all* theological understandings is required in order to hold things in balance. The tactical response of the Church must be to broaden its theological outlook else it will simply be cast to one side *as* a fundamental discourse. In as much as the Anglican Church is seen as comprising of three main constituents, high, low and liberal church, it should be 'liquid modern ready,' allowing parity between the differing theological voices. Yet, until it appreciates how and why historical forces shaped these three distinct voices it will struggle to understand the need for parity.

(4) As much as Western society is fluid in nature, so the Church needs to give space for public expressions of restlessness. The wider cannon of scripture provides a wide range of feelings, from lamentation to the erotic love contained in the Song of Songs, all feelings about what it means to be human. There has, though, been what Warner describes as Evangelical "vision inflation" in which "conservative Christians evoke a promised land of imminent and epoch-changing advance, in defiance of the secularizing trends that result in diminishing returns for religious recruitment drives."[168] While a vision of

---

167. Lynch, *Sacred in the Modern World*, 3–13.
168. Warner, *Secularisation and Its Discontents*, 4.

LYRICAL CONTENT, TRANSCENDENCE, AND SHALOM   145

hope is entirely laudable, such hyper-sentiment becomes perceived as inauthentic. This becomes translated within the Church as a fear that to express feelings of dissonance is to challenge aspects of its discourse, especially the model offered by the reduced discourse to four key themes.[169] Unless liturgical expression is first given to this existential angst, the Church will not be able to reach out to show an authentic discourse of ontological security.

From a practical point of view we can speak here of two stages. Firstly, in the same way that our musical cultures express feelings of restlessness, liturgical space ought to be given to help express feelings of restlessness. Secondly, we have noted the potential in songs considered to be transgressive,[170] through which we can begin to construct a "conflict of narrative programs" between feelings of restlessness and a discourse of hope.[171]

5. To build on that, within the Christian tradition that hope is expressed in Jesus' call that "I have come that they may have life and have it to the full" (John 10:10). His ontological presence brings fulfilment, which is to characterize Jesus as one who holds no dissonance. Bauman's stance is that it is highly unlikely that existential restless can be resolved, partly from fear that the longed for security will not ultimately be found if a new identity were to be taken on.[172] Ultimately, such restlessness, however sociologically explained, needs to be recognized as an ontological concern.

The argument here is that it is through encountering Jesus' presence, his *Geist*, his Logos that we begin to encounter one who holds no dissonance. Jesus speaks of his shalom being with us (John 14:27). The biblical tradition speaks of how encountering Jesus brings, what effectively is the antidote to dissonance, his shalom, his peace. Shalom (שָׁלֹם): the Hebrew understanding means wellbeing, covering one's health, prosperity, friendship, salvation and security. It is a communal as well as an individual experience and is possible because of God's presence.[173]

The term 'peace' (εἰρήνη, eiréné) is also found in the New Testament and while the Greek can be translated as an absence of war, it still carries its Old Testament connotations. While shalom is an eschatological hope, its presence is ushered in through Jesus' presence (i.e., Luke 1:79). The first words spoken to his disciples following his resurrection is that of "Peace" (John 20:19). While this is a typical Hebraic greeting, that it is repeated in this verse gives is added impetus. Shalom had been attained between

---

169. E.g., Ward, *Liquid Ecclesiology*.
170. Kahn-Harris and Moberg, "Religious Popular Music," 90.
171. Ricoeur, *Figuring the Sacred*, 239.
172. Bauman, *Community*, 3.
173. Geddert, "Peace," 604; Carson, *Gospel according to John*, 505.

humanity and God. Peace is central to the notion of the Kingdom of God, which Jesus ushers in (e.g., Mark 1:15). Within the bible texts, Jesus' death brings reconciliation between God and humanity and peace heralds in the coming of the Kingdom of God.[174]

Yet, it is the presence of Jesus which brings his peace. In this sense, Jesus's presence will bring ontological security. This can be seen as both a sublime as well as an immanent experience, so echoing Jesus' words: "For where two or three gather in my name, there am I with them" (Matt 18:20). As the Church gathers, so shalom should be experienced, not as a lengthy talk that brings episteme to a situation, rather simple recognition of Jesus' presence as the answer to our ultimate concerns, our need for ontological security. Within liquid modernity the Christian understanding of shalom should be viewed as a key theological and missiological theme.

To develop this, there may not seem much difference, practically speaking, in hearing a knowledge based talk (episteme) about Jesus, and simply recognizing that Christ's Being is present as two or three meet together in Jesus' name (Matt 18:20). Yet, it is the acknowledgment of such presence through which we may go on to find ontological security. We will consider this further in the next chapter when we consider how we use our feelings to check whether we feel an experience is real or not. It is through our emotional reactions where we ultimately decide whether our cognition is correct and whether we should risk incorporating the story that our emotions are reacting with into our own biography.

From drawing out these five points we move from the functional nature of popular music to that of how we engage with songs emotionally.

---

174. Carson, *Gospel according to John*, 506.

5

Music and Emotion

LADY GAGA'S SONG 'SHALLOW' (2018) expresses her wish to be far away from the "shallow area" of superficial relationships.[1] The song expresses her need for greater meaning in life, again reflecting the restless, liquid-modern zeitgeist. The musical exchange between Lady Gaga and Bradley Cooper begins with Cooper asking Lady Gaga if she is content with her life experience or searching for more? In response, Lady Gaga asks Bradly if he is tired of filling the emptiness he felt in life.

From a sociological perspective, this theme is commented on by Bauman: "Human life is . . . an incessant effort to fill the appalling void, to render life meaningful."[2] He speaks, too, of our use of language,[3] self-performance,[4] self-realization[5] and effort to make sense of the world around us. However, little mention is made about how our emotions affect our meaning-making. Yet, as we will see, it is our emotional work *alongside* our cognitive deliberations that contribute to the construction of the self. We will return to 'Shallow' to see how two listeners reflect on this song in their own meaning-making in due course.

According to Bauman, for liquid moderns to fulfil a secure life project, they must have a "'confidence to dwell in disorder' and the ability to 'flourish

---

1. SMF, "Meaning of 'Shallow.'"
2. Bauman and Raud, *Practices of Selfhood*, 5.
3. Bauman and Raud, *Practices of Selfhood*, 21.
4. Bauman and Raud, *Practices of Selfhood*, 40.
5. Bauman and Raud, *Practices of Selfhood*.

in the midst of dislocation.'"[6] We noted in chapter 1 how feelings of confidence are a valuable part of our decision-making processes.[7] Alongside that, we can use our musical appreciation to help regulate our sense of self, to increase feelings of self-confidence, especially, to use Tia DeNora's term, when using popular music to form an "asylum" within which we may consider aspects of our self.[8] In short, our emotional connection with popular music can affect our sense of self, our self-confidence, and even our feelings of ontological security. We will explore this through this chapter. Additionally, we will work towards a deeper understanding of the opportunities presented in purposefully forming an affective space within which aspects of the Christian discourse may be explored. Here, this is the purposeful formation of a space where, using sound, symbol, aesthetics and story, aspects of the Christian story can be engaged with intellectually and emotionally.

Music has long been recognized within musicology as a language of emotion.[9] Moreover, within the psychology of music there has been much work done on the significant links between music and our emotional well-being.[10] We now know that even from before birth we are drawing on musical-like encounters that can stimulate our emotions positively. To follow Rolls' model, these encounters influence our behavior and security. In other words, we become drawn to music that somehow makes us *feel* confident and ontologically secure. Hence, more specifically, there is good evidence to suggest that music is able to engender para-religious experiences.[11]

If the previous chapter explored some of the different forms of information that may be drawn from popular music, so this chapter explores how we may draw this information into our meaning-making. The aim here is to explore this relationship between music, emotion, and religion across four broad areas: (1) We will examine the musical communicative process, termed here as communicative musicality.[12] Influencing us from before birth, this process sets the structures through which we begin to find meaning in the world around us. In considering this we will see how our emotional response to music affects our cognitive reflections and, therefore, the social construction of the world around us. We will also consider how

---

6. Bauman, *The Individualized Society*, 39.
7. Rolls, *Emotion and Decision-Making*, 417.
8. DeNora, *Music Asylums*, 1.
9. E.g., Meyer, *Emotion and Meaning in Music*.
10. E.g., Juslin and Sloboda, *Handbook of Music and Emotion*; DeNora, *Music Asylums*; Gabrielsson, *Strong Experiences*.
11. E.g., Gabrielsson, *Strong Experiences*; Ward, *Gods Behaving Badly*.
12. Gratier and Apter-Danon, "Improvised Musicality of Belonging," 301.

sound, particularly when it is composed, can cause us to feel emotion. (2) This will help us to understand how we have learned to use music in everyday life to regulate our emotions.

(3) This, in turn, will inform our understanding of how we may make good use of our interiority.[13] We should view this, and the purposeful creation of affective space, as helpful in helping to explore the Christian story within liquid modernity. (4) Within musically constructed affective space we are able to encounter a "strong experience with music" (SEM).[14] While not exclusive to the use of affective space, SEM can powerfully affect and change our patterns of behavior, even our whole outlook on life. For some, these experiences are interpreted as being strongly transcendent, religious in nature. This, of course, makes them particularly important for understanding the relationship between popular music and religion.

1. Musical Communication

While there are still those who would suggest that popular music is a lesser form of musical expression,[15] popular music leaves an indomitable mark on many. Tom Beaudoin, for example, notes how popular culture, including popular music, is a "shared generational experience" and causes formative moments of shared collective meanings. In other words, music can help to anchor particular moments of our life's journey: the music to a first romantic dance, the song on the radio as a key family event happens. As he notes, "Pop culture provides the matrix that contains much of what counts as 'meaning' for our generation."[16] A good example in popular music would be the Live Aid concert of 13th July, 1985, which, over thirty years later is still referenced as a key musical event that sought to challenge third world hunger, although there are mixed views concerning its legacy.[17] The term communicative musicality helps us to see that such musical meaning-making begins before birth.

Communicative Musicality

Mlaya Gratier and Gisele Apter-Danon note how the spontaneous interaction between mother and new born child communicates understanding and

---

13. Bauman and Raud, *Practices of Selfhood*, 21.
14. Gabrielsson, *Strong Experiences*, 2.
15. E.g., Scruton, *The Aesthetics of Music*, 496.
16. Beaudoin, *Virtual Faith*, 22.
17. E.g., Jones, *The Eighties*; Grant, "Live Aid," 310.

knowledge, alongside feelings of security. This, they term as the "essence of communicative musicality."[18] In further describing the nature of the term, Stephen Malloch and Colwyn Trevarthen see three important parameters: pulse, quality and narrative.[19] They view pulse as the regular pattern of behavioral events which communicate vocal or gestural information. It is through the pulse that infants begin to anticipate what is happening in the world around them. Quality includes the timbre, pitch and volume of the pulse. The combination of pulse and quality create a narrative of expression and intention through which adult and infant, and subsequently adult to adult can begin to share meaning and gain a sense of passing time. Such narrative structure in infants may be viewed as the "poetic form of protoconversations."[20]

We can see this in action in the poetic nature of 'motherese' and 'baby talk,' whereby the infant responds to the melodic, timbrel and rhythmical quality, often with exaggerated intonation, in the language used primarily by the mother.[21] This can be understood in terms of what the theologian Hans Urs von Balthasar discussed as the awakening of the child: "the little child awakens to self-consciousness through being addressed by the love of his mother."[22] From our perspective, the human reaction to music finds its roots from the earliest experiences with our significant care-providers, while the poetic and aesthetic quality of motherese influences our aesthetic encounters as we grow. It is part of the awakening of our self-consciousness as persons in relation. Our values and virtues are reinforced through this mother/child dyad, particularly so for religious feelings where potent symbolism used in adulthood can most often be traced to early childhood experiences.[23]

In this early mother-child relationship there is, argued Balthasar, the beginnings of a "movement toward God."[24] This highlights the importance of familial socialization into Christian belief. Strategically, not only is the support of that relationship an important responsibility of the wider Church family, but music can be key. It is argued here that it can constitute an important element of the growing person's movement towards God.

---

18. Gratier and Apter-Danon, "Improvised Musicality of Belonging," 301.
19. Malloch and Trevarthen, "Musicality," 4. See also Levitin, *World in Six Songs*, 149.
20. Malloch and Trevarthen, "Musicality," 4.
21. Hodges, *Human Musicality*, 49.
22. Balthasar, *Explorations in Theology III*, 15.
23. Riis and Woodhead, *Sociology of Religious Emotion*, 99.
24. See Balthasar, *Explorations in Theology*, 15–55.

Our ability to respond to emotion begins before birth. In vitro, a baby can distinguish both musical and non-musical sounds from around the seventh month,[25] enabling Raymond North and David Hargreaves to suggest that infants responding to music may be considered as showing an aesthetic response.[26] Again, significantly, an unborn child can respond to the feelings of the birth mother, including the mother's stimulation by sound.[27] Most people can remember a song/music from their very-early childhood. The memory is particularly acute, significant, and often moving if the tune/song was sung to them regularly by their mother. Popular music which reflects childhood memories, such as Aqua's 'Barbie Girl' (1997) are often negatively critiqued, yet the humor of the song connects with listeners precisely because good memories of childhood can be called to mind.

Malloch and Trevarthen develop the link between cultural appreciation and young age by further defining communicative musicality as the

> expression of our human desire for cultural learning, our innate skill for moving, remembering and planning in sympathy with others that makes our appreciation and production of an endless variety of dramatic temporal narratives possible—whether those narratives consist of specific cultural forms of music, dance, poetry or ceremony; whether they are the universal narratives of a mother and her baby quietly conversing with one another; whether it is the wordless emotional and motivational narrative that sits beneath a conversation between two or more adults or between a teacher and a class.[28]

They suggest it is this common musicality that enables us to share meaning-making time together. Likewise, Merlin Donald reinforces the importance of mimesis in enabling humans develop language.[29] Here we are arguing that we draw on these processes in our ongoing search for ontological security. For example, what we hear can resonate with those early experiences of finding safety with our principle care-givers.

Children can interpret such musicality as a form of playfulness,[30] which, we will see, is a helpful concept in understanding how to explore the Christian story within liquid modernity. Play triggers the release of opioids

---

25. Mazokopaki and Kugiumutzakis, "Infant Rhythms," 187.
26. Hargreaves and North, "Experimental Aesthetics," 533.
27. E.g., Malloch and Trevarthen, "Musicality," 2.
28. Malloch and Trevarthen, "Musicality," 4–5.
29. Donald, "Evolutionary Approach to Culture," 56.
30. Malloch and Trevarthen, "Musicality," 7; Donald, "Evolutionary Approach to Culture," 58.

and dopamine in the brain, bringing feelings of pleasure that make the event memorable and a positive learning experience. It strengthens trust while building an attitude that you are safe.[31]

Playful songs such as Los Del Rio's 'Macarena' (1993) will cause all ages to get on the dance floor, enacting a particular set of dance moves which have become almost ritually remembered, even though the song is about the singer's unfaithfulness to her boyfriend. We should also note that somatic interaction helps reinforce the discourses we engage with.[32] The Macarena works precisely because of the dance-moves connected with it. This is further borne out in how communicative musicality helps babies to fulfil aspects of their ritual learning, such as "ceremonial movements" which help build up trust and attachment between child and carer.[33] Through such activity the child learns about shyness and shame as the sense of self develops. This, again, provides the foundations for an adult's future relationships and negotiating skills.

Ulrik Volgsten also makes a strong case in linking music with the early non-verbal communication of a child,[34] where a young child will attune her feelings to the parent's style of song. He, too, notes how the self is developed through such "protonarrative envelopes, articulating the child's earliest sense of desire and motivation, which adds a narrative-like structure to the perceived world."[35] While Volgsten uses the term "protonarrative,"[36] Ellen Dissanayake sees this as a child developing "protomusical" abilities.[37] She also describes this as a baby's ability to attune himself or herself to the carer's sense of rhythm, be that through soft, gentle, rhythmic speaking (*motherese*) or expressions of anger. 'Attunement,' here, is an important aspect of a child finding peace and security with their carer.

Julie Nagel views musical encounters in early childhood acting as a transitional object, akin to a baby's soft toy that brings comfort when the parent is not around. In particular, the mother's voice in motherese tones, becomes associated with gratification, tension reduction, and pleasure, while silence may be threatening and anxiety inducing.[38] Such kinesthetic attunement enables self-soothing and the management of anxiety, even,

---

31. Baylin and Hughes, *Neurobiology of Attachment-Focused Therapy*, 112–94.
32. Malloch and Trevarthen, "Musicality," 6.
33. Also, Levitin, *The World in Six Songs*, 193.
34. Volgsten, "Between Ideology and Identity," 74; see also Brown, "Introduction," 38.
35. Volgsten, "Between Ideology and Identity," 82.
36. Volgsten, "Between Ideology and Identity," 82.
37. Dissanayake, "Root," 22.
38. Nagel, *Melodies of the Mind*, 3.

Dissanayake suggests, enabling interpersonal coordination and conjoinment with others.[39] Tia DeNora notes how we make use of what she terms the "asylum-pod" with the ability to now construct playlists of music on iPods and the like precisely for self-soothing,[40] a point echoed by Daniel Levitin.[41] Such understanding undergirds the practice of music and dance therapy, with its ability to energize and facilitate communicative meaning, especially for those whose lives are characterised by social difficulties.[42] It should also inform our discussions as how someone may become socialized into Christian belief.

These theorists all conclude in differing ways how our earliest experiences are musical in nature and how the contribute to our negotiation of the world as adults. As Dissanayake seeks to convey, "musicality is a psychobiological capacity that underlies all human communication, including music." She additionally notes that the influence of the Enlightenment has been that "more 'scientific', quasi-evolutionary sources and functions for music were proposed."[43] We have already noted aspects of this in the Arnoldian attempts to shape culture.

To reflect this into our developing understanding of 'affective space' we can see that from birth an infant seeks to regulate their feelings in relation with their principal care-provider in order to feel secure within the world as they experience it. The relationship between child and usually the mother then sets the way for secure relationships to be established with others. Because of this we can relate to others and are able to kinaesthetically attune our feelings with them.[44] Affective space, therefore, can be viewed as a space where attunement to a particular discourse around issues of ontological safety can occur.

From Musical Control to Enchantment

That said, as we grow and develop, we also become aware of the emotional power of music to coerce and direct us. Stephen Brown, for example, notes how music can be used to coerce a group of people in at least three discrete forms which he terms tradition, government and industrial control.[45] These

39. Dissanayake, "Root," 26.
40. DeNora, *Music Asylums*, 65.
41. Levitin, *World in Six Songs*, 127.
42. Malloch and Trevarthen, "Musicality," 6; Alderidge, "Music," 10.
43. Dissanayake, "Root," 17.
44. E.g., Dissanayake, "Root," 26.
45. Brown, "Introduction," 1.

particular forms of music can draw on sedimented discourses which hold agency on us.[46] For some, this agency brings security, such as a patriot hearing a national anthem, while, for others, music can act as a symbol which needs to be resisted, such as the "moral panic" experienced in some adults wanting to understand the reasons behind fights between mods and rockers in the 1960s.[47]

The cognitive and discursive power of music and emotion to control and direct can be evidenced too in further ways. North and Hargreaves, for example, are often quoted for their experiment of playing a national style of music with increased wine sales. When French music was played in an off-license, so more French wine was purchased and when German styled was played, more German wine was purchased.[48] North and Hargreaves have also noted how playing fast music can help clear congested areas.[49] Brian Eno wrote his 'Music for Airports' (1978) as environmental music "intended to induce calm and a space to think" and to encourage reflection on one's mortality.[50] However, as Partridge notes, its effects were not positively received, probably because airport users did not want to consider their possible demise through flying![51]

This negative example, though, still underlines the ability of music to influence our individual affective states in differing ways. Similarly, to recall Brown's triad of musical control,[52] we can see the use of musical cultures in forming boundaries of distinction between nation-states, through the use of traditional styled folk music and in employing national anthems.[53] One of the controversies of the Eurovision Song Contest is precisely because, as Paul Jordan observes, it is a "discursive tool in nation building and, in more recent years, nation branding."[54] Volgsten goes as far as noting how "Once sound-making becomes related to verbal discourse and turns into music it is also transformed from a merely social activity into an ideological expression. Musical sound thereby becomes a very subtle ideological manipulator

---

46. E.g., Dissanayake, Root," 34.
47. Cohen, *Folk Devils and Moral Panics*, 2.
48. North and Hargreaves, "Music in Business Environments," 111.
49. North and Hargreaves, "Musical Communication," 409.
50. Eno, "Music for Airports Liner Notes."
51. Partridge, *The Lyre of Orpheus*, 52.
52. Brown, "Introduction," 11.
53. See also Bauman, *Culture*, 54.
54. Jordan, *The Modern Fairy Tale*, 49.

in that-by utilizing the earliest means for human socialization—it *affectively articulates* the discursive contents to which it is bound."[55]

Brown notes how musical stimulation reinforces any association that has made with the symbolic, such as words or rituals used. Such reinforcement helps to persuade individuals to conform to expected attitudes.[56] Here, music semiotically conveys what has previously been denoted as the appropriate response.[57] For example, quiet, solemn music in a sacred space usually causes people to speak quietly. Such activity will also occur as we encounter the cultural milieu of popular music, reacting to it in, often, pre-described ways—the slow romantic dance; the excitement of the mosh-pit.

Brown additionally notes that those who use culture in this manner often unite musical structure to semantic meaning. He, however, argues that a more fruitful way to look at the communicative value of music is via communication studies.[58] The difference is that to consider music semantically focuses on how the receiver interprets music as a sign, whereby, to consider it as part of a wider communication process is to emphasize a wider dynamic of the relationship between the performer (sender), the listener (receiver) and the context within which this occurs.[59] This is also reflected in Clive Marsh's and Vaughan Roberts' argument that popular music communicates something of our ritual needs.[60]

Importantly, Brown maintains that when music is related to either religious or political discourse its influence will maintain and reinforce present values over constructing new beliefs.[61] Alongside that, Marsh and Roberts note a difference in how religious and non-religious listeners relate to political themes expressed in music where justice issues become magnified by religious listeners due to their beliefs.[62] At face value this runs contrary to Hopps' suggestion that music can be a force for re-enchantment. However, the argument throughout has been that once dissonance is experienced it needs resolution.[63] In other words, (re)enchantment remains a possibility when someone feels dissonance with the worldview they hold and seeks resolution.

55. Volgsten, "Between Ideology and Identity," 74.
56. Brown, "Introduction," 14.
57. Middleton, *Studying Popular Music*, 220.
58. Brown, "Introduction," 14–17.
59. See also Raffman, *Language*, 55.
60. Marsh and Roberts, *Personal Jesus*, 9.
61. Brown, "Introduction," 23; see also Volgsten, "Between Ideology and Identity," 75.
62. Marsh and Roberts, "Listening as Religious Practice (Part One)," 133.
63. E.g., Lawler, *Identity*, 1.

Christopher Partridge notes the particular opportunity provided in the relationship between music, spiritual practice and the religious, which is used in our creative use of affective space: "Through its peculiar ability to construct affective space as a site of 'meaning-making,' music encourages psychosomatic states that much spiritual practice seeks to cultivate. . . . In other words, it is used as a prosthetic technology in the construction of sacred space."[64] By that he means that music has the ability to extend the natural abilities of our minds and bodies.[65] As he further asserts, "An appreciation of such noncognitive dimensions of agency is enormously important for understanding the relationship between popular music and religion" be that functional or transcendent in nature.[66]

However, one cannot contrive a space where postemotionalism may occur, that is, where "emotionally charged collective representations [may] be abstracted from their cultural contexts and then manipulated in artificially contrived contexts."[67] This is positive, as it means that should an individual feel some sense of enchantment, it will be from their own interpretation over that of a falsely constructed experience.

Before we can further consider (re)enchantment we need to additionally note other social forces which interpolate us. Marsh and Roberts schematically describe their understanding of this in their *Magisteria-Ibiza Spectrum* (Fig. 19). In seeking to ascertain whether listening to popular music can specifically sustain and shape religious (Christian) belief they seek to explore the relationships between differing sources of authority (*Magisteria*) and that which reflects "a culture characterised by diversity and tribalism but also by the importance of the individual and of personalized autonomy," which encapsulates what is often communicated by the word 'Ibiza', a Balearic island known for its club scene and alternative culture.[68] The center of their spectrum is termed affective space, which is where identity work in relation to the numerous forces suggested in within the Magisteria can be explored. As they note, "authority structures (often as hidden factors) are always at work."[69]

---

64. Partridge, "Emotion," 31.
65. Partridge, "Emotion," 29.
66. Partridge, *Lyre of Orpheus*, 37.
67. Riis and Woodhead, *Sociology of Religious Emotion*, 183.
68. Marsh and Roberts, *Personal Jesus*, 5–18.
69. Riis and Woodhead, *Sociology of Religious Emotion*, 21.

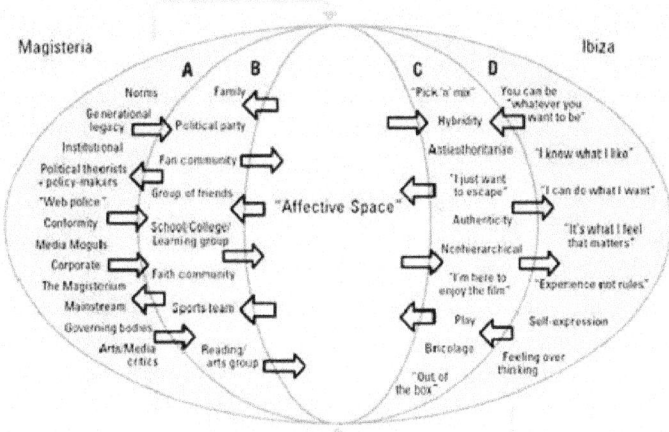

Figure 19: Marsh and Roberts' Magisteria-Ibiza Spectrum[70]

Their model is helpful. It not only emphasizes the fluid nature of liquid modernity by identifying numerous social forces at work, it also reflects something of how identity is expressed at differing levels of the self. However, their schema reflects the idea that 'Ibiza' is about personal choice and hedonism rather than, to follow Bauman, the pursuit of survival of the self. For example, the phrase "You can be whatever you want to be" is used alongside the metaphoric title of Ibiza, reflecting the hedonistic nature of the holiday destination. However, identity construction needs to become understood at a more critical level. Certeau's need to 'make do', and Bauman's 'to cut up' from what sources are available to gain some level of ontological security shows a deeper, more fundamental need for security. It is too superficial to simply say 'we can do what we like.' Rather, restlessness is present because of wider society's inability to resolve the conundrum of what the purpose of life is for or how best to attain that.

Marsh's and Roberts' work does not go deep enough to explore why people are being *coerced into* making the choices they make. This is what Bauman's work helpfully explores. Their schema also notes the place of emotion and authority in constructing affective space, so creating a space where a sense of wonder may become experienced, yet its superficiality masks the need as to *why* identity work is so important to complete.[71] Again, it is not about simplistic lifestyle choices, it is fundamentally about the need

70. Marsh and Roberts, *Personal Jesus*, 19.
71. Marsh and Roberts, *Personal Jesus*, 79.

to feel ontologically secure in a world where so many social forces pull you in differing directions and where dissonance needs resolution.

Rather than framing affective space as an individualistic, momentary emotional space, it ought to be understood as a place for learning, even informing a pedagogy within which identity work can be completed. In purposefully creating a space that is aesthetically and emotionally driven, those who experience cognitive dissonance can begin to attune to a differing narrative and to interrogate it to see if its offer is robust enough to offer ontological security. This is to recognize the spatial turn, the awareness of the value of place and space, noting John Corrigan's comments that "The experience of space and the process of place-making are central elements of how communities develop codes that order emotional life."[72] Such space can encourage the formation of emotional regimes which can help someone to experience the divine.[73] Our emotions become the fuel that enables such learning. This emotional energy can be induced in us through our aesthetic encounters. In considering popular music we will briefly cover differing theories of music and emotion, building to how music can induce emotion in us.

Differing Theories of Music and Emotion

There are a number of theories which seek to explain the relationship between music and emotion. For example, music has been said to act symbolically in the same way that language is a set of symbols through which emotional content is conveyed. However, music does not intrinsically hold semantic content, the ability to convey the subtle differences in the meaning of related words, or the ability to convey predication such as linguistically affirming or proclaiming something. Neither can it express prepositional closure, that is to help describe the relationship between differing objects.

Akin to symbolic theory lies synesthetic theory, which suggests that certain timbres transmit emotion, such as a saxophone's tone conveying a particular ambience and feeling. Yet, while ambience can be expressed, there is no evidence to show that this generates emotion.[74] There is wider agreement that the easiest emotions to convey through music are those seen as 'basic emotions,' such as happiness, sadness, anger, fear and love. Yet there are often coinciding non-vocal cues given, such as the performer's

---

72. Corrigan, "Introduction," 158.
73. Riis and Woodward, *Sociology of Religious Emotion*, 47.
74. Davies, "Emotions Expressed," 25–26.

facial expressions, or the tone of the radio presenter's voice, which can give rise to the perception of an emotion.[75]

A further suggestion is that composers and songwriters simply express their own emotions that then cognitively arouse emotion in the listener.[76] However, a performer (and listener) need not follow the writer's original intentions, interpreting the composition in their own manner. Therefore, a musical piece's emotional character is interpreted by the way we have previously indexed the genre of music against past events.[77]

Stephen Davies' contour theory suggests that rather than music expressing emotion, it presents emotional characteristics. In other words, expressiveness is a property of the music itself, which is decoded by the listener in the same manner that a person can decode the expression on another's face by looking at them. This enables Davis to assert "when we attribute emotions to music, we are describing the emotional character it presents, just as we do when we call the willow sad or the car happy."[78] Akin to this, Robert Beckford speaks of the "semiotics of sound" in describing how we decode music to make sense of it within a spatial setting.[79] Colin Martindale and Kathleen More also note how one's aesthetic preference is based on prior cognitive understandings of their emotional expectations. Therefore, having listened to a good example of something that provides aesthetic pleasure, one is able to ascertain if future encounters elicit the same of more intense results.[80]

Juslin suggests that our understanding of musical expression echoes how we express our state of mind in real life. Yet, he suggests that while music holds the ability to express and induce emotions the listener must first be able to understand something of the music's symbolic content, be it in understanding the composer or performer's intention for the song, or awareness of how the listener may respond.[81] In other words, to what level we are able to decode the expressive intention of the composer or the performer of a piece, or the affect of a live performance and how that is responded to. While this does not demonstrate how emotion becomes induced in an individual it does help to show that the more intensely a listener

---

75. Juslin, "From Mimesis to Catharsis," 100.

76. Davies, "Emotions Expressed," 29.

77. Lipscomb, "Cognitive Organization of Musical Sound," 139; Dowling and Harwood, *Music Cognition*, 204.

78. Davies, "Emotions Expressed," 31–33.

79. Beckford, *Jesus Dub*, 26.

80. Martindale and More, "Priming," 661.

81. Juslin, "From Mimesis to Catharsis," 85–88.

draws from a particular genre or repertoire the more that they are likely to emotionally draw from it.

Vladimir Konečni favors what he describes as the "royal road," the "aesthetic trinity," as the way music elicits emotional states. He asserts that for music to produce emotions, its effects must be cognitively mediated by memories and associations concerning powerful real-world events.[82] He does not favor the argument that emotions are induced, which we will consider below, arguing that research in its favor "can be seen to be sizable variety of linguistic and methodological pitfalls for researchers in the music to emotion area, which have sometimes resulted in dubious conclusions that emotion has been directly induced by music."[83]

Music and Induced Emotion

There is, though, a growing body of work that does favor music's ability to induce emotion in a listener, in some way bypassing aspects of cognition and providing a direct stimulus to the brain. However, there is, again, no consensus as to how music is able to do this. For example, Judith Becker argues that while emotion may be induced, emotions relating to music are culturally embedded and socially constructed.[84] In contrast, Isabelle Peretz opines that basic emotions such as happiness, sadness, fear and anger are assumed to be innate, driven by reflex-like circuits, but that induced musical emotions are more nuanced.[85] Martindale and More also note that emotion can be induced when a listener's expectation is met or violated, such as a climatic outcome of the music, or an unresolved musical suspension finding resolution.[86]

While Becker suggests that musical emotions are different from life-experience emotions, being experienced through tears, chills or shivers, goose bumps and perspirations, which she terms as aesthetic emotions,[87] Patrik Juslin and Daniel Vastfjall[88] argue that there is no evidence to suggest that musical emotions are any different from others forms of emotional response. This wider body of work supports Rolls' work on emotions and

---

82. Konečni, "Does Music Induce Emotion?," 123.
83. Konečni, "Does Music Induce Emotion?," 127.
84. Becker, *Deep Listeners*, 145.
85. Peretz, "Neurobiology of Musical Emotions," 100. Also, Starr, *Feeling Beauty*, 43.
86. Martindale and More, "Priming," 565.
87. Becker, *Deep Listeners*, 45.
88. Juslin and Vastfjall, "Emotional Responses to Music," 572.

reinforces the argument that music holds the ability to induce emotion. Juslin and Vastfjall reflect Rolls' theory arguing additionally that

> research on music and emotion has failed to become cumulative because music researchers have either neglected underlying psychological mechanisms or assumed that musical emotions reflect a cognitive appraisal. We argue that it is important to look beyond appraisal theory and consider alternative but less obvious ways in which music might induce emotions. While appraisal may be important for many forms of art, there are other mechanisms that are far more relevant in the case of music. We claim that if these additional mechanisms are taken into account, there is nothing particularly strange about results that suggest that music induces all kinds of emotions.[89]

Juslin and Vastfjall consider six mechanisms through which emotions become induced. That is through the brain stem reflex via one or more acoustical characteristics of the music; emotion may also be induced as the acoustic stimulus has been repeatedly paired with other positive or negative stimuli; emotional contagion may happen as the emotion of a piece of music is perceived by a listener who then mimics this expression internally, which leads to an induction of the same emotion.[90] Again, this reflects Baylin and Hughes' work with traumatized children.[91] As they note, "emotions are contagious largely because their bodily affective expression tends to evoke a similar affective expression in the person who perceives them."[92] Again, this adds support to Roll's understanding of brain construction together with how music may positively affect us.

Emotion may also be induced as the listener imagines visual images while listening to the music, such as a beautiful landscape. Likewise, where music causes the listener to remember a particular event, an episodic memory, so emotion may also become induced. Juslin and Vastfjall note that while music theorists often regard such episodic events as less "musically relevant," it probably is one of the most frequent and subjectively important sources of emotion in music.[93]

---

89. Juslin and Vastfjall, "Emotional Responses to Music," 561.
90. Juslin and Vastfjall, "Emotional Responses to Music," 564.
91. E.g., Baylin and Hughes, *Neurobiology of Attachment-Focused Therapy*, 246.
92. Baylin and Hughes, *Neurobiology of Attachment-Focused Therapy*, 118.
93. Juslin and Vastfjall, "Emotional Responses to Music," 565–67.

Cognitive, Discursive and Induced Emotional Engagement with Music

The argument here is that music does induce emotional energy which we process as either a reward or a punisher. It is this energy which we can positively use in the formation of places where the stimulation of our own affective space can be encouraged. Reflective practice holds value, too. This is not to downplay the relationship between cognitive and social constuctionist approaches to music and emotion, rather it simply highlights the importance of our emotional work as we appraise our musical encounters.[94] As Gabrielle Starr notes, musical experience is "cognitive, sensory and emotional."[95]

To draw this together, both Rolls' work and the theory of communicative musicality demonstrate that our need for ontological security is not simply governed by our cognitive reasoning alone. It is not the case whether one 'offer' from the holistic milieu is rationally stronger than another. Rather, from birth we have a *felt* need for ontological security. For the majority this is established through a strong, positive emotional bond with our principal carer. As we grow, mature and make sense of the world around us we still employ the same processes in order to stay in-tune with our experiences of the world around us. As adults, for example, when we feel stressed we may make use of peaceful music to attune our feelings on anxiety to that of the restful emotion that can be induced from the music, mirroring the troubled infant finding attunement with its principal carer by drawing on their tone of voice, breathing and heart-rate. The music we listen to can help us recall positive memories from past times.[96] This is central to constructing our identities and narratives about ourselves.

Likewise, the need for a 'big story' to help us frame both our lifeworld experiences and that which may lie beyond its horizon can be viewed in the terms of communicative musicality. As already discussed, before the Enlightenment the West sought to do this through the Christian discourse. Within liquid modernity with its various offers of ontological security which we "saw up" and "make fit,"[97] we are drawn to those aesthetically expressed narratives in the world around us, the pulse and quality of which helps us to attune ourselves to the wider discourses that may be being expressed. Such a process is enacted between writers such as Mel C and her song 'Dear life' and those who listen to her song finding themselves attuning to her thinking.

---

94. See also Robinson, *Deeper than Reason*, 26.
95. Starr, *Feeling Beauty*, 16.
96. E.g., Partridge, *Mortality and Music*, 72.
97. Bauman, *The Individualized Society*, 142.

This is evidenced by the comments on the video's YouTube page (discussed earlier), such as one fan who expresses "I absolutely love this song. It is intoxicating. I find myself singing it out of the blue. Great song Mel. Thank you for this wonderful blessing. May you be as blessed in return."[98]

Such an emotionally driven response, the need to attune to what is felt to be authentic, seemingly ontologically real, is a challenge to an epistemologically driven rational world. Yet, we can argue that we are hard-wired from birth to respond in this way. When listening to a lyric that expresses ontological security we are offered the opportunity to attune our self away from feelings of dissonance towards feelings of security.

To apply this to the purposeful construction of space where we can stimulate our own affective space, it can be argued that such space should be a managed safe place which enables the exploration of differing discourses. This will, of course, be governed by our own emotional responses, yet we are influenced, too, by those we seek to relate to. It is a place where sonic and physical symbols interact. It is a potent space, where, as Riis and Woodhead note, both emotionally explicit and implicit regimes may provide agency.[99] An explicit regime may be a Christian experiencing a moment of revelation whilst prayerfully reverencing a cross; an implicit regime could well be an encounter with a beautiful sunset which brings feelings of peace which we in turn attribute to the divine. The creation of places where the use of our affective space is encouraged can allow feelings that are not otherwise socially permitted to become expressed. We use such methodology in our use of music in everyday life. Here, we are applying this to particular places to explore thoughts concerning what may lie beyond the horizon of the lifeworld.

2. Music in Everyday Life

DeNora, whose sociological work has focused on our use of music in everyday life, has expressed surprise that this has not been extensively explored in the constitution of self.[100] As she notes, music's aesthetic quality is all too often ignored in favor of its cognitive and discursive content.[101] She further comments "Using music as a resource for creating and sustaining ontological security, and for entraining and modulating mood and levels of distress, is by no means unique to the purview of the professional music therapeutic encounter. In the course of daily life, many of us resort to music, often in

---

98. See John Pitharas' comment in Melanie C., "Melanie C – Dear Life."
99. Riis and Woodhead, *Sociology of Religious Emotion*, 169.
100. DeNora, *Music in Everyday Life*, 46.
101. DeNora, *Music in Everyday Life*, 109.

highly reflexive ways. Building and deploying musical montages is part of a repertory of strategies for coping and for generating pleasure, creating occasion, and affirming self and group identity."[102]

At a basic level, this reflexive process is reflected in two comments made in connection with Lady Gaga's song 'Shallow.' One fan notes how "Shallow by Lady Gaga really pulled on my heart strings for several reasons. For me, this is a song that everyone can relate to at some point in life. Change is scary, and the bad times can really make us question our own sanity.... [It] makes me reminisce about the journey I travelled not only for love, but also to find myself.[103] A further comment highlights "Lady Gaga and Bradley Cooper really explore the idea of the "deep and troubled" artist in this song. They sing about how ill content they are with average, everyday life and can't settle for living "in the shallow." As a young millennial who just entered the workforce and has fallen into a steady routine, I can relate."[104]

However, simply listening to music in an unstructured manner will not alone resolve feelings of dissonance. Indeed, it may amplify such feelings. For example, in speaking of the Emo subculture Partridge notes, "Its music seeks to evoke dispositions that often reflect an exaggerated sense of vulnerability, nostalgia, despair and social dislocation." Where death is viewed as the resolution of life's struggles, so this musical community can, perversely, find an element of ontological security in a discourse of mutual self-harm.[105]

Resolution of existential restlessness still requires discussion, cognition and even political resolve to facilitate resolution.[106] David Hesmondhalgh makes this point in critiquing DeNora's work by noting that music provides only a "constrained agency" and that the music-in-everyday-life-approach does not take sufficient note of social and psychological dynamics that may limit individual freedom. Yet he does observe how "We should not underestimate the psychic difficulties that individuals face in constructing a coherent and healthy self-identity."[107] He even suggests that her (and John Sloboda's) approach to the effects of music is too positivistic, leaving little

---

102. DeNora, *Music in Everyday Life*, 16.
103. See sphinxsnake's comment in "Lady Gaga – Shallow."
104. See ReonataO's comment in "Lady Gaga – Shallow."
105. Partridge, *Mortality and Music*, 100–109.
106. I.e., Bauman, *Culture*, 69.
107. Hesmondhalgh, *Why Music Matters*, 40. See also Lynch, "Role of Popular Music," 486.

room for the "dark side of human nature."[108] Indeed, it is too "middle-class," thus leading to an incomplete sociology of music.[109]

Where Hesmondhalgh and DeNora concur is how music is "powerfully" linked to memory, drawing links between the cognitive, emotional and sensory aspects of our being.[110] The link between memory and music is important. Our musical memories can help us to recall positive life experiences precisely because of the holistic nature of listening to music which affects us emotionally, cognitively and sensory,[111] even spatially.[112] From a spiritual perspective, memory can help us recall past moments when we have particularly recognized the divine.

Dido's 'You Don't Need a God' (2019) provides an example of her everyday encounter with music. Of particular note are her reflections on immanent and transcendent understandings of spirituality. Very poetically she notes how even the sound of a song from a vehicle driving by can, as it were, move her from one place to another. Very interestingly, she speaks of her need for the immanent resourcing of the self, which, for her, can be fulfilled through popular music rather than a transcendent encounter with the divine. For Dido, such musical encounters can result in strong experiences with music, which we will subsequently discuss. One fan recounts via YouTube how the song has affected him both cognitively and emotionally: "Such an awesome addition to the soundtrack of this so called life of mine! Here's to spanning your collection that transforms me and rescues me from fear . . . and keeps me anticipating the next song to boot up while each moment possible can be peacefully cherished!"[113]

Something of the movement and rhythm of the music helps sustain us and draws us to the song.[114] Hesmondhalgh notes the importance of dance in expressing emotion and its value in play.[115] Our internal processes become affected by the music's rhythm.[116] Starr, like DeNora, also identifies the link between emotion and the need *for* motion. For her, rhythm is even able to drive individuals forward, helping them to seek hope through

---

108. Hesmondhalgh, *Why Music Matters*, 40.
109. Hesmondhalgh, *Why Music Matters*, 52.
110. Hesmondhalgh, *Why Music Matters*, 53; DeNora, *Music Asylums*, 4.
111. Starr, *Feeling Beauty*, 16; Partridge, *Mortality and Music*, 71.
112. Brown, *God and Enchantment*, 153.
113. See Brett Golightly's comment in Dido, "Dido – You Don't Need a God."
114. E.g., Middleton, *Popular Music Analysis*, 106.
115. Hesmondhalgh, *Why Music Matters*, 32.
116. DeNora, *Music in Everyday Life*, 95; DeNora, *Music Asylums*, 3, see also Starr, *Feeling Beauty*, 88.

encountering fresh poetic experiences that may offer ontological security. She notes how neuro-mapping identifies how viewers who describe their response to an artwork as extremely moving, brain regions often implicated in self-assessment, forward planning, autobiographical memory, and ideas of self, were triggered.[117]

Significantly, these parts of the brain lay alongside those which are engaged with movement.[118] To follow George Lakoff and Mark Johnson's thinking, that we primarily make sense of our life experience through our bodies[119] suggests that the movement and emotion of a sung worship event is a learning opportunity that may help to close the gap between espoused and operative beliefs, a moment for reinforcing Christian identity and of embodying God's story. Ironically, the formal learning activity within such a service is predominantly passive, often in the form of a lengthy preachment. Grace Jones' 'Slaves to the Rhythm' (1985) helps make the point that the rhythm, the pulse of the songs we encounter in daily life significantly affect what we may draw from it overall, hence it is useful as a prosthetic technology.[120] This does emphasize the elementary processes of communicative musicality seen in the pulse and quality of the fundamental relationship between carer and infant. In short, rhythm and movement become avenues through which differing narratives can become entrained within us, even when heard 'in the background.' Music can provoke individuals to react, by disturbing, motivating and inspiring them as one attunes themselves to the rhythmic patterns of the music.

3. Affective Space as an Asylum

In using Erving Goffman's term, *asylum*, DeNora's work becomes more focused in looking at music as a resource for the self. In particular, she explores how music can form an affective space that facilitates respite from distress. Indeed, such space provides opportunity to flourish where one finds the ability to "feel as if one is in the flow of things, to be able to feel creative and to engage in creative play, to enjoy a sense of validation or connection to others, to feel pleasure, perhaps to note the temporary absence or temporary abatement, of pain."[121]

---

117. Starr, *Feeling Beauty*, 47.
118. Starr, *Feeling Beauty*, 81.
119. Lakoff and Johnson, *Metaphors We Live By*, 56.
120. Partridge, *The Lyre of Orpheus*, 51–55.
121. DeNora, *Music Asylums*, 1.

In drawing on Michel Foucault's term, music listened to in the asylum acts as a "technology of the self." It helps to regulate our sense of self, as much as it may allow for a collective gathering of emotion.[122] In contrast to Brown's musical control, DeNora views music as a stimulant for social development, formed by the way the listener interacts with the music and their surroundings.[123] This allows it to become a personal "musically reconfiguring agency,"[124] so facilitating the "cultural construction of subjectivity."[125]

DeNora notes, too, that music can, in certain situations, be used so that pharmacological and other medical interventions are not needed.[126] Indeed, she argues that such wellbeing enables both ontological security and flow,[127] albeit if only in the affective space of the asylum. Such creative use allows her to see music "as a meaningful and aesthetic form, [which] affords the creation of pathways toward or away from desirable and undesirable environmental matters. Music is simultaneously meaningful and functional."[128]

Likewise, Benjamin Koen notes this activity enables the "human certainty principle" which he describes as the "certitude or knowing that resides deep within a person's being and can effect transformations and healing therein and beyond."[129] Essentially, it is through communicative musicality that music holds agency within this space.

Edmund Rolls' work additionally reflects this by highlighting that we positively respond to stimuli, so affecting our behavior, our cognitive reasoning and ultimately our meaning-making. We will see this in particular in our subsequent understanding of strong encounters with music (SEM). However, that is not to say that musical encounters that are less intense hold diminished value, simply they affect our decision making in a less intense manner.

Again, to reflect this into our discussion around affective space, the ability to use music for self-regulation, together with the opportunity to discursively discuss aspects of life with trusted individuals, provides the opportunity to road-test differing feelings towards ontological security, even providing the opportunity to playfully try out aspects of a new discourse. However, as we will see, aspects of this process can become fast-tracked

---

122. DeNora, *Music Asylums*, 5.
123. DeNora, *Music in Everyday Life*, 41.
124. DeNora, *Music in Everyday Life*, 53.
125. DeNora, *Music in Everyday Life*, 73.
126. DeNora, *Music Asylums*, 31.
127. E.g., Csikszentmihalyi, *Flow*.
128. DeNora, *Music Asylums*, 73.
129. Koen, "Music-Prayer-Meditation," 95.

when one encounters a strong experience with music, or, to recall Paul Tillich's experience, a strong experience with art.[130]

4. Strong Experiences with Music

There are many accounts of individuals being overwhelmed by a musical experience. Gabrielsson terms this a "strong experiences with music"—SEM,[131] while Thomas Schäfer, Mario Smukalla and Sarah-Ann Oelker classify this as an intense musical experience—IME.[132] There is agreement that these experiences can profoundly affect a listener. Such experiences can be characterized by an altered state of consciousness, leading to feelings of harmony and self-realization. Such experiences can change personal values or motivate individuals to attain the same harmony in their daily life.[133] We begin our discussion in noting Marghanita Laski and Maslow's contribution to strong aesthetic experiences.

There are clear links between Maslow's "peak-experiences,"[134] which mark a point of self-actualization and SEM. Such experiences provide insight into "the psychology of the fully evolved and authentic Self and its ways of being."[135] If a peak-experience is to speak of human fulfilment, then Maslow equally recognizes it is human nature to move away from the unfulfilment of illness in all its forms, including feelings of dissonance such as discussed in chapter 1. He is also keen to note the importance of creativity in attaining self-actualization. In contrast to both Gabrielsson and Schäfer, Smukalla and Oelker's understanding of SEM, Maslow saw peak-experiences occurring primarily with older people who are at peace with themselves towards the end of their lives.[136]

As Maslow describes it, "The peak-experience is felt as a self-validating, self-justifying moment which carries its own intrinsic value with it" which will, more or less, permanently change one's outlook on life, releasing creativity and spontaneity.[137] The experience can make life feel more worth-while, bringing peace to the individual and the world around them,

130. Tillich, *On Art and Architecture*, 235.
131. Gabrielsson, *Strong Experiences*, 2.
132. Schäfer et al., "How Music Changes Our Lives," 525.
133. Schäfer et al., "How Music Changes Our Lives," 525; Gabrielsson, *Strong Experiences*, 4.
134. Maslow, *Toward a Psychology of Being*, 83.
135. Maslow, *Toward a Psychology of Being*, 24.
136. Maslow, *Toward a Psychology of Being*, 26–30.
137. Maslow, *Toward a Psychology of Being*, 67.

even bringing a fresh innocence to life.[138] We can begin to note here, the similarities between SEM and aspects of the Christian understanding of shalom, which is about discovering wholeness in body, mind and spirit (We will return to this in the next chapter).

Laski also sought to investigate such peak-experiences, although her preferred terminology was that of ecstasy which she drew from the Catholic tradition of mystic experience.[139] While her respondents described their experiences as either sacred or secular in nature, she argued that such experiences were entirely secular and biological in nature. She particularly noted that when an individual described a religious experience they already held the language to be able to describe it as such[140] and, therefore, to borrow William James's term, showed overbelief.[141] For her, drawing on Nietzsche, "we hear only the questions to which we are capable of finding an answer."[142] She was keen to argue that religious experiences could hold "an alternative possibility" yet still be as "awe-inspiring as earlier interpretations."[143] Yet, she falls into her own interpretative understanding of overbelief, in that she provides no space for alternative interpretations to be listened to.

Laski identified several settings which could trigger an ecstatic moment, such as encountering natural beauty, art, poetic or scientific knowledge,[144] deducing that such moments could fall into three categories: tumescence and release (e.g., 'like a great climax which has built up—this thing has been seething inside you and suddenly it comes out'), tumescence only (e.g., 'something wells up, grows like a spring'); or release only (e.g., 'it sort of overwhelms you, it hits you . . . , and it's all powerful.'[145] She even describes one set of recorded experiences as "adamic," that of encountering a feeling of agape, with "especial warmth" for those on the edges of society. The lens that she interprets this though is not that of religion, rather, she posits that "those who pursue adamic values are often lowly educated and wanting to keep things simple.[146]

There are clearly many similarities between Laski and Maslow's work, with Robert Panzarella, whose research we will consider in a moment,

138. Maslow, *Toward a Psychology of Being*, 87.
139. Laski, *Ecstasy*, 5.
140. Laski, *Ecstasy*, 8.
141. Laski, *Ecstasy*, 20.
142. Laski, *Ecstasy*, 339.
143. Laski, *Ecstasy*, 373.
144. Laski, *Ecstasy*, 17.
145. Laski, *Ecstasy*, 19.
146. Laski, *Ecstasy*, 228.

suggesting that Maslow was influenced by Laski in arguing that a peak experience would only be transformative when there was self-recognition of the cognitive aspect of the experience, over that of, simply, an emotional response.[147] To turn to Panzarella, by drawing on his respondent's thick narratives he identified what he saw as four phenomenological aesthetical stimuli: renewal, motor-sensory, withdrawal and fusion-emotional experiences. Renewal experiences are more associated with visual encounters while motor-sensory experiences correlate with music. Such renewal experiences are linked with feelings of self-actualization. He noted, too, a very high correlation between those who experienced visually driven peak experiences and those who either paint or complete other visual art forms and, likewise, between audio experiences and those who play music.[148]

That Panzarella widened the range of stimuli from simply our emotional responses to music to include the visual, so reminding us again of the Renaissance notion of *ut pictura poesis*, of the similarity in emotional and poetic affect between the visual, aural and poetic based arts. With reference to the creation of an affective space within which spirituality can be explored, it emphasizes that scholars have to understand more than simply the sonic characteristics. Affective space makes use of all our senses.

Alongside four key stimuli Panzarella additionally noted four forms of ecstasy. Renewal ecstasy allows for the cognitive renewal of past experiences, such that the world becomes viewed with added beauty. He deducts that such experiences are experienced by those with musical or visual abilities.[149] By his categorizations, high feelings or floating sensations, which may include somatic reactions such as increased in heartbeat, are termed motor-sensory ecstasy. Yet, he comments that such experiences are "rarely described as satisfying, fulfilling, renewing or the like." This shows the emotional response hold less agency, where the physical reactions are more localized in parts of the body that are, in some way, more detached from the 'self.' Withdrawal ecstasy involves a sense of withdrawal from one's physical and social environment, where one's attention becomes deeply focused on the aesthetic stimulus. Lastly, he notes a fusion-emotional ecstasy, which, drawing on Laski's terminology, is primarily drawn from religious experiences.[150]

Panzarella views these experiences occurring in three stages. Initially, cognitive judgements regarding the aesthetical content are made, leading to

---

147. Panzarella, "The Phenomenology of Aesthetic," 70.
148. Panzarella, "The Phenomenology of Aesthetic," 69–72.
149. Panzarella, "The Phenomenology of Aesthetic," 75.
150. Panzarella, "The Phenomenology of Aesthetic," 76–77.

a climax stage where an individual may either loose or gain motor experience, before a more emotional response was felt towards the end of the musical or visual experience, where subsequent motivational responses would begin to be felt.[151]

Of note is that 90 percent of his respondents attribute long-lasting, usually permanent effects to their peak experiences, often recalled in a vivid memory from which the respondent can again draw from. In particular, Panzarella reported a wider range of triggers than that of Maslow, including that of popular music and popular art. In other words, encountering popular music or popular music videos can leave a profound mark on you which can affect your sense of ontological security. Interestingly, he concludes that music is becoming more sensory while visual art is becoming more intellectual.[152] Panzarella's work is particularly helpful in that it emphasizes the emotional responses from a wider field of stimuli from that of simply musical experiences, while he also emphasizes the life affirming nature of ecstatic moments which are non-cognitively, emotionally driven.

To move to Gabrielsson's significant research, he reviewed one thousand, three hundred and fifty differing accounts of SEM from which he drew out one hundred and fifty different reactions, further refined into a three levels.[153] His work validates much of his predecessors work, yet he further draws out the long lasting effects that SEM may have on people. He notes, too, that individuals of all ages may be surprised by the intensity of such emotions.[154] We will draw on just some of his differing reactions.

Interestingly, those who remembered musical experiences from early life were seen to hold secure attachments within the family, further reflecting the effects of communicative musicality. Such young experiences were expressed in the language of wonderment and being overwhelmed,[155] with these feelings being recalled in later life. Our use of affective space can draw on this, to help recall positive past experiences of spirituality in childhood, reimagining them for later age. Again, this reflects the important link between music and memory. Gabrielsson additionally noted that around 25 percent of his sample reported an SEM during their teenage years, although he deduces that this higher percentage may simply be because older people were not exposed to the level of music that younger

---

151. Panzarella, "The Phenomenology of Aesthetic," 79.
152. Panzarella, "The Phenomenology of Aesthetic," 80–83.
153. Gabrielsson, *Strong Experiences*, 373.
154. Gabrielsson, *Strong Experiences*, 13.
155. Gabrielsson, *Strong Experiences*, 13.

people are.[156] He notes, too, how our encounters with music in teenage years often becomes decisive for how we continues to engage with music in the future.[157]

In noting how our visual sense usually dominates our other senses,[158] Gabrielsson also noted that SEM encountered at popular music concerts are more than the result of simply encountering the music. It speaks again of our encounter with a whole aesthetic, through styles of dress, the lights and atmosphere of the venue, dancing and being with likeminded individuals, akin to Durkheim's "collective effervescence." This is noted, too, in Graham St John's observations on the political and aesthetical details of the early underground dance scene.[159]

In contrast, Gabrielsson's research makes interesting links with music that DeNora would describe as 'music in everyday life.' He provides examples of people encountering SEM while performing household chores with music only being listened to in the background. We should at this point recall the example of Dido's song 'You don't need a God'. While such experiences may seem surprising, Starr suggests that all powerful aesthetic experiences involve an element of the unexpected.[160]

In Gabrielsson's thinking, SEM can range from strong and intense feelings, positive feelings, sometimes negative feelings, even contradictory feelings.[161] Such feelings may cause the respondent to try and recreate the experience. Like DeNora and Juslin, he concludes that music "can be perceived as mirroring what it means to be a human being, the conditions for life in it; its various phases, what life can offer, and how one ought/can take advantage of its possibilities," such that some experiences are so intense the individual recognizes the moment cannot be recaptured, leaving the experience to be 'unrivalled,' 'ultimate,' or 'holy' in nature.[162]

These experiences may, ultimately, profoundly affect the individual's outlook on life. Some of Gabrielsson's respondents interpreted such experiences as religious in nature. Again, he notes that such experiences result from the mixture of music, the context of where the serious encounter with music SEM occurred and the language already held by the respondent to

---

156. Gabrielsson, *Strong Experiences*, 36.
157. Gabrielsson, *Strong Experiences*, 59.
158. See also Clarke, "Music," 90.
159. John, *Tecnomad*, 28.
160. Starr, *Feeling Beauty*, 119.
161. Gabrielsson, *Strong Experiences*, 120.
162. Gabrielsson, *Strong Experiences*, 144.

describe it.[163] For example, he records a middle aged woman as stating how a musical concert affected her: "I had been deeply moved in my soul and I felt very inspired. I think that I can say without exaggeration that this music gives me the courage to face life. It gives me strength when I feel that I need it, it brings to life joy and a fighting spirit and inspiration."[164]

Or, a lady encountering a concert of Finnish Tango, who reported: "Afterwards I was bouncy, giggling, lively, and filled with deep joy. It was really about a life-kick. . . . It was so bewildering that it almost felt like a salvation. It was as if I was selected to take part in such an experience when I needed it the most."[165] A man describing his experience of religious music recited how "I was absolutely enchanted, shocked. In a way that I shall never forget. More than 50 years have passed since that time. I remember how I thought then—and always when I have thought about it later—that if any worldly song could give a vision of heavenly song, this was it. My experience is indescribable. During my long life I have of course had the time to have many experiences of music, positive as well as negative. But no experience came anywhere near this."[166] Or, again, Gabrielsson recounts how one man's experience at a Christian rock concert left him feeling: "Straight afterwards I felt deeply touched. I was touched by God through the music and God can touch us in all situations. I think the biggest reason for the experience depended on God's presence during the concert."[167]

This is echoed by accounts of SEM which occur in the EDM scene. While not using the term SEM, both Sylvan and Jimi Fritz record their own experiences on the dance floor in such manner. Both Fritz[168] and Sylvan[169] describe these experiences as spiritual, while, in their reflections on the scene, Lynch[170] and St John[171] speak of such experiences as liminal dance-floor experiences which allow for self-realization. Yet, to purposefully create a space where liminal experiences may occur does not mean that an SEM can be manufactured. SEM simply happen as and when they do, yet they can have profound effects.

163. Gabrielsson, *Strong Experiences*, 172.
164. Gabrielsson, *Strong Experiences*, 197.
165. Gabrielsson, *Strong Experiences*, 205.
166. Gabrielsson, *Strong Experiences*, 175.
167. Gabrielsson, *Strong Experiences*, 178.
168. Fritz, *Rave Culture*, 179.
169. Sylvan, *Trance Formation*, 79.
170. Lynch, *After Religion*, 88.
171. John, "An Overview," 15.

The experience of the dance floor is that liminality, at the very least, helps to reinforce the narrative that is being told there. For example, Tim Olaveson describes rave as "timeless places, removed social spaces where utopias are both imagined and lived."[172] The dance-floor functions as, to use Hakim Bey's term, a "Temporary Autonomous Zone" (TAZ), a liminal and marginal space where many hopes and fears are expressed.[173] The overall aesthetic of the dance floor aids liminality and self-expressive spiritual encounter. Sarah Thornton notes this defining attitude as "the buzz, vibe, mood or atmosphere created in interaction with the DJ and the crowd in space."[174]

St John, in considering the Underground EDM scene suggests that the underground clubs in Nazi Germany created a 'rebellious aesthetic' which the Underground sought to keep going.[175] Hillegonda Rietveld acknowledges that "amplified dance music carries me into another plane of experience, in regular beat comforting me while a world of musical textures, rhythms and visual impressions whirls around me. I forget how I arrived here, about my usual daily life, myself. My body seems to have shed its burdens of human existence, its limitations reduced: free at last."[176]

For her the soundscape becomes a place for spiritual energizing.[177] Here we again see music acting as a prosthetic technology. Within EDM mainly wordless songs are used to prevent distraction,[178] alongside the DJs' 'tricks' of filtering to change the sonic quality of the music, the use of 'EQ' to drop the bass when beat matching songs and the depth of narrative between clubber and DJ.[179] In addition, the scene's use of drugs such as MDMA (ecstasy) aids liminal attainment.[180] Such space is transgressive, therefore adding to the potential of the affective space.

Schäfer, Smukalla and Oelker's work reinforces that of Maslow's, Panzarella's and Gabrielsson's. Simply, SEM hold positive impact. They also note that, to use their terminology, an IME is characterized by altered states of consciousness which can lead to experiences of harmony and self-realization, where the experience leaves the individual with a strong motivation

172. Olaveson, "Connectedness and Rave Experience," 95.
173. Bey, *Temporary Autonomous Zone*, 96.
174. Thornton, *Club Cultures*, 65.
175. John, *Tecnomad*, 21.
176. Rietveld, "Ephemeral Spirit," 46.
177. Rietveld, "Ephemeral Spirit," 47.
178. John, *Global Tribe*, 122.
179. Gerard, "Selecting Ritual," 175.
180. John, *Global Tribe*, 273; John, "An Overview," 8.

to maintain feelings of harmony in daily life. This experience becomes a resource to the self, affecting understandings of the meaning of life. The music we listen to can cause us to feel both harmony or disharmony, which acts as a resource, providing agency that can affect our values, relationships and how we draw meaning from different situations. As they postulate "Results suggest that music can indeed change our lives—by making it more fulfilling, spiritual, and harmonious."[181]

Valorie Salimpoor, Mitchel Benovoy, Kevin Larcher, Alain Dagher, and Robert Zatorre's research shows that such musical experiences also release dopamine into parts of the brain,[182] which, they note, is pivotal for establishing and maintaining behavior. They see this as being a key reason why music is used ritually, in marketing or films as well as in affecting hedonic states,[183] such as within EDM. Levitin makes a similar comment concerning enjoying music and increased levels of serotonin production.[184]

Randy Thornhill's reflections are that the immediacy of affective response can generate subsequent imagination and fantasy, so creating an imaginative space that the respondent can move forward into, which echoes Paul Ricoeur's idea of a "conflict of narrative programs" from which we may begin to discover new ways of looking at the world around us.[185] From Thornhill's perspective, this is an evolutionary activity of looking into the future. From a Christian perspective one could also speak of such experiences as having a prophetic function. As Starr shows. "It is not just that ideas and perceptions, however, become newly linked in aesthetic experience but that the hedonic value assigned to those perceptions and ideas at a neural level enables powerful connections that had not existed before. Aesthetic experience thus makes possible the unexpected valuation of objects, ideas, and perceptions and enables new configurations of what is known, new frameworks for interpretation, and perhaps even a new willingness to entertain what is strange or to let the familiar and the novel live side by side. We may then acquire new knowledge, which enters into our lives differently—by showing us undiscovered similarities or contrasts, and opening new room for comparison and evaluation."[186]

Starr further posits that such aesthetic experience may bring new moral ideas and perspectives into view: the greater the sense of reward is felt

---

181. Schäfer et al., "How Music Changes Our Lives," 525.
182. Salimpoor et al., "Anatomically Distinct Dopamine Release," 260.
183. Salimpoor et al., "Anatomically Distinct Dopamine Release," 262.
184. Levitin, *World in Six Songs*, 99.
185. Ricoeur, *Figuring the Sacred*, 239.
186. Starr, *Feeling Beauty*, 20.

to be, so new connections within the brain may be made and new epistemic possibilities discovered that were "not just absent but even unpredictably beyond the horizon of our knowledge."[187] Frith also explores the relationship between aesthetics and ethics, noting how one's appreciation of a popular music aesthetic can reinforce particular ethical values precisely because "it places us in the social world in a particular way."[188]

From this we should note that as much as the need for ontological security is fundamental to our existence, our aesthetic engagement with cultural artefacts such as popular music helps us to become more aware of what is of true importance to us. This again reinforces popular music as a significant theological resource. When we encounter something in what we hear which speaks into our need for security, which aesthetically resonates with us, it provides a positive reward in the brain and we will want to connect ourselves with that experience. We will then draw from that experience discursive and semiotic properties which shape our sense of self, while very strong musical experiences will significantly reinforce, even short-cut this process.

5. Theological Response

Greater theological reflection and appreciation of the work of scholars such as Bowlby, Rolls, DeNora and Gabrielsson is needed to help us understand how our brain's physiology provides the processes through which we may emotionally encounter the divine. Again, terms such as attunement and SEM need theological grounding, not to superficially spiritualize them, but rather to understand how these processes can help us to make more sense of possible divine encounters. Popular songs such as Mel C's 'Dear Life' and Henderson's 'Ghost,' are drawn into a listener's affective space and used to explore other discourses than those currently considered. They can function as prosthetic technologies enabling a broadening of the listener's horizon.

This certainly happened during the counterculture of the 1960s when protest music and psychedelic music encouraged a range of new religious, political and cultural interpretations of the world.[189] To consider for a moment the opportunity for white middle-class society to express religious or social hopes and concerns through music (e.g., George Harrison's 'My Sweet Lord' (1969) and his hopes to promulgate the Hare Krishna movement) in comparison to black Americans whose ability to express themselves

---

187. Starr, *Feeling Beauty*, 53.
188. Frith, "Music and Identity," 120.
189. See Partridge, "Psychedelic Music," 294–305; Peddie, "Music," 32–42.

was much more limited helps to demonstrate why hip-hop's relationship with religion, politics and power, as Joseph Winters describes, "reflect and trouble power relationships, especially around race, gender, class and sexuality."[190] Likewise, dance and ambient music which expresses alternative, often Eastern spiritualities further demonstrates that many are looking beyond society's concrete lifeworld.[191] An example of this is Goa Trance, a genre centered on Goa in India, with performers such as Total Eclipse, Hallucinogen and Astral Projection. Yet the affect of popular music culture is generally overlooked within ecclesial circles.

We have argued how music and its related discourses can reflect and affect our emotional state. Popular music helps us to make sense of the world around us. By identifying how we experience emotional feelings as a reward and so begin to draw something of the connected discourse into our need for ontological security suggests there is a liturgical need to bring popular cultural experiences into our worship experiences in order to help those looking to make sense of the Christian story to ground it within wider life. This is not to suggest some form of worship karaoke where a congregation sings along to a pop song. Rather, for example, it can be used within a liturgical setting to explore feelings of dissonance. Neither is it to suggest a particular 'Christ *and* Culture' perspective,[192] as one's understanding of this will be affected by a particular church community's understanding of the purpose of Christ *within* culture, whether that is couched in the language of redemption, conflict or synthesis. Rather, it is simply to recognize that, as sentient beings, we need to make sense of the world around us, which popular music culture is very adept at doing.[193] While some will view such an approach as profane, we are arguing that the poetic content of popular music acts as a connection point between belief and wider society. To follow Hopps' line of thought, it can facilitate the "epiphanic expansion of vision."[194]

The Church needs to draw on this dynamic and purposefully facilitate the stimulation of affective space both within its sacred spaces and well beyond its four walls to facilitate telling its discourses. This requires an understanding of the differing social dynamics taking place: how cultural texts such as popular music help express ultimate reality; the agency of aesthetics; our need to attune away from restless feelings to resolve cognitive

---

190. Winters, "Rap and Hip Hop," 313.
191. E.g., Partridge, "Psychedelic Music," 302; John, *Global Tribe*, 18.
192. See Niebuhr, *Christ and Culture*.
193. See also Keuss, *Blur*.
194. Hopps, "Theology," 87.

dissonance, together with an appreciation of Ricoeur's "conflict of narrative programs."[195] We have ascertained that such an approach to story-telling cannot be considered as emotional coercion as our musical appreciation is seen to reinforce present feelings over forcefully replacing them with a differing discourse.[196] Rather, it is helping those who recognize a sense of restlessness to find a narrative that may support them in their quest to make more sense of the world around them.

Some of these processes do already occur within the Church's worship repertoire, although the language of attunement, or of the possible effects of SEM are not used. Two examples are the intentional use of popular music culture within worship and in particular, charismatic worship, which seeks to attune individuals towards a heavily aestheticized Christian discourse.

Marcus Moberg, for example, has noted the effects of "popular music divine service formats" in Finland.[197] Here, religious services utilize popular music culture to explore the divine. The Evangelical Lutheran Church of Finland (ELCF) are developing "niche" services which, for example, include services that substitute traditional church music with various forms of popular music, yet are otherwise recognizable as traditional Lutheran worship.[198] He notes three particular genres, pop, metal, and 'dance-and-pray,' are enabling primarily young people to connect with a divine discourse, albeit the majority of attendees identified already as Christian.[199] However, whilst these niche services are seen as valuable to those who attend, this approach is not so successful in embedding new belief. We will, see, in the concluding chapter how this rationale can be developed.

We can see the Christianized purposeful pursuit of an SEM within the charismatic worship scene and similarly within cathedral worship, albeit that such language is not encouraged. To focus on the charismatic scene, a worshipper's affective space becomes centered around those biblical discourses which are espoused by that community, such as the use of spiritual gifts through which God can communicate with humanity (e.g., 1 Cor 12). Through the rhythm of its worship the community seeks to attune to its ultimate care-giver, God, which, to follow DeNora, it symbiologically achieves through the emotion and movement of the worship event.

Tom Wagner draws on the work of Kahn-Harris and Moberg in his exploration of Charismatic worship at Hillsong, a large Charismatic church

---

195. Ricoeur, *Figuring the Sacred*, 239.
196. E.g., Brown, "Introduction," 23; Volgsten, "Between Ideology and Identity," 75.
197. Moberg, "Popular Music Divine Services," 46.
198. Moberg, "Popular Music Divine Services," 35.
199. Moberg, "Popular Music Divine Services," 44.

MUSIC AND EMOTION   179

in London. His critique is that worship sets are very structured and that worshippers both know the semiotic code and what is expected of them. He draws on Sloboda's work to note that popular worship music widely uses suspended chords to provoke strong physio-emotional responses such as tears or goose pimples.[200] We have already established that emotional responses are significant in affirming the discourses around which they are set.[201] Within their affective space a worshiper's understanding of God can become strengthened.[202] To follow Brown's musical hierarchy (Fig. 20), the more intense someone engages with the music and aesthetic, the more positive stimulation the brain will receive helping the discourse to be affirmed.

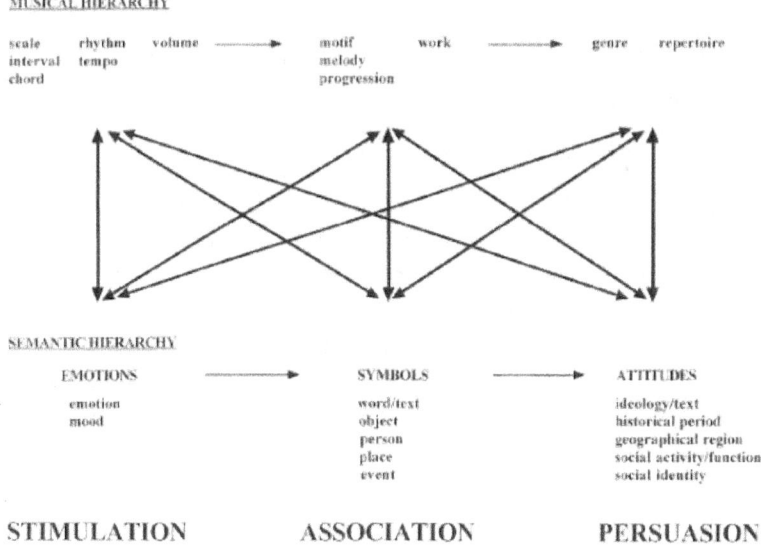

Figure 20. Brown's Hierarchical View of Musical Semantics[203]

As worship ebbs and flows there will be moments when the movement and rhythm suddenly become stilled. In such moments many worshippers attest to sensing something of God's presence, echoing what Herbert Marcuse referred to as the "aesthetic power of silence."[204] In such moments

200. Wagner, "Christianity," 95; cf. Miller and Strongman, "Emotional Effects of Music," 10.
201. See also Miller and Strongman, "Emotional Effects of Music," 9.
202. See Ingalls, "Singing Heaven."
203. Brown, "Introduction," 15.
204. Marcuse, *The Aesthetic Dimension*, 117.

feelings of transcendence and revelation may be experienced which become interpreted against the symbolism and narrative employed in that space. This is affective space in action. The experience of a SEM in sung worship can be profound. Tillich's own ecstatic experience, albeit through visual media, emphasizes this. The place where the SEM is experienced, alongside the discourse that the recipient has in mind is crucial in decoding what has occurred and often reinforces Christian experience at a deep level.

Such worship experiences can become predictable and, as such, lose intensity. Practically, that may simply be that dopamine levels have become less intense. While dopamine is seen as the 'reward' drug, when the same situation is re-lived over time, levels of dopamine decrease.[205] Hence, the same level of pleasure is not achieved. Wolfram Schultz notes that "In learning situations governed only by experienced rewards, consecutive unrewarded trials lead to progressively decreasing reward prediction," However, this can become interpreted as a sense of a lack of God's presence—compared to previous experiences. The loss of such a heavenly encounter can lead to what Warner has described as "vision inflation,"[206] possibly leading to disillusionment with belief, rather than evolution of the learning opportunity.

While the charismatic scene encourages SEM to occur it would be best placed to go beyond the language of divine encounter alone to that of an SEM as providing a learning opportunity which may help someone who is already aware of the Christian story to be further drawn into its discourse. The purposeful use of affective space becomes pedagogy. It is too reductionistic to suggest that such religious experience is simply emotional hype and should be discarded as such. To do so is to reduce all emotional experience such as enjoying the beauty of a sunset, to that simply of electrical activity in the brain. The focus, though, should be that of a learning opportunity, a Kairos moment, where the movement and emotion of the worship experience helps embody the discourse over that of divine encounter. The problem is that when sung worship is interpreted as divine encounter alone rather than in terms of education, the individual is not able to decode it as such. The focus remains on the experience rather than what may be learnt from it.

A similar dynamic occurs within a cathedral setting, where Christian popular music is replaced with classical music and where the sign-system of sound-system, lights and TV screens is replaced by the aesthetic of the building's architecture. In the same way, divine encounter can be said to occur as the choir sings and the recipient, staring at a stain-glassed window,

---

205. Schultz, "Updating Dopamine Reward Signals," 230–39; Rolls, *Emotion and Decision-Making*, 277.

206. Warner, *Secularisation and Its Discontents*, 4.

encounters a SEM. The process of encounter is the same, which is to again highlight the translucent nature of the boundary between 'high' and popular culture. While at aesthetical opposites, the same musical communicative process is at work. Anecdotally, the Dean of Lichfield Cathedral, Adrian Dorber has drawn a link between increased attendance over the Christmas period by young people, and the wider attendance at music festivals. He views young people as being more "spiritually inquisitive" than in previous generations.[207]

6. Summary

There is a clear link between our engagement with music, our emotional well-being and our need for human flourishing. This is evidenced through both our use of 'music in everyday life' and our reaction to strong experiences with music. Such experiences do leave their mark on us for the better. There is evidence that our musical encounters help to bring order to disordered lives, be that through attunement as we listen to music generally or in the use of affective space that acts, to use DeNora's language, as an asylum. Our musical engagement can provide a life-enhancing encounter that simply overwhelms, which the listener may want to recapture time and time again. Yet, our musical encounters, or, to again draw on the notion of *ut pictura poesis*, our aesthetic encounters, provide the stimulus that may cause as to feel rewarded. This can enable aspects of the narrative that supports a SEM to be drawn into our own biography, strengthening our ontological security.

To return to popular music alone, it can act as an interface between our inner self and the outer world which we use to helps us to make sense of who we are. To recall the theory of communicative musicality, proto-musical communication has helped us feel the security of our primary carers and we utilize these processes to form relationships with others. Music's aesthetic and sonic quality enables us to give expression to parts of ourselves that we simply are unable to find words for and for it to help us attain aspects of ontological security. Our affective space within a musical asylum or the experience of an SEM provides a metaphorical space through which we can begin to find ways to make sense of who we are in life. SEM in particular can act as a fast-track way to reflect on who we are.

From such experiences we begin to build up a wider narrative that helps us to make more sense of ourselves, poaching and making do from the differing discourses we encounter as we go along. This is not to reduce musical experiences to that of us simply using music as a symbol to reflect something

207. Wright, "Christmas."

of our sense of self, rather, our musical and aesthetical experiences provide us with tools which help us make more sense of our experience of life. The need for aesthetical encounter is real and is not frivolous. Rather, aesthetical appreciation resources our wellbeing and pursuit of ontological security. Such aesthetical experiences are often viewed as secondary experiences. Clearly, food and shelter may hold greater value than the symbols we may use to express our needs. Yet, the way we do physically react to a discourse's aesthetical content shows its importance in resourcing ontological security.

Starr precisely notes that the unpredictable value of aesthetic rewards are set apart from the rewards of sex, food, water and the like, but, importantly, she believes that "that aesthetic experience helps us understand a world we cannot fully predict, helps us value things that are new and learn how to compare what seems, at first, incommensurable." Remembering the unstable and fluid nature of society, it can be of no surprise that our need to engage aesthetically has increased. In an environment that is forever changing, our aesthetical response "enables the comparison and integration of novel kinds of reward in a process that makes these rewards particularly meaningful for inner life and opens up possibilities for new knowledge, or new ways of negotiating the world."[208] The more fluid society becomes, so the more we should take note of our aesthetical experiences as ways to exploring fresh opportunities and of making sense of what we truly value in life.

In the last two chapters we have shown the discursive and emotional processes by which we poach symbolism and the psychological systems through which we manage such stimuli. What, in particular, may help us in telling the Christian story as affectively as possible within liquid modernity? In focusing on how we use our emotions, we can conclude that:

1. The playful nature of communicative musicality emphasizes the importance of a secure relationship between carer and child, alongside how this influences our meaning-making into adulthood. Childhood experiences of engaging with the Christian story should be viewed with greater significance and strategic focus given to nurturing spiritual encounters through music with as young an age children as possible, alongside their carers. Likewise, to follow Baylin and Hughes' work, those who have become disenchanted with Christian belief may well benefit from playful approaches to Christian spirituality as part of the process of regaining trust in it, which the use of affective space encourages.

---

208. Starr, *Feeling Beauty*, 26.

2. Liquid moderns need a high level of consumable symbols to draw on. However, this bricolage is one of the reasons that fuels feelings of insecurity. The Church would do well to highlight this and, to use Laski's turn of phrase, to show "an alternative possibility,"[209] to root oneself to a traditional discourse.

3. Aesthetic encounter is an important component in our search for ontological security. In as much as aesthetical reactions highlight the immanent self's need to understand the world around us, so such experiences provide opportunity for discursive engagement and theological reflection. Experiences such as the shivers need not be viewed as a one-sided transcendent, divine encounter, rather, they can be seen as our need to make sense of who we are, which should include making more sense of the divine.

4. The dynamic of purposefully using affective space needs to be drawn into the Church's pedagogy to encourage the heuristic exploration of Christian belief. This is far more than simply creating a welcoming space, or a tidy place. It is about intentionally creating space where epiphanic moments may occur through sounds and aesthetics, while giving opportunity for individual response. We have noted that postemotionalism does not occur with those who feel secure with their identity. Individuals must first feel dissonance with the world around them for affective space to provide opportunity for (re)enchantment.

5. This does emphasize the value of our emotions which, as a hangover from the Enlightenment, have not been given as much value as our cognitive reasoning.

6. One thing that is key is the discursive work that happens around our musical consumption, which is how we make sense of such experiences, such as resulting from a SEM. All these moments are primarily learning opportunities, providing opportunity for what Baylin and Hughes term as "affective-reflective dialogue."[210] As Starr views it, while evolutionary approaches can provide the mechanism that help us understand how we function, such approaches cannot deal with the poetic quality of art, which she views as operating on a different level.[211] This is the space where Logos, where Geist can be at work. While her approach is humanistic, Starr's rationale does provide fresh

---

209. Laski, *Ecstasy*, 373.
210. Baylin and Hughes, *Neurobiology of Attachment-Focused Therapy*, 118.
211. Starr, *Feeling Beauty*, 28.

opportunity to understand the opportunities provided by affective spaces as places where issues of belief can be discussed.

Of course, one cannot go back to past corporate understandings of resourcing ontological security, such as a communal sufficiency in the Christian story alone. Rather, within liquid modernity a more fluid and less boundaried approach to sharing the Christian discourse is required. Our use of affective space is a helpful way of framing how telling the Christian story may be done. Yet, by employing such an individualist starting point emphasis becomes placed on a variety of understandings of the Christian discourse.

This, however, should not be viewed as either a case of watering down the Christian experience, or of needing to anchor the Christian story to one past moment of time, such as the Reformation. Rather, the fluidity of liquid modernity requires these differing understandings to reside alongside one another. Even within one particular stream of the Church, be it liberal, Evangelical or Catholic, individuals are influenced by their own emotional response to the story they have heard and how they have tried to make sense of the world around them within that particular tradition. The post-Enlightenment Church may have felt the need to maintain two key understandings of belief (e.g., evangelical and catholic). However, within liquid modernity, liberal pluralism highlights the need for a wider appreciation of the nuances of Christian belief. This would help the institutional church in the West to promulgate its discourses. The final chapter will explore how this may practically be achieved.

7. Music, Restlessness, and the COVID-19 Pandemic

Some initial comment ought to be made at this point about our musical consumption during the coronavirus pandemic, especially in relation to dealing with the existential threat the disease poses. The psychologist Mark Yang observes, "The COVID-19 pandemic is a powerful border experience awakening us to our existential predicament. Such a predicament includes transience and impermanence, unpredictability, emptiness (existential vacuum), and the interdependence of life and death. The anxiety aroused by the pandemic can awaken us to an ontological mode of existence in which we are authentic, aware, responsible, and transcendent." These are certainly issues we have sought to consider through this book. He follows the model that human existence places anxiety at its center, and he suggests that "our experience of living is never certain, never predictable, never secure," albeit that anxiety may be alleviated, but never eliminated.[212] As such, the pandemic has sharply brought into focus many of the issues we have been considering. This helps emphasize why the theology of shalom that was discussed earlier is so valuable, indeed, a somewhat unique narrative to explore today.

Many have felt fearful of the pandemic and, no doubt, will continue to do so for years to come, even when the initial phase has fully passed. Yet, the angst that the pandemic brings is political as much as viral. As a personal observation, Yang notes that how differing countries are managing this situation is helping him to "appreciate the complexity of this dialectic between conformism/totalitarianism and freedom and individuality," a sentiment that, again, will resound for a long time.[213] Again, this emphasizes how important it is to understand the social forces which shape our communities. Our consumption of popular music during this time also reinforces its values as a threptic resource as much as a theological or sociological resource. In other words, the micro nature of the pandemic mirrors the macro nature of the issues we have discussed thus far.

It may, therefore, seem somewhat surprising that Spotify saw a decline in the streaming of the world's biggest hits by some 11 percent as the pandemic and lockdowns took hold.[214] With live performances suddenly stopped one may have expected an increase in streaming services. It suggests that the initial shock of the pandemic required processing before that could then become expressed through music that could then be listened to. It highlights how music enables us to express our emotions towards events *once* time has been allowed to cognitively process them. Such a process is often observed at funerals and during times of mourning, where music can facilitate a strong emotional response which can help someone to process the enormity of death.[215]

Having noted a reduction in streaming at the beginning of the pandemic, by the end of 2020, the recorded music business saw a 7 percent increase in its revenues over 2019, primarily through streaming, which, overall, grew by almost 20 percent.[216] Spotify's own 'The Sound of the Virus' playlist, compiled by Glenn McDonald, one of the company's statisticians, shows how much we made use of streamed music to help us deal with the ongoing nature of the pandemic. Over three months his playlist considered

212. Yang, "Resilience and Meaning-Making," 662–64.
213. Yang, "Resilience and Meaning-Making," 668.
214. Cooper, "Change the Tune."
215. Viper et al., Music as Consolation, 3–15.
216. Ingham, "Global."

all the song titles held by the site which used words common in dealing with the pandemic, alongside their popularity of play. At the lower end of the 8000 song playlist are many songs by amateur musicians expressing differing emotions towards world events, while the top of the list includes song titles which express a certain level of irony and humor, such as 'Stuck with U' (2020) by Ariana Grande and Justin Bieber, or Luke Comb's 'Six Feet Apart' (2019). More reflective feelings found expression in songs such as Twenty One Pilots' 'Level of Concern' (2020), or the American rapper Lil Baby's 'Social Distancing' (2020), which does speak of the insecurity the writers felt towards events.

The expression of humor as a way of dealing with the pandemic is notable, with songs such as The Police's 'Don't Stand So Close to Me' seeing an increase in being listened to by 130 percent over the preceding period.[217] That the song was originally released in 1980 shows how even the title of a lyric can resonate in such a way as to express our existential concerns. Well-known artists changed particular lyrics when streaming live songs during this period. For example, Neil Diamond, changed the well-known lyric from 'Sweet Caroline' of touching hands to washing hands, bringing humor into a challenging situation.[218] Yet, Spotify also noted an increase in listening to 'Chill Music' and music without vocals as a way of helping to manage the immanent self.

The site also noted an increase in collaborative playlists, emphasizing, that whilst so many found themselves in lockdown and isolation, music was a way to enhance community, drawing people together. In countries such as Italy and Spain, individuals leading singing from balconies of flats and apartments found themselves subjects of international interest, with the songs they sung equally finding an increased in being streamed. One example being 'Abbracciame,' which following a news report about it being sung saw an 820 percent increase in the number of times it was streamed.[219] As Nisha Gupta noted, such use of music strengthened communal resilience, yet at the same time was able to help the autonomic nervous system through rhythm and melody, reflecting comments made earlier about attunement.[220]

With the opportunity for live music curtailed, artists turned to virtual events, both as a way of drawing income, and also, in some way, to interact with fans. The need for virtual events emphasizes that our aesthetical needs are important when seeking to find a level of equilibrium within our sense

---

217. "Don't Stand So Close to Me."
218. Lehman, "Washing Hands."
219. "Don't Stand So Close to Me."
220. Gupta, "Social Distancing Blues," 596.

of self. While for some fans it raised issues around authenticity, it also allowed some to feel greater intimacy between the performer and themselves, giving opportunity to engage virtually through emojis or on-screen chat.[221]

What this demonstrates is how much popular music is a resource to managing the immanent self and it provides insight into how people are seeking to make sense of their inner conservations, their self-talk as they process events which affect their existential wellbeing. It again emphasizes popular music as both a technology of the self and as a prosthetic technology. Far more scrutiny of our consumption of music during the pandemic is needed. Yet this very brief look at the way we are utilizing our musical consumption at this time does emphasize how important our music listening is when making sense of the existential risks we continue to face. The pandemic has magnified the issue of restlessness in society.

The pandemic has also shown that spirituality holds capital. The Economist noted that at the beginning of the first lockdown around 25 percent of Britons had attended an online religious service,[222] although that initial increase has settled down as regular patterns for daily living again take hold. Yet this does highlight the value of the relationship between popular music, the aesthetical and the theological. It is to this which is the is the focus of the final chapter.

---

221. Rendell, Staying in, Rocking out," 6–12.
222. "Your Own Personal Jesus," lines 12–14.

6

A Theology of Emotion and Popular Music

THE ENDING OF CHRISTENDOM and its replacement with liberal pluralism renders implausible any suggestion that the Christian worldview can, once again, become a hegemonic ideological discourse. Historically, the telling of the Christian story was reinforced by this ideology. Outside of that framework the Church needs to be confident to tell its story in fresh ways. Our exploration of popular music has shown how it might provide one of these ways. In reflecting on society's relationship with popular music, the Church can learn how it might best tell the Christian story within liquid modernity.

For example, we have noted how communicative musicality informs the development of the self from before birth and also how our aesthetic appreciation and the value of our emotions will influence our decisions around ontological security. We have noted, too, that despite living in a predominantly secularized age popular music has much to say about immanent and transcendent spiritual beliefs, alongside what may lie beyond the horizon of the Western lifeworld. It is logical to suggest, therefore, that we can draw on these various components to help tell the Christian story today.

Having highlighted throughout how popular music is a theological resource, we will focus on four specific points. Firstly, a greater appreciation is needed of the role emotions play in deciding whether to accept a discourse that offers ontological security. Such appraisal is not an intellectual process alone, rather, our consideration of communicative musicality shows that it is influenced by how we learn to emotionally attach to our initial caregivers.

Secondly, our use of an intentionally constructed space where our own affective space can be challenged should be viewed pedagogically. This is not, therefore, to set out a model for wholesale conversion, rather it is to purposefully provide opportunities for small groups of liquid moderns already experiencing existential restlessness to explore Christian spirituality through popular music. All music can be used for this process even if the recipient does not 'like' a certain piece. What is of importance here is *how* the music affects you, providing an opportunity for affective-reflective dialogue around the self and, in this context, our spiritual and theological outlook.

As Paul Tillich observes, a correlation can be made between our existential questions (such as we have seen highlighted in popular music) and theological answers,[1] which for him found expression in viewing Botticelli's 'Madonna with Singing Angels.' Such space can be intentionally constructed, not in order to force moments of revelation, but to provide a safe place for such correlation through affective-reflective dialogue. We will refer to this space as a Creative Space for Spiritual Reflection (CSSR). Such space draws on the differing aesthetical and emotional dynamics we have noted throughout. It provides a practical model for how popular music may be utilized to help tell the Christian story within liquid modernity.

Thirdly, having explored how the dynamics of such space can work we will focus on Baylin and Hughes' PACE parenting method in helping traumatized children to reframe their emotional wellbeing.[2] Their methodology, which holds a particular emphasis on playfulness, provides a helpful analogy to further explore how individuals may (re)connect to the Christian story and we will draw this into our intentional formation of affective space.

Lastly, we will conclude by outlining a theology of emotion and popular music to frame our effective telling of the Christian story today.

1. Liquid Belief and Flowing Emotions

In 'Big God' (2018), Florence Welch sings that our need for God is substantial (Fig. 21). The song can purposefully be interpreted as both a deep love song or a cry asking why God has not answered her prayers. She wistfully comments that the song reflects "obviously, an unfillable hole in the soul, but mainly about someone not replying to my text."[3] Welch is keen that the song, together with its enigmatic video, can be interpreted in several ways, noting that: "I quite like the idea of putting really big, unanswerable spiritual

---

1. Tillich, *Systematic Theology*, 1:60.
2. Baylin and Hughes, *Neurobiology of Attachment-Focused Therapy*, 194.
3. Ryzic, "I Never Thought."

questions in pop songs. We can be together in this moment, and celebrate the not-knowing, and perhaps feel closer to each other."[4]

Figure 21. Florence and the Machine, 'Big God'

The chorus of Welch's song, with its angry, repeated rendition of 'Jesus Christ,' is sung in a way to grab the listener's attention—a purposeful crossing of the sacred-profane divide. It is, as Partridge argues, that words and symbols can be used to deliberately "piss others off," to provoke an emotional reaction so that listeners are forced to consider fresh opinions.[5] Welch's song expresses both a need to attain ontological security and openness to religious belief, albeit couched with ambivalence. That is not too far removed from Bauman's skeptical yet open-mindedness towards the religious.[6]

In commenting on this song, Melena Ryzik sees that "In real life and in performance, Ms. Welch is looking for connection."[7] While there is purposeful ambiguity in Welch's lyrics, she is expressing the conundrum experienced by many: God may not be there, but then again, he might be. Whether he is or not, however, we need to *feel* a connection to the divine in our search. The rapper DMX's 'Lord, Give Me a Sign' (2006) captures this need with his plea for divine revelation. We will use Welch's song to explore how the purposeful formation of a place where our affective space may attune to new discourses can be helpful for sharing the Christian discourse.

Within the Church, this more subjective response is seen as individuals wanting to "suit their own desires, . . . gather round them a great number

4. Ryzic, "I Never Thought."
5. Partridge, *Mortality and Music*, 45.
6. E.g., Bauman and Obirek, *Of God and Man*, 56.
7. Ryzic, "I Never Thought."

of teachers to say what their itching ears want to hear" (2 Tim 4:3–4). Yet, our approach is sociologically observed, recognizing the fullness of our personhood including our neurological physiology.[8] Our feelings are integral to our decision-making, especially when evaluating the authenticity of the discourses we listen to—what Middleton would term as the fidelity of what we listen to.[9] While our emotions show us how we feel and can help us to gain deeper understanding of our personhood, such as described by DeNora's 'asylum'[10] and Partridge's use of 'prosthetic technology,'[11] we are not so keen to affirm that the same emotions play an active role in our decision making, especially when affirming discourses supporting ontological security.

While we have seen that Roll's work does emphasize the function of our emotions in our decision making, there is little reference in the Church's theological repertoire to how our emotions help us to feel safe—a significant measurement of ontological security. As Riis and Woodhead note, emotion has long been seen as being unruly: "Christian culture supported a biblical view in which the 'heart' is the seat of knowledge, and the cultivation of sentiment is an essential part of the quest for wisdom and truth. In a long tradition of practical and theological reflection, unruly and uncontrollable 'passions' are seen as the enemy of both knowledge and righteousness, and a right ordering of feeling—particularly of loves—as essential for discernment and discrimination."[12]

The theological theme of *shalom* (chapter 4) should, therefore, include a robust understanding of emotional peace. The experience of peace is holistic: body, mind and spirit. This is not to suggest that feelings must trump intellect, but it certainly highlights the need to recalibrate the balance between felt, ontological truth and epistemological understanding, what Andrew Tallon also describes as the difference between religion of the "head" and that of the "heart."[13] A positive emotional connection between person and discourse is required else the individual will simply look for other discourses which can be emotionally related to.[14]

What is being suggested here is the formation of places where the emotional and sensory input will stimulate our interiority, will impact our

---

8. E.g., Rolls, *Emotion and Decision-Making*.
9. Middleton, "Faith," 293.
10. DeNora, *Music Asylums*, 5.
11. Partridge, *The Lyre of Orpheus*, 196.
12. Riis and Woodhead, *Sociology of Religious Emotion*, 15.
13. Tallon, "Christianity," 111.
14. I.e., Bauman, *Community*, 3.

affective space, helping us to connect with fresh discourses.[15] We are seeking to encourage what Baylin and Hughes term as "affective-reflective dialogue" which is to recognize that we are affected by what we hear, see and feel *and* that we need to account for this.[16]

This is not promoting emotional manipulation, rather it is to draw on the value of play in learning, what Rikke Nørgård, Claus Toft-Nielsen and Nicola Whitton see as the development of a signature pedagogy. Here, they describe the formation of a "magic circle," a physical or ideational space within which learning can occur. Playfulness engenders feelings of security. This, they observe, helps create a positive learning environment.[17] For Whitton such a circle provides a space for "how people construct relationships and realities during play."[18] The notion of learning, rather than being taught is something that Bauman would commend as a necessity within liquid society.[19] The Church, in contrast, favors the use of the term teaching.

2. CSSR and Pedagogy

Nørgård, Toft-Nielsen and Whitton affirm playfulness as a "fundamental part of human experience and learning." It can "support spontaneous learning, facilitate social interaction, develop emotional resilience, stimulate imagination, support problem-solving, reduce stress, and increase happiness," issues which can affect the resolution of existential restlessness.[20] For Baylin and Hughes, "playfulness conveys the attitude that you are safe" and triggers opioids and dopamine in the brain which bring feelings of pleasure, making the event memorable, even a positive learning experience.[21] Play increases trust,[22] while it can also help establish a strong care-bond between carer and infant.[23]

While the strategy of playfulness has, in more recent times, been focused on digital game-based learning, its appeal is far wider. It can make use of techniques such as role-play and performance, alongside attributes

---

15. Bauman and Raud, *Practices of Selfhood*, 36.
16. Baylin and Hughes, *Neurobiology of Attachment-Focused Therapy*, 118.
17. Nørgård et al., "Playful Learning in Higher Education," 273.
18. Whitton, "Playful Learning," 2.
19. Sarid, "Self-Critical Appropriation," 463; Bauman, "Education in Liquid Modernity," 316.
20. Nørgård et al., "Playful Learning in Higher Education," 273.
21. Baylin and Hughes, *Neurobiology of Attachment-Focused Therapy*, 112.
22. Baylin and Hughes, *Neurobiology of Attachment-Focused Therapy*, 194.
23. Malloch and Trevarthen, "Musicality," 7.

which engender playfulness including surprise, humor and storytelling.[24] These can all be well utilized in the purposeful setting up of space—CSSR— which can encourage the use of our affective space for connecting with the Christian discourse. While helpful for learning in general, the term 'magic circle' is not so congenial within ecclesial circles. However, as John Corrigan points out, following the *spatial turn* the terms sacred or holy space have become outdated.[25]

Drawing on what we have observed from our use of popular music, CSSR is an emotional space where someone may connect with the music that is played alongside others who are listening to it. It is an 'asylum' where spiritual reflection can occur; where the aesthetics of the space together with the music can act as a prosthetic technology, helping the individual to attune to an alternative discourse. It is a managed, safe place where a "conflict of narrative programs" can be explored.[26] It is not deliberately seeking to cause a SEM, rather, to draw on Baylin and Hughes' work with traumatized children, to note that "the child's inherent potential for engagement needs reawakening."[27] In other words, a restless, hurting child can be helped to attune towards positive care.

The analogy here is simply that, from a faith perspective, if humanity has felt the trauma of restlessness by moving away from the divine, which the Christian tradition reveals as Father, then the manner in which traumatized children can again find trust and resolution to their inner angsts can become a model for encouraging a spiritual awakening and possible socialization into belief. It makes sense, therefore, that, if God can be viewed as our principal carer (e.g., as creator, revealed as Father), how we physiologically, as well as theologically, relate to the divine can be considered in a like manner. When such moments of connection occur, however briefly, one can speak of a Kairos moment. While this does not necessarily imply a connection with the divine, nevertheless, a moment has occurred which requires greater self-reflection to understand what our emotions are telling us. Theologically, this may be understood as recognizing the presence of *Geist*.[28]

Why should such modelling be effective? The popular music we encounter is not listened to in a vacuum. Rather, as we have explored, it holds agency (see chapters 4 and 5) and evokes memory,[29] all which we

24. Whitton, "Playful Learning," 5.
25. Corrigan, "Introduction," 158.
26. Ricoeur, *Figuring the Sacred*, 239.
27. Baylin and Hughes, *Neurobiology of Attachment-Focused Therapy*, 155.
28. E.g., Tillich, *Systematic Theology*, 3:21.
29. I.e., Hesmondhalgh, *Why Music Matters*, 53.

use to express what we hold as sacred or affect our well-being.[30] We can imaginatively engage with music and music video to explore this, in some cases helping us to find language we may otherwise be unable to express.[31] Simply, we react to music. While the emergent church has long made use of the arts to explore belief, or to use Jonny Baker's terminology, to curate worship which may facilitate epiphanic moments,[32] here, we are seeking to explore more directly *how* popular music may alter our affective state. Having argued for a recalibration of the value of our emotions in making sense of the self, CSSR seeks to draw on the importance of our affective state while employing insights from Dan Hughes' therapeutic parenting work to interrogate our spiritual biography.

Reflective practice and person-centered counselling have long been acknowledged as methods for facilitating personal change. Mustafa Kur, for example, notes how the application of reflective thinking to "relatively complicated and unstructured thoughts [can] help to process already possessed knowledge, perceptions and emotions."[33] Similarly, from Carl Rogers's person-centered counselling to "offer help in bringing to modern man an increased peace of mind,"[34] to more recent strategies such as play therapy[35] or Dan Hughes' Dyadic Developmental Psychotherapy,[36] reflective dialogue has facilitated positive change in many lives.

Similarly, akin to Christopher Partridge's prosthetic technology[37] or Tia DeNora's "asylum,"[38] David Hesmondhalgh notes how popular music encourages human flourishing evoking strong emotions where "some might find that it opens a door to their inner lives."[39] CSSR seeks to purposefully create environments where reflective dialogue between music and Christian spirituality can take place. In the spirit of Paul Tillich, we seek to assimilate insights from communicative musicality and therapeutic parenting with missiology.

Through reflective-affective dialogue, using the questioning style of Hughes' PACE parenting model (see below), aspects of the Christian story

30. E.g., Robinson, *Deeper than Reason*, 405.
31. E.g., Robinson, *Deeper than Reason*, 359.
32. E.g., Baker, *Curating Worship*, xiii.
33. Kur, "Quality in Reflective Thinking," 248.
34. Rogers, *Client-Centered Therapy*, 15.
35. E.g., Robinson, "What Play Therapists Do."
36. Hughes, *Attachment-Focused Family Therapy*.
37. Partridge, *The Lyre of Orpheus*, 196.
38. DeNora, *Music Asylums*, 1.
39. Hesmondhalgh, *Why Music Matters*, 24.

may become freshly explored and embodied. Kur, for example, notes how affective-reflective actions can result in what he terms exaltive, appreciative or discontentive behaviors within the learning environment. Here, language such as expressing pleasure taken from learning or expressing positive opinions about one's academic abilities is viewed as an exaltive reflective act, making negative comments about the instructor's teaching style, or showing dissatisfaction about general learning in the group is viewed as a discontentive act, while appreciative comments about the learning experience are viewed as positively engaging with the reflective process.[40] By listening out for similar affective-reflective language concerning spirituality we can gain insight into the effectiveness of such pedagogy.

CSSR should be a space for movement. Hesmondhalgh notes the value of musical somatic experiences, including dance which can be viewed as a valuable form of play.[41] Movement can encourage entunement and empathy, shaping the environment within which reflective-affective dialogue can occur. While empathy alone will not bring about therapeutic change,[42] Dan Hughes, Kim Golding and Julie Hudson observe that "neuropsychologists are increasingly aware of how non-verbal 'mirroring', interpersonal resonance and empathic attunement are central in social/emotional development at all ages."[43] While music is a prosthetic technology its effects can be more fully utilized to create spaces where issues of spirituality and belief can be examined.

Jenefer Robinson argues that in order to make good use of such emotional musical encounter we need to be "'qualified listeners,'" that is, to hold some understanding of the aesthetic and stylistic variables shaping the music being listened to.[44] However valuable though such knowledge may be, Hesmondhalgh counters that "even the fragments that one might pick up, listening to the song on the radio, or dancing to it at a party, might elicit versions of these various emotions in response to the song,"[45] echoing Dido's song 'You don't need a God' (2019). By focusing on one's affective state, by purposefully reflecting on how one feels towards Christian spirituality and interrogating what such feelings may mean, one can "guide individuals to perform structured, efficacious and successful reflective acts in order to

---

40. Kur, "Quality in Reflective Thinking," 256.
41. Hesmondhalgh, *Why Music Matters*, 28–30.
42. Robinson, "What Play Therapists Do," 214.
43. Hughes et al., "Dyadic Developmental Psychotherapy," 360.
44. Robinson, *Deeper than Reason*, 349.
45. Hesmondhalgh, *Why Music Matters*, 25.

improve the quality of their reflective thinking and learning."[46] Such appraisal, Robinson affirms, will "give way to cognitive evaluations," encouraging therapeutic change.[47]

We will use Welch's 'Big God' as an example of how popular music may be used within CSSR. The video constructs a specific aesthetic, where dancers wear clothes in primary colors against a black background (Fig. 22). Creating a space that echoes that colour scheme can set the scene. Attunement can begin through exploring the space that has been set aside—a physical way to make sure that one's affective space is a safe space.

Figure 22. Florence and the Machine, 'Big God'

To recall Stephen Brown's point that musical stimulation reinforces associations between symbol and ritual, there is good reason for religious symbolism to be placed amongst the colour scheme.[48] For example, as the video is set within "an open ocean,"[49] the colored fabrics could be placed around a baptismal font, helping to also make connections with the lyric that speaks of her lover, or God (remembering the dual nature of the song's lyrics) to let that fondness to be experienced and the theological idea of baptism as a sign of new life. Likewise, to follow Brown's musical hierarchy

---

46. Robinson, *Deeper than Reason*, 247.
47. Robinson, *Deeper than Reason*, 364.
48. Brown, "Introduction," 14.
49. Lanigan, "Director Autumn de Wilde."

(Fig. 20.), listeners who are aware of Welch's views on music and spirituality will be more intuitively aware of the opportunities for such affective-reflective dialogue. This does not mean that listeners must know a detailed background to any music that is listened to, although a brief summary can be given to highlight certain points that an unknown artist may bring.

Baylin and Hughes speak into the restless feelings held by a traumatized child. For example, they note how a child in an emotionally aroused state, for example, angry, can begin to attune those feelings towards a more peaceful outcome. This can be achieved by a caregiver purposefully matching the intensity of the child's angry energy, almost imitating the child vocally. This helps to demonstrate empathy. Then the carer begins to calm their own voice, helping to lower the emotional energy of the child until a more restful state is found[50] thus enabling attunement.[51] To draw on the analogy, CSSR can become a place where spiritual attunement can occur. By watching the song's video and asking individuals to explore their own need for God or times when it has felt that prayer has and has not been answered, even encouraging the verbalization of disappointment, we are using Baylin and Hughes' idea of matched intensity to help with the symbiological attunement[52] of the group as a whole.[53]

It is worth, here, also noting Hans Urs von Balthasar's comments on what he terms 'Christian attunement.' Simply, there is "attunement to Being on the part of the feeling and experiencing subject."[54] His thinking reflects that of communicative musicality and of what we have seen concerning how we attune to music in order to manage our feelings. Balthasar goes to the extent of arguing that "The creature is ontologically resonant to God and for God; it is this in its totality and prior to any differentiation of its faculties into spiritual and sensuous, active and passive. This is why this primal attunement to him is not an intuition in the epistemological sense, nor is it the result of a purely logical inference from the finite to the infinite. The nonfriability of this primal experience is but the noetic reflection of the ontic indeterminateness of Being in its totality over against God. Being as such, and everything it entails, continually directs us to the inaccessible Fount."[55]

---

50. Baylin and Hughes, *Neurobiology of Attachment-Focused Therapy*, 125.
51. E.g., Dissanayake, "Root," 26.
52. E.g., Dissanayake, "Root," 17.
53. DeNora, *Music in Everyday Life*, 142.
54. Balthasar, *Glory of the Lord*, 244–45.
55. DeNora, *Music in Everyday Life*, 45.

It is this attunement that, for Balthasar, leads to divine love.[56] CSSR, I want to argue, provides an opportunity for this to take place.

The desire for symbiological attunement often lies in the construction of modern worship songs, albeit that such language is not used to describe this. A good example is Hillsong's 'Oceans' (2013). Hillsong holds a particular arena style aesthetic with lots of musicians present on stage, alongside strong lighting and staging. Notwithstanding Wagner's comments around Hillsong,[57] this song is both a call to explore who God is, while it also speaks of moments in life when we can feel overwhelmed by events, as the storms of life overcome you.

It is an extension of the Bible story of Jesus calling Peter out of his fishing boat to walk on water (Matt 14:22–33). Our interest here is not just in the lyrics, but in the musical break between the second verse and the bridge section of the song, where a musical storm is enacted. Having sung of being overwhelmed, an open-ended image that can speak of failing faith or of facing a calamitous life-event, a sixteen bar interlude is played where the drums echo a restless ocean. Suddenly, the waves cease and the music becomes calmer, before the vocalist expressively calls on the Holy Spirit to draw the worshipper forward, to echo the biblical image of Peter walking on the water in the storm with Jesus by his side. It is a moment of attunement, of speaking down the over-aroused restless soul through musical matched intensity. It is a *break with the familiar*. This is the asylum in operation.

Having attuned to the music and wider discourse being explored within our CSSR we can move to creating a conflict of narrative programs,[58] providing narratives which "offer modes of redescribing life."[59] We can note the similarity between this and early EDM, where the dancefloor allowed for conversations about a new world order to be embodied as the rave took place.[60] This can be achieved through discursive questioning rather than providing apologetical argument. In relation to Walsh's song, again remembering the dual nature of the lyrics, she contrasts the differences between her lover not returning her calls with that of God not answering her prayer requests which can elicit a non-threatening discussion around themes of prayer (i.e., Matt 6:9), omnipotence (i.e., Ps 139), indeed our wrestling in understanding God (e.g., Gen 32:22–32).

---

56. Balthasar, *Glory of the Lord*, 249.
57. Wagner, "Christianity," 95.
58. Ricoeur, *Figuring the Sacred*, 239.
59. Ricoeur, *Figuring the Sacred*, 43.
60. John, *Global Tribe*, 26; John, "The Difference Engine," 22.

It is about engaging with the Bible story in imaginative ways. Other playful tactics can be employed such as, in this instance, role playing differing prayerful techniques—Ignatian prayer, for example. While Whitton notes that such a playful technique enables "learners to suspend their disbelief and immerse themselves in the spirit of play,"[61] she equally notes that "Associations with play as an activity that is childish, frivolous or inauthentic may limit the motivation for learners."[62] Authenticity, again, is a significant attribute that shapes people's response.

We can also use CSSR metaphorically. For example, in using Walsh's song, we can draw the distinction between darkness and colour to explore feelings of emptiness contrasted with a colorful different styled life; to explore what may be meant when Jesus declares that "I have come that they may have life, and have it to the full" (John 10:10). As Riis and Woodhead note, "an additional part of what makes an emotional regime religious is the way in which it represents its emotional programme as relating to an 'alternate ordering' that goes beyond the orderings of everyday life."[63] Likewise, exploring objects within this space which convey something of the subject being discussed can be helpful. As Motti Regev notes, artistic objects can convey what he terms as epistemic culture, as aesthetic culture.[64]

CSSR is largely about discovering *how* to playfully encounter God. To follow Balthasar's attunement to God's love, CSSR awakens what Baylin and Hughes refer to as the "inherent potential for engagement" in a manner that allows for reflection.[65] It is not enough simply to present facts, rather this allows differing possibilities of re-ordering to be probed and felt. It is the felt nature of this experience that helps someone to connect with, to embody the narrative that is being explored.

Clearly, this is far more than offering a warm welcome or the space looking tidy where apologetic argument can be listened to. This is not about creating a Shaferian soundscape where recorded music is mediated in as lifelike manner as possible. Rather, it is about recognizing the potential presented by a space within which both sonic and visual may interact. The prominence of aesthetics will be a challenge to the wider Church. As Kahn-Harris and Moberg note, the religious music scene is usually "aesthetically timid," while "There is little idea of an aesthetic 'for its own sake', that would drive innovation. This lack of a theology of the aesthetic is often related

---

61. Whitton, "Playful Learning," 4.
62. Whitton, "Playful Learning," 9.
63. Riis and Woodhead, *Sociology of Religious Emotion*, 70.
64. Regev, *Pop-Rock Music*, 129.
65. Baylin and Hughes, *Neurobiology of Attachment-Focused Therapy*, 155.

to a firm commitment to the 'middle of the road', based on a view of mass culture that seeks the benefits of a mass audience but does not wish to contribute to its development."[66]

Such opportunity can be further reinforced by drawing on Baylin and Hughes' use of the acronym, PACE, used to help primary carers connect with a traumatized child, often through adoption. As mentioned, the acronym stands for key values which a parent needs to express towards a traumatized child: playfulness, acceptance, curiosity and empathy. The analogy of a traumatized child needing to emotionally reconnect with a caregiver correlates with that of a restless liquid modernist (re)connecting to a discourse such as the Christian discourse. These values can frame our formation of CSSR. Furthermore, we will draw links between playfulness and poetics, between acceptance and socialization into belief, curiosity and beauty and, lastly, empathy and wisdom. Effectively, we are seeking to stimulate what Baylin and Hughes see as an "affective-reflective dialogue."[67]

3. Theologizing PACE

Playfulness and Poetics

The initial value is playfulness,[68] the positive nature of which we have already highlighted. Within popular music, a playful attitude can be seen visually in the editing of music videos, both in their cut and content.[69] We have seen this, for example, with the imagery of cowboys and motorbike in the video for Jonas Blue's 'Fast Car'. Bauman has emphasized how individuals are fearful of commitment to a particular life-style in case it does not meet expectations.[70] In other words, where there is a lack of trust around a particular life discourse, playfulness can be a significant value to help rebuild trust. As discussed, our approach to constructing CSSR must engender playfulness.

Playfulness, though, is not a theme that is often cited theologically. Kevin Vanhoozer's approach to theology does seek to express levels of playfulness by exploring what he terms the theodrama of scripture,[71] yet his work also inadvertently highlights the tension that liquid moderns feel around religious language and doctrine. Vanhoozer views scripture as a

66. Kahn-Harris and Moberg, "Religious Popular Music," 98.
67. Baylin and Hughes, *Neurobiology of Attachment-Focused Therapy*, 118.
68. Baylin and Hughes, *Neurobiology of Attachment-Focused Therapy*, 131.
69. Vernallis, *Unruly Media*, 35.
70. Bauman, *Community*, 3.
71. Vanhoozer, *Pictures at a Theological Exhibition*, 169.

form of dramaturge. This is a term used by dramatists in America, whereby a researcher helps a director to make sense of an old script in order to make the production as authentic to the original as possible.[72] He suggests that "The canon is less a textbook than playbook. It does not preserve a set of ideas so much as patterns of speech and action,"[73] reflecting aspects of Habermas' communicative action.[74] Vanhoozer's hope is that his theological method will allow for a plurality of images to be processed over that of a single propositional understanding,[75] while that process will encourage communities to pursue and understand doctrine. He claims that: "Only the imagination—the ability to grasp meaningful patterns or conceive unified wholes out of apparently unrelated elements—enables us to "see" God and the kingdom of God at work in the world. It is faith that enables this imagination—and faith comes by hearing, and hearing from the word of Christ."[76]

Our imaginative encounter with popular music, especially within CSSR, can help us to "see" something of God. Vanhoozer again speaks of wanting to stand "in the breach" between theology and ministerial praxis,[77] where he wants to make a link between doctrine and what he terms as "theodramatic systematics,"[78] that is the difference between espoused and operative theologies. Vanhoozer even goes as far as noting that the imagination is "not less than cognitive"[79] and that to view scripture as simply a collection of propositional statements is to de-dramatize it, which risks losing its figurative ability.[80]

However, he does this with a view to sustaining the traditional social dynamics of Christian belief, which, we have argued, is not sustainable within liquid modernity. Vanhoozer faces a dilemma. He longs for traditional dogma to be retained, yet he notes how, "ossified, formulaic knowledge that will either wilt on the vine or, another plausible scenario, be used as a shibbolethic instrument of power."[81] He acknowledges that "Narratives make story-shaped points that cannot always be paraphrased in propositional

---

72. Vanhoozer, *Pictures at a Theological Exhibition*, 244.
73. Vanhoozer, *Pictures at a Theological Exhibition*, 145.
74. Habermas, *Theory of Communicative Action*, 8.
75. Vanhoozer, *The Drama of Doctrine*, 386.
76. Vanhoozer, *Pictures at a Theological Exhibition*, 27.
77. Vanhoozer, *Pictures at a Theological Exhibition*, 10.
78. Vanhoozer, *Pictures at a Theological Exhibition*, 11.
79. Vanhoozer, *Pictures at a Theological Exhibition*, 25.
80. Vanhoozer, *Pictures at a Theological Exhibition*, 87.
81. Vanhoozer, *Pictures at a Theological Exhibition*, 88.

statements without losing something in translation."[82] This is one of the key issues that liquid moderns are concerned about—the shibbolethic use of doctrine.

We have noted the helpfulness of *ut pictura poesis*. Vanhoozer also notes the value of the medieval view of poetry, which does not express the poet's experiences, rather "poets are merely ministers of the things—real presences—that truly matter."[83] This is a poetic pursuit of ontological realness. The evidence here points to a playful, poetic engagement of the bible story as a highly significant opportunity for liquid moderns to explore differing worlds. The point is that to tell the Christian story today it needs to be done poetically and playfully to help demonstrate where a new world, the Kingdom of God, may be encountered. Simply, as Dyrness points out: "God's participation in creation and creation's embrace by the Trinitarian presence of God—these together constitute theological grounds for the potential inherent in the symbolizing inclination of the poetic imagination."[84] Therefore, within our CSSR we can use of the differing sounds, lyrics and imagery of popular music to playfully and poetically re-describe life.

Acceptance and Socialization

Children who have suffered trauma, especially if caused at an early age, are likely to act out behaviors related to that original trauma as they grow older. Yet, it is in the caregiver accepting such acted out behaviors—not condoning them but being accepting of them however socially unpleasant they may be—that the hurting individual begins to find security.[85] With acceptance grows trust which may encourage attunement to a caregiver. Here, the analogy is that existential restlessness can be viewed akin to early trauma while feelings of restlessness represent acted out behaviors.

Bauman accepts that it is the loss of grand-narratives which have caused instability resulting in us needing to saw up pieces of differing narratives, pulling them together in our search for ontological security.[86] Ironically, this is not too far removed from Augustine's assertion that "because you have made us for yourself . . . our hearts are restless, until they find rest in you."[87] To reflect this into ecclesial praxis, there is a need for the Church

---

82. Vanhoozer, *The Drama of Doctrine*, 88.
83. Vanhoozer, *Pictures at a Theological Exhibition*, 22.
84. Dyrness, *Poetic Theology*, 24.
85. Baylin and Hughes, *Neurobiology of Attachment-Focused Therapy*, 133.
86. I.e., Bauman, *Liquid Modernity*, 23.
87. Augustine, *Confessions*, 1.1.1.

to first acknowledge identities that it would once have found troublesome, as it is in firstly accepting *how* someone feels that individuals can begin to see the positive outcomes of the Christian discourse for themselves.

As noted, the need for acceptance is seen in Sia's 'Cheap Thrills' (2016) and Avicii's 'Wake Me Up' (2014). Avicii's video makes it clear that when a mutual connection is recognized, seen in the main protagonists recognizing the same tattoo on other individuals, people feel secure and belong. Liquid moderns need to feel truly accepted for who they are. Bauman makes the specific point concerning fear in committing to a particular identity in case it does not provide security.[88] Where there resides an element of doubt over acceptance, so someone will simply seek an identity where they do feel accepted. Yet, acceptance leads to socialization into that community's discourse.

Curiosity and Beauty

In asking a traumatized child in a playful manner a question such as "I wonder why you expressed that behavior?" or, "I'm curious as to why you did that?" it is possible that the answer given will begin to give insight into how they really feel and to discover why certain behaviors are being expressed. As much as playfulness engenders confidence, Baylin and Hughes note, "Curiosity is a not-knowing position, with no assumptions, no expectations, no judgements about what is being discovered."[89] Once a child begins to recognize for themselves why they act as they do, or find the language to describe how they feel, so the caregiver can begin to speak into that and, together, repair the damage of past traumatic events, enabling beauty to replace brokenness.

A similar curiosity should be encouraged in exploring Christian belief. This is different from the traditional apologetic, didactic and epistemological approach, rather, it is helping someone to find the words for themselves as to how they truly feel. Questions concerning aspects of belief can simply be "I wonder why you feel that way?" or "I wonder how this might help?" It is in raising curiosity that an alternative discourse can become offered. To return to the video of Avicii's 'Wake Me Up,' it is fair to ask people questions such as "I wonder what it feels like to feel so unsettled that you need to find an identity that truly connects with you?" Or Welch's 'Big God,' curiosity can explore emotions around how we feel connected with God. For example, should you interpret the lyric referencing messages as simply

88. Bauman, *Community*, 3.
89. Baylin and Hughes, *Neurobiology of Attachment-Focused Therapy*, 135.

being about unanswered voicemails or the frustration felt around seemingly unanswered prayers?

A key aspect of Christian belief is to invite others to be curious enough to step into the new world of the Kingdom of God and within that to find beauty and shalom. To quote Balthasar, beauty is "being identical with Being, spirit, and freedom."[90] This is to suggest that in encountering beauty, there is an opening to encountering something divine. Central throughout has been how aesthetics and our emotional response can help us to identify those discourses which enable us to feel ontologically secure. This reflects the belief that deeper meaning, ontological meaning is to be found in art,[91] or akin to the Deleuzean understanding of spirituality found in film (or in popular music videos). For Balthasar, beauty becomes equated with truth: *kalokagathon*—the 'beautiful-and-true'.[92]

Balthasar argues that "In fact, God's Incarnation perfects the whole ontology and aesthetics of created Being."[93] While Vanhoozer argues that his poetic journey is to find doctrinal truth in scripture, Balthasar considers the need for ontological truth from a different angle in asserting "We must, then, repeat that Scripture is not the Word itself, but rather the Spirit's testimony concerning the Word." Rather than simply affirming doctrinal facts about Jesus, the gospels reveal Jesus' character to whom we give ourselves over to.[94] As Balthasar asserts "The mystery of God proclaimed by the Church is his doxa become visible."[95] Our curious exploration of popular music and its use within CSSR becomes a place to encounter the beauty of doxa.

Empathy and Wisdom

"Empathy," Baylin and Hughes note, "is often the intervention that enables the dialogue to continue, that begins the process of the mistrusting child beginning to sense the possibility of trust."[96] Within CSSR, empathy is the language that says "I understand why you feel as you do and I accept that without judgement." We have also noted how through the process of emotional induction we can find ourselves deeply connected with a piece of music, enabling us to empathize with the writer's intentions. Such emotional

90. Balthasar, *Glory of the Lord*, 22.
91. cf. Tillich, *On Art and Architecture*.
92. Balthasar, *Glory of the Lord*, 22.
93. Balthasar, *Glory of the Lord*, 29.
94. Balthasar, *Glory of the Lord*, 31–33.
95. Balthasar, *Glory of the Lord*, 174.
96. Baylin and Hughes, *Neurobiology of Attachment-Focused Therapy*, 138.

connection is often reflected in the comments often placed by fans on the internet. For example, a fan expresses via the YouTube page of "Big God" how Welch "has this innocent speaking voice but when she sings it's like some heavenly god has taken over. It's incredible."[97]

This helps to explain why CSSR can feel an empathetic space. It is about feeling connection. If empathy is the ability to understand and share the feelings of another, then wisdom becomes the way to help move empathetic feelings forward. It is moving the conversation from "I understand why you feel as you do" to "I wonder if this can help you?" This is affective-reflective dialogue in action.

Wisdom can be found in the wisdom tradition of the Bible. What is offered it is the wisdom of lived experience. The wisdom tradition holds poetic content that allows someone to explore a concept over simply being told what you should believe. It is often practical as well as anticipatory. The potential for wisdom to act poetically alongside its ability to provide wise advice is of huge potential to the liquid modern church. It becomes a resource to the Church and wider society as it reflects both accumulated life-experience which has been sedimented over many generations. Appropriately, Vanhoozer views wisdom as "the virtue that orders all other virtues—is intrinsically linked to the imagination and beauty via the theme of fittingness. The wise person perceives and participates fittingly in the ordered beauty of creation. Wisdom thus integrates the good, the true and the beautiful. Works of art and music provide the lighting on the stage of human existence."[98]

Wisdom, as found in scripture, is often employed metaphorically. Again, metaphors can help us to view situations in new ways.[99] Ricoeur observes that where there is an element of movement within a metaphor, it can help to move us from one idea to another *through* the metaphor. Examples could be, Proverbs 25:20: "Like one who takes away a garment on a cold day, or like vinegar poured on a wound, is one who sings songs to a heavy heart." Or Proverbs 22:26–27: "Do not be one who shakes hands in pledge or puts up security for debts; if you lack the means to pay, your very bed will be snatched from under you."

Paul Fiddes highlights the potential for wisdom to be a positive resource for late-moderns. Indeed, its potential to connect with liquid modernity should be all the greater due to the variety of style of wisdom and

---

97. See Clayton Moore's comment in florencemachine, "Big God."

98. Vanhoozer, *Pictures at a Theological Exhibition*, 136.

99. I.e., Ricoeur, *From Text to Action*, 11; Lakoff and Johnson, *Metaphors We Live By*.

the opportunity for this to be interpreted in a variety of ways. Here, Fiddes helpfully draws on Augustine to make the point that biblical texts are often polysemic.[100] He describes the Hebrew wisdom literature has having been drawn together by a class of people called 'the wise,' who, through time and effort observed how people coped with life's experiences.[101] This wisdom assumes a divine connection, one which may remain hidden, yet which also gives up something of itself, which we glimpse of as real, yet which becomes voiced in a hidden fashion, again, in the form of riddles and the like. As we noted in the video of New Order's 'Restless' or in the lyrical content of Mel C's 'Dear life,' there is a hunger to look for that which often feels hidden.

Yet, the wisdom tradition is seen as the poor relative in the wider biblical cannon. Fiddes draws out why the traditional church is suspicious of wisdom. In noting the differences between wisdom as *techne* (technical wisdom), *phronesis* (practical wisdom) and *Sophia* (theoretical wisdom), Aristotle saw that *Sophia* enabled one to discern what is ultimately real and true, by using one's *nous* (intelligence) and *episteme* (reasoning). Fiddes additionally notes the link between the Greek use of the word wisdom and that of the Hebraic understanding of *hokmah* (wisdom), which subsequently becomes translated as Sophia within the Greek New Testament.[102] Such a conflation of understandings has led to sections of the Church viewing wisdom with suspicion due to this entanglement and leanings with Greek philosophy.

The picture becomes further muddied in that the counterpart of Aristotle's Sophia in the Western, Latin Christian tradition became termed as *sapientia*. By the Middle Ages, *sapientia* became seen as the binary opposite to *Scientia*.[103] Yet, to peel away these differing layers one can rediscover, as Fiddes expresses, that wisdom becomes the "codification of life experiences."[104] Hebraic wisdom, he argues, offers a "unique integration of phronesis and Sophia."[105]

The point here is that we have already seen a strong differentiation between ontological understandings of the world and those which are epistemologically considered. With such engrained roots it cannot be a surprise that parts of the Church will view anything that critiques its epistemologically governed discourse as a threat. Fiddes is right, therefore, to seek to redress that balance. To do so would clearly help to redress that imbalance

---

100. E.g., Augustine, *Confessions*, 31.42.
101. Fiddes, *Seeing the World*, 96.
102. Fiddes, *Seeing the World*, 5–6.
103. Fiddes, *Seeing the World*, 6–7.
104. Fiddes, *Seeing the World*, 16.
105. Fiddes, *Seeing the World*, 9.

between a society which express itself ontologically (as we have noted within popular music) and with a Church that views such expression as, at best, theologically weak, or at worse, simply postmodern bricolage. He draws the contrast between epistemological understanding of the world and wisdom, noting: "The priests bid their worshippers to hear' the commandments of God (Torah) which they hold as guardians from the past, or which they formulate in their own day as they reflect on their tradition. The wise, however, bid their disciples to cultivate the art of 'looking at the world around.'"[106]

Whether intentional or not, one can see similarities between a Church that is keen to hold on to its traditions and those, such as the poets and lyricists of popular music who would simply challenge us to 'look at the world around us.'[107] Yet, wisdom considers what lies hidden in the world and brings it into the open.[108] As Fiddes is keen to note: "God is the final (though collaborative) author of the text of the world and is present in the text in a hidden way, it is empathetic participation in the movement of the triune God that actually enables us to interpret the signs of the world."[109]

This is precisely what the religious/spiritual content that we find within popular culture is ultimately about, yet it operates beyond the majority of structures of the institutional church. It describes an empathetic and curious participation with the movement of the triune God. In this sense, CSSR can be governed by our playful attitude, our acceptance of one another, our curiosity towards a new discourse and our growing empathy towards one another.

4. Outlining a Theology of Emotion and Popular Music

We began by linking feelings of existential restlessness with what Bauman saw as the ending of religious narratives as shaping society. We have also noted how individuals long for an identity which makes them feel ontologically secure, albeit that Bauman does not feel that is plausible in liquid modernity.[110] Now, living within the hegemony of liberal pluralism, the social forces which structure such ideology restrict our understanding of religion and spirituality.[111] While there is the opportunity to consider dif-

---

106. Fiddes, *Seeing the World*, 13.
107. See also Keuss, *Blur*.
108. Fiddes, *Seeing the World*, 106.
109. Fiddes, *Seeing the World*, 288.
110. Bauman, *Community*, 142.
111. Bauman, *Community*, 3.

fering worldviews, there is a point when looking beyond the limits of the lifeworld becomes epistemologically and ideologically frowned upon.

However, there is growing awareness of these social forces as there are clear expressions within popular music culture which highlight deeper ontological needs. We can view this as Certeau's tactics in action. The key point here is that such bricolage should not be understood simply as consumer choice, rather a deeper ontological need is being addressed, for individuals to attain an identity that ends feelings of restlessness. Yet, the institution of the Church seems reluctant to actively respond to these ontological needs. It also remains suspicious of identity issues when all that individuals are seeking is ontological security.

Rather, the Church's evangelistic response to favor epistemological apologetics is in response to modernity's need for rational thinking. This is currently evidenced in its strategy of encouraging churches which actively promote an apologetically driven evangelism focused on what Ward has identified as a reduced doctrine of belief.[112] This is not to criticize such an approach, but to point out a lost opportunity which will become ever more pronounced as liquid modernity becomes more established.

Ironically, churches which favor such an epistemological approach often use worship which is contemporary in style and which does make use of emotions to 'bring people into God's presence.' Such moments encourage what Gabrielsson would call a serious encounter with music (SEM). This is not to discredit such worshipful experiences, yet a more robust theological understanding of our emotional life would enhance our understanding of what is truly going on here. With a wider appreciation, the aesthetical quotient in all ecclesial or spiritual settings can be more robustly utilized. Essentially, years of enlightenment thinking have repressed subjective understanding. The relationship between religious discourse and our affective state is significant. This is to recognize the 'turn to the self' and that affective-reflective dialogue is a valuable component of our meaning-making.

Yet, how may one believe in God in a world which is suspicious of looking beyond that which may be described concretely? One thing which our consideration of popular music identifies is that many do seek understanding, even if at a rudimentary level. It is, rather, that Enlightenment values still subvert our understanding of Christian spirituality today. The whole point of considering popular music, the way we functionally make use of it, the poetic nature of the lyrics and the emotional quotient of the music, is that it can be transgressive, helping us to express what we may feel but cannot see. Telling the Christian story today must be able to draw on

---

112. Ward, *Liquid Ecclesiology*, 66.

this. We have argued that by using the values of playfulness, acceptance, curiosity and empathy can purposefully create affective space within which the Christian story can be told. We have noted, too, how beauty and wisdom can be part of this process.

The more the Church can tactically highlight the detrimental effect of the social forces which restrict belief, so more within the Church may gain confidence to overtly express Christian belief. Likewise, a key issue for the institutional Church to address is the need to find the confidence to rebalance its own reliance on epistemological approaches to evangelism and find fresh ways that allow for felt expressions of belief. This is an area for greater research. The fear for the Church is that any change in tactical direction will be seen as a revision of what has gone before. Yet, the poetic content of the Jesus story, of the wisdom held within the wider cannon of scripture is more robust than the fear held by many in the institutional church that such an approach would simply lead to doctrinal chaos.

We have considered the Hebraic understanding of Shalom, of wholeness in body, mind and spirit. This is of particular significance within liquid modernity as that is the antithesis to existential restlessness. Alongside Shalom, wisdom as in 'lived experience' can be drawn on with which to explore the new world of the Kingdom of God, helping to demonstrate that the Christian worldview has depth and resilience. We have also spoken of Geist and Logos, of the divine nature woven within the fabric of the cosmos. It is against these theological concepts which feelings of transcendence and revelation need to be interpreted, albeit more as highlighting learning opportunities about God.

We have noted that SEM hold a particular potency in changing or reinforcing a particular worldview, albeit that some understanding of that outlook is required for a particular interpretation to be foregrounded. This is to support that high quality and authentic music production is needed within our church communities to enhance such moments. This is not the same as supporting expensive production techniques. It is rather to emphasize the authenticity of music production within a particular church community. However, the place where such occurrences may happen will gain from a strong aesthetic schema.

It will never be a straightforward journey to socialize people into Christian belief. A fluid society will require a less boundaried approach to matters of spirituality for the simple reason that anything too rigid in approach will be more likely to scare liquid moderns away from considering the Christian world view. Such a conclusion is drawn from Bauman's understanding that liquid moderns are reticent to commit to an identity in their pursuit of ontological security, although the premise of this book has also been that it is still possible to develop a strong attachment with the Christian story.

How might such a broad approach work in practice? As a methodology for engaging liquid moderns, a theology of popular music and emotion requires the awareness that we are all cultural poachers and that we use our culture to express something of our existential needs and ultimate hopes. Such bricolage is part of our affective-reflective dialogue. Biblically, we see that artistic endeavor should be valued (i.e., Exod 35:30–35), albeit that historically the Church has not felt able to do so. In looking at the biblical tradition we could note that when Judah was taken into captivity in Babylon by King Nebuchadnezzar the artisans were deemed important enough to be led away, too (2 Kgs 24:12–14). While not stated, it can be assumed that this is precisely because their work could express forbidden existential needs and ultimate hopes that needed to be ideologically repressed with Judah's confinement. Clearly, how a nation expresses itself culturally is a highly significant factor, the ramification being that how the Church expresses itself culturally should be held with equally as high a value. Again, this is not to suggest form over substance, but that importance should be given to the aesthetics that are used to communicate the Church's message.

The Church needs to be open to a far more robust conversation between popular culture, wider society and itself.[113] If, as Certeau describes, there are few with the ability to create art that purposefully speaks into a cultural situation, then we need to encourage the majority who "make do (*bricolent*)" with "everyday art."[114] Pressingly, to follow St. Paul's Areopagus moment (Acts 17:16–34), it needs those who see themselves strongly immersed within the Christian subculture to openly show interest with wider popular culture. Here, we have considered popular music.

Alongside this, we have also noted how musical traits are set in place from birth through the playful *motherese* attitude of the central care provider, noting how this holds a strong influence on our decision making through one's life. Tactically, this should mean that work with young children should be greatly encouraged, especially that which is musically and aesthetically expresses Christian spirituality.

We have also argued that the local church can purposefully make use of CSSR. This is not holy or sacred space by a different name, rather it is providing a place where individuals can purposefully complete identity work. This is an emotional and heuristic space which utilizes aesthetics, as well as a safe space within which an individual can begin to explore a different world

---

113. E.g., Niebuhr, *Christ and Culture*.
114. Certeau, *Practice of Everyday Life*, 66.

described before them. Again, it is a place for affective-reflective dialogue. While one always needs awareness that there are many hegemonic forces at work,[115] there is a certain level of neutrality that can be found between people in looking at popular cultural objects—one can simply agree with what another says or turn away. CSSR is a playful space where reparative and playful spiritual work can be undertaken.

Those who are wary of such approach could consider the positive role that traditions can play in enabling key facets of a discourse to be retained over time. As David Brown asserts: "Instead of thinking of tradition as purely human reflection added on to an original and unchanging divine disclosure, or even of it as small, but significant, divinely added supplements, we need to see that continuing human reflection as itself an indispensable part of the process of divine disclosure. Revelation is mediated to the community of faith through a continuous stream of developing tradition."[116]

Rather, he asserts that we should see "the hand of God in a continuing process," noting that even stories found within scripture "have not stood still," becoming reworked in order to make specific theological points suited towards particular communities.[117] One can see such a process within the cannon of scripture in comparing the Gospel of Matthew, with its strong Jewish feel, to that of John's Gospel, which is not only more theologically nuanced and written later, but written for a Hellenized audience.[118] Brown helpfully identifies the issue is about how a particular narrative works and what it is, therefore, seeking to say in a particular context. As he further notes: "For to my mind, so far from undermining the search for knowledge and understanding, being aware of the traditions upon which one inevitably draws is what makes progress possible, provided that these traditions are allowed to function as open, both towards their past and to the wider context within which they are set."[119]

Now, within liquid modernity, a key factor that allows tradition to continue is that of emotional connectivity, to recognize further the 'turn to the self.' To draw on Ward's observations, what is required is "a cultural theology in the sense that it seeks to interact with patterns of practice and thinking that are operant in the lived expression of the Church."[120] The lived expression is seeking to make Christ *real* in the liquid modern age. What

---

115. I.e., Marsh and Roberts, *Personal Jesus*, 19.
116. Brown, *Tradition and Imagination*, 169.
117. Brown, *Tradition and Imagination*, 1–5.
118. See also Tillich, "Theology and Symbolism," 4.
119. Brown, *Tradition and Imagination*, 111.
120. Ward, *Liquid Ecclesiology*, 111.

needs to be remembered is that liquid moderns "saw up and make fit" differing narratives to feel ontologically secure not because they want to, but out of fear that they need to.[121]

Whatever our taste in popular music, we have seen that our listening and reflecting will profoundly say much about who we are and our need for ontological security. We have also seen that the spiritual expression of who we are is a significant aspect of what it means to be human and cannot be discounted by the processes of secularization. Instead, we have seen how pluralism's hegemonic forces subtly, but effectively prevent many from clearly hearing the Christian story. Yet, restlessness will remain unless we take seriously the needs expressed by popular culture and are prepared to look beyond the horizon of our lifeworld to resolve feelings of cognitive dissonance. This is a call to all those who seek to tell stories about what may lie over the horizon of our lifeworld to create places where such tactical story-telling can be listened to. The Christian story is still as potent as it was two thousand years ago. The key contents of the story stay the same, rather the manner that it is told must adapt accordingly.

5. Postscript—Bauman's Heritage

Bauman's reflections have been most helpful. From his Marxist beginnings, his sociological thinking led him to engage with post-modern thinking,[122] ultimately criticizing it for its ethics in dealing with others. He identified the fluid nature of modernity and how individuals negotiate this space[123] concluding that the demise of the Western telos of religion would lead to the *fate of identity* where existential restlessness would result.[124] However, Bauman's later writings appreciated the ontological nature of the world around us, arguing there was more than he could account for sociologically. His journey took him to move from celebrating that religious beliefs were "now out of the way"[125] to that of viewing religious language in the public sphere as enriching.[126]

There is something profound in Bauman's thinking which does reflect the spirit of our age. Especially so as we reflect on aspects of Woodhead's

---

121. Bauman, *The Individualized Society*, 142.
122. Bauman, *Postmodern Ethics*.
123. Bauman, *Liquid Modernity*; Bauman, *The Individualized Society*; Bauman, *Community*; Bauman, *Identity*.
124. Bauman, *Liquid Modernity*, 34; Bauman, *The Individualized Society*, 46.
125. Bauman, *Liquid Modernity*, 23.
126. Bauman and Obirek, *Of God and Man*, 44, 56.

work on 'the rise of the nones,' with her description of a typical 'none' as younger, liberal in ethics and morals, not necessarily atheist, suspicious of organized religion yet still open to that which resources the spiritual side of our being, be that immanent or transcendent in nature. While Woodhead notes that the liberal pluralist nature of British society is enshrined within our laws, the social forces of our day, such as the suspicion of needing to look beyond the horizon of our lifeworld, still make it challenging to express transcendent belief in God.[127] However, we have seen that popular music is very open to asking questions about what may lie beyond the horizon, even if such comments cannot be considered as epistemologically concrete.

Bauman concluded that the Christian worldview was the "most radical and egalitarian of all the alternative suggestions I can think of."[128] The social forces of liquid modernity make it highly unlikely that, at the present time, the Christian discourse will be able to recapture the veracity of previous ages. Yet, by drawing on both Bauman's thinking and what we may learn from how we make use of popular music we can see that there is hope for the Christian story to be told well within liquid modernity, if only the Church will be broader in its approach, accepting of why society is restless and understanding how the dynamics of popular music help to quell that existential storm. Time will tell if the institutional Church is courageous enough to step fully into liquid modernity.

6. Conclusion

The positive link between historic religious belief and popular music will, for some, remain tenuous. Yet, as Paul Tillich has established, dialectic relationships exist between religion and culture.[129] We have seen how popular music, its functional uses, the effects of its sonic qualities alongside the song's interpretation through video can express structural and existential disquiet, all which the Church has historically spoken into. Society also expresses a need for spiritual connection in both its immanent and transcendent understandings. This is significant as it reinforces our understanding of popular music as an important theological resource.

We have also noted how liquid modernity articulates an ideological preference for postmetaphysical, rationally driven argument which does place it at odds with those who hold to non-secular discourses. This does place the Church on the back-foot and it does not know how best to

---

127. Woodhead, "The Rise of 'No Religion,'" 252–55.
128. Bauman and Raud, *Practices of Selfhood*, 5.
129. I.e., Church, "Aspects of a Religious Analysis," 103.

tactically respond. That popular music expresses many credible references to life beyond secular constructions of reality (e.g., Mel C's 'Dear World' or Drake's 'God's Plan') simply reinforces our present disconnect between religion as the substance of culture and culture as shaping religion. Such songs are examples which express disconnection between individuals and society as well as society and the Church. The need for ontological security, though, is fundamental to our thriving.[130]

The issue of restless disconnection will remain until there can be a significant reordering of society's views towards what may lie beyond the horizon of Western secularity. Presently, the Church does not find itself at the crossover point of Tillich's dialectic, where it should most effectively reside. This is partly because it has lost the ability to speak into our culture in a constructive and meaningful way. Whereas, Tillich's post-war dialectic was, from the Church's perspective, balanced in a culture still familiar with core Christian values, within liquid modernity it is not.

Popular culture, with its bottom-up dynamic, is able to authentically highlight the values embedded in society. One thing which this demonstrates is the need for dialogue focused on feeling a connection with the divine as opposed to reliance on rational apologetics alone. That we use popular music to express our spiritual needs shows that wider society is very open to wrestling with the divine. Woodhead's work around 'the nones' further shows that society is still prepared to wrestle with God albeit that it feels constrained by organized religion.[131] The issue, rather, is the need for the Western Church to understand more the sociology of our era and how to communicate something of God's story within this environment. The pursuit of a secure identity which offers ontological security must not be viewed as someone simply making a consumeristic choice. A secure identity is needed for survival.[132] Again, the Church overly favors rational argument in its offer of security, when popular music expresses its angsts emotionally, effectively expressing a differing form of language, craving authenticity and ontological reality over apologetic argument.

Feelings of ontological security, which are shaped by our early life-experiences, hold significant importance. Tia DeNora's work does, of course, articulate this with her notion of music as an asylum.[133] Here, though, we are describing a link between our need for ontological security and

---

130. E.g., Maslow, *Toward a Psychology of Being*; Bowlby, *A Secure Base*; Laing, *The Divided Self.*

131. Woodhead, "The Rise of 'No Religion,'" 252.

132. E.g., Bauman, *Community*, 3.

133. DeNora *Music Asylums*.

the sound of security. This holds both a metaphoric quality to express our need for security, as well as the sonic reality that we bricolage from cultural artefacts in order to find security, which we are hard-wired from birth to achieve.[134] The restless frustration of liquid moderns feeling unable to find ontological security can be viewed as a child who struggles with issues of attachment towards her carer. The child may seem ambivalent, avoidant or disordered towards the need for security and in need of support to see this necessity. This, again, becomes an issue of communication and we have presented some practical pointers to aid this affective-reflective dialogue. This is to note that our story-telling holds a therapeutic quality, which is a point often overlooked by the established Church.

The Church does struggle to accept that significant social forces affect the reception of its discourses, employing argumentation instead to reinforce its rationally based methodologies over actively wanting to communicate with liquid moderns 'where they are.' Missiological writing usually makes the point of listening to society and contextualizing accordingly.[135] The tactical response of the Western Church must be to broaden its theological outlook else liquid moderns will, indeed have, cast its narratives to one side as a fundamental discourse.

One significant theological theme which will connect with liquid moderns is the need for shalom, peace being the antithesis of restlessness. Perhaps this is the most significant reason why more impetus should be placed on feeling connection with the divine. Jesus' peace is there to be experienced. His ontological presence is the theological antidote to existential restlessness. This is why Hans Urs von Balthasar's talk of Christian attunement is valid in our generation, its process affirmed by therapeutic musicology,[136] together with scholars such as Baylin and Hughes' work with traumatized children, who reinforce the importance of attunement and wellbeing.[137]

Creative Space for Spiritual Reflection (CSSR), which is not related to past understandings of sacred space, is purposefully creating emotional space where individual affective space is stimulated to engage in affective-reflective dialogue around the Christian discourse.[138] The fact that this is such an emotional space clearly sets it apart from places where the focus lies on God's story being cognitively expounded. Of course, the aesthetics of

---

134. E.g., Certeau, *Practice of Everyday Life*; Willis, *Common Culture*.
135. E.g., Donovan, *Christianity Rediscovered*.
136. E.g., DeNora, *Music Asylums*.
137. E.g., Baylin and Hughes, *Neurobiology of Attachment-Focused Therapy*.
138. E.g., Corrigan, "Introduction," 158.

emotion are evident in preaching and this is not to decry that methodology. However, within liquid modernity our emotions need to be given greater credence than in the past and our personal use of popular music provides the ideal medium with which to encourage this. Instants when affective-reflective dialogue does occur are valuable Kairos moments. Against a worldview which does make space for Logos and Geist, such moments can and should be interpreted as divine encounter, seeking, to misquote Baylin and Hughes to reawaken our "inherent potential for engagement" with the divine. However, these are moments not just to celebrate divine connection, but to learn from the discourse that supports these events.

We have highlighted the value of playfulness, which is underrated as both pedagogy and theological tool. We can include, too, the lived experience of the wisdom tradition, all devices which can accentuate the affective-reflective dialogue needed to communicate the Christian discourse within liquid modernity. We have noted how liquid moderns need a high level of consumable symbols to draw on, which can fuel feelings of insecurity. We can finally draw several strands together. When our affective space is challenged by the aesthetics of both sound and place, a process which can be accentuated with the prosthetic technology of, say, transgressive popular music, so we may even feel a serious encounter with music (SEM) which can profoundly affect our behaviors towards the divine. CSSR is not seeking to force such moments, rather to promote reflection on both our affective state and the Christian story being told at that moment. Again, our playfulness, acceptance, curiosity and empathy are all reflective tools to help in this process, helping to embody the Christian story. This thesis, therefore, seeks to develop a theological understanding of affective space, grounding it within present thinking in terms of child trauma-based therapies to help liquid moderns become socialized into the Christian discourse.

It, therefore, brings new thought into the conversation between therapeutic musicology and theology, especially concerning feelings of existential dissonance and discourses which offer ontological security. Sociologically, it also brings fresh insight to the structural forces which restrict the telling of the Christian discourse today against the backdrop of how popular music expresses society's need for spiritual resourcing. It reinforces the value of popular music as a theological resource, providing a pedagogy that can both help redress the balance of the Church's overreliance on rational thought while helping individuals to reflect on their affective experiences.

These outcomes help identify several areas that would be good to build on in the future. The links between SEM and transcendent experiences opens up fresh discussions around charismatic sung worship and embodied changes to lifestyles, which should help close the gap between espoused and operant theologies at work within a church community. While Tia DeNora focuses on the therapeutic value of the asylum[139] and Christopher Partridge demonstrates the positive value of affective space,[140] further work would also be fruitful in further considering the therapeutic value of affective space and theology, especially in helping the Church to understand how best to tell its discourses within our fluid, liquid society. Finally, greater discussion should be given to the interface between theology and studies such as religion-as-attachment research.

The lyrics of New Order's 'Restless' do not just reflect the existential angst of many within society; they express angst which many within the Church, who long to help people connect with its discourses, hold too, but who do not understand why it is so sociologically challenging to do so. CSSR, though, can provide a theology and sociology with which to help individuals to find shalom, the peace they crave.

139. DeNora, *Music Asylums*.
140. Partridge, *The Lyre of Orpheus*.

Bibliography

Abercrombie, N., and B. Longhurst. *Audiences: A Sociological Theory of Performance and Imagination.* London: Sage, 1998.

Abraham, I. "Postsecular Punk: Evangelical Christianity and the Overlapping Consensus of the Underground." *Punk & Post Punk* 4 (2015) 91–105.

Adorno, T. *The Culture Industry.* Abingdon, England: Routledge, 1991.

Alderidge, D. "Music, Consciousness and Altered States." In *Music and Altered States: Consciousness, Transcendence, Therapy and Addictions,* edited by D. Alderidge and J. Fachner, 9–14. London: Kingsley, 2006.

Allen, L. "Lily Allen | The Fear." *YouTube,* December 3, 2008. https://www.youtube.com/watch?v=q-wGMlSuX_c.

Althusser, L. *Lenin and Philosophy and Other Essays.* New York: Monthly Review, 2001.

Angelo, M. "Waywardtales." http://waywardtales.wordpress.com.

Archer, M. *Making Our Way through the World: Human Reflexivity and Social Mobility.* Cambridge: Cambridge University Press, 2007.

———. *The Reflexive Imperative in Late Modernity.* Cambridge: Cambridge University Press, 2012.

Arnold, M. *Culture and Anarchy.* Oxford: Oxford University Press, 2006.

Augustine. *Confessions.* Translated by H. Chadwick. Oxford: Oxford University Press, 1992.

Avicii. "Avicii – Wake Me Up (Official Video)." *YouTube,* July 29, 2013. https://www.youtube.com/watch?v=IcrbM1l_BoI.

"Avicii Premieres 'Wake Me Up' Music Video." https://www.aceshowbiz.com/news/view/00062720.html.

"Avicii – Wake Me Up! lyrics." https://www.lyricsmode.com/lyrics/a/avicii/wake_me_up.html.

Bailey, J. "Existentialist Transvaluation and Hip Hop's Syncretic Religiosity." In *Christian Metal: History, Ideology, Scene,* edited by M. Moberg, 38–53. London: Bloomsbury, 2015.

Baker, J. *Curating Worship,* London: SPCK, 2010.

Balthasar, H. *Explorations in Theology, Volume III: Creator Spirit.* Translated by B. McNeil. San Francisco: Ignatius, 1993.

———. *The Glory of the Lord: A Theological Aesthetics, Volume 1: Seeing the Form.* Edinburgh: T&T Clark, 1982.

Barrett, L. "Variety Is the Spice of Life: A Psychological Constructionist Approach to Understanding Variability in Emotion." *Cognition and Emotion* 23 (2009) 1284–306.
Bass, D. *Christianity after Religion.* New York: HarperOne, 2012.
Baudrillard, J. *The Consumer Society: Myths & Structures.* London: Sage, 1998.
Bauman, Z. *Community: Seeking Safety in an Insecure World.* Cambridge: Polity, 2001.
———. *Culture in a Liquid Modern World.* Cambridge: Polity, 2011.
———. "Education in Liquid Modernity." *Review of Education, Pedagogy, and Cultural Studies* 27 (2005) 303–17.
———. *Identity.* Cambridge: Polity, 2004.
———. *The Individualized Society.* Cambridge: Polity, 2001.
———. *Liquid Modernity.* Cambridge: Polity, 2012.
———. *Postmodern Ethics.* Oxford: Blackwell, 1993.
Bauman, Z., and S. Obirek. *Of God and Man.* Cambridge: Polity, 2014.
Bauman, Z., and R. Raud. *Practices of Selfhood.* Cambridge: Polity, 2015.
Baylin, J., and D. Hughes. *The Neurobiology of Attachment-Focused Therapy: Enhancing Connection & Trust in the Treatment of Children & Adolescents.* New York: Norton, 2016.
Beaudoin, T. *Virtual Faith.* San Francisco: Jossey-Bass, 1998.
Beck, U. "The Reinvention of Politics: Towards a Theory of Reflexive Modernization." In *Reflexive Modernization: Politics, Tradition and Aesthetics in the Modern Social Order,* edited by U. Beck et al., 1–55. Cambridge: Polity, 1994.
———. *Risk Society.* London: Sage, 1994.
Beck, U., and D. Levy. "Cosmopolitanized Nations: Re-imagining Collectivity, World Risk Society." *Theory, Culture & Society* 30 (2013) 3–31.
Becker, J. *Deep Listeners: Music, Emotion and Trancing.* Bloomington: Indiana University Press, 2004.
Beckford, R. *Jesus Dub.* Abingdon, England: Routledge, 2006.
Beilharz, P. *Socialism and Modernity: Modernity and Communism: Zygmunt Bauman and the Other Totalitarianism.* Minnesota: University of Minnesota Press, 2009.
Begbie, J. *Resounding Truth: Christian Wisdom in the World of Music.* London: SPCK, 2008.
———. *Voicing Creation's Praise: Towards a Theology of the Arts.* Edinburgh: T&T Clark, 1991.
Bellah, R., and H. Joas. "Introduction." In *The Axial Age and Its Consequences,* edited by R. Bellah and H. Joas, 1–6. Cambridge: Harvard University Press, 2012.
Bennett, A. *Cultures of Popular Music.* Maidenhead: Open University Press, 2001.
Bennett, A., and P. Hodkinson. *Aging and Youth Cultures: Music, Style and Identity.* London: Berg, 2012.
Bennett, A., and K. Kahn-Harris. *After Subculture: Critical Studies in Contemporary Youth Culture.* Hampshire: Palgrave MacMillan, 2004.
Berger, P., and T. Luckman. *The Social Construction of Reality: A Treatise in the Sociology of Knowledge.* London: Penguin, 1966.
Bey, H. *The Temporary Autonomous Zone, Ontological Anarchy, Poetic Terrorism: Anarchy and Conspiracy.* London: Forgotten, 1999.
Beyoncé. "Beyoncé – Video Phone (Extended Remix featuring Lady Gaga)." *YouTube,* November 18, 2009. https://www.youtube.com/watch?v=CGkvXpovdng.

Björnberg, A. "Structural Relationships of Music and Images in Music Video." In *Reading Pop: Approaches to Textual Analysis in Popular Music*, edited by R. Middleton, 347–78. Oxford: Oxford University Press, 2003.

Black Eyed Peas. "The Black Eyed Peas – #WHERESTHELOVE ft. The World (Video)." *YouTube*, September 1, 2016. https://www.youtube.com/watch?v=YsRMoWYGLNA.

———. "The Black Eyed Peas – Where Is The Love? (Official Music Video)." *YouTube*, June 16, 2009. https://www.youtube.com/watch?v=WpYeekQkAdc.

"Black Eyed Peas Remake 'Where Is the Love?' for 2016." *CNN*, 2016 http://edition.cnn.com/videos/world/2016/09/05/will-i-am-remake-where-is-the-love-2016-gorani-intvw.cnn.

Blankenship, C., and S. Renard. "Pop Songs on Political Platforms." *Journal of Popular Music Studies* 29 (2017) 1–36.

Blood, A., and R. Zatorre. "Intensely Pleasurable Responses to Music Correlate with Activity in Brain Regions Implicated in Reward and Emotion." *PNAS* 98 (2001) 11818–23.

Bohlman, P. "Introduction: World Music's Histories." In *Cambridge History of World Music*, edited by P. Bohlman, 606–33. Cambridge: Cambridge University Press, 2013.

———. "Music Inside Out: Sounding Public Religion in a Post-Secular Europe." In *Music, Sound and Space: Transformations of Public and Private Experience*, edited by G. Born, 205–23. Cambridge: Cambridge University Press, 2013.

Boniwell, I. "What Is Eudaimonia? The Concept of Eudaimonic Well-Being and Happiness." http://positivepsychology.org.uk/the-concept-of-eudaimonic-well-being/.

Bossius, T., et al. "Introduction." In *Religion and Popular Music in Europe: New Expressions of Sacred and Secular Identity*, edited by T. Bossius et al., 1–10. London: Taurus, 2011.

Bourdieu, P. *Distinction*. Abingdon, England: Routledge, 2010.

———. *The Logic of Practice*. Cambridge: Blackwell, 1990.

Bowlby, J. *A Secure Base: Clinical Applications of Attachment Theory*. London: Routledge, 1988.

Brant, J. "Music and How We Became Human—A View from Cognitive Semiotics: Exploring Imaginative Hypotheses." In *Communicative Musicality Exploring the Basis of Human Companionship*, edited by S. Malloch and C. Trevarthen, 31–44. Oxford: Oxford University Press, 2010.

Braider, C. "The Paradoxical Sisterhood: 'Ut Pictura Poesis.'" In *The Cambridge History of Literary Criticism*, edited by C. Knellwolf and C. Norris, 168–75. Cambridge: Cambridge University Press, 2008.

"British Social Attitudes: Record Number of Brits with No Religion." http://www.natcen.ac.uk/news-media/press-releases/2017/september/british-social-attitudes-record-number-of-brits-with-no-religion/.

Brown, C. *The Death of Christian Britain: Understanding Secularisation 1800–2000*. London: Routledge, 2009.

Brown, D. *God and Enchantment of Place: Reclaiming Human Experience*. Oxford: Oxford University Press, 2004.

———. *Tradition and Imagination: Revelation and Change*. Oxford: Oxford University Press, 1999.

Brown, F. *Good Taste, Bad Taste and Christian Taste: Aesthetics in Religious Life*. Oxford: Oxford University Press, 2000.

———. *Religious Aesthetics: A Theological Study of Making and Meaning*. Princeton: Princeton University Press, 1994.

Brown, S. "Introduction." In *Music and Manipulation: On the Social Uses and Social Control of Music*, edited by S. Brown and U. Volgsten, 1–27. Oxford: Berghahn, 2006.

Brown, S., and T. Theorell. "The Social Uses of Background Music for Personal Enhancement." In *Music and Manipulation: On the Social Uses and Social Control of Music*, edited by Brown, S. and U. Volgsten, 126–60. Oxford: Berghahn, 2006.

Bruce, S. *God Is Dead*. Oxford: Blackwell, 2002.

Butler, D. *Christianity after Religion*. New York: HarperOne, 2012.

Callaway, K. *Scoring Transcendence: Contemporary Film Music as Religious Experience*. Waco: Baylor University Press, 2013.

Carlin, S. "New Music to Know: Ella Henderson Is Coming for America." http://radio.com/2014/08/07/new-music-to-know-ella-henderson/.

Carson, D. *The Gospel according to John*. Leicester: Apollos, 1991.

Castells, M. *Communication Power*. Oxford: Oxford University Press, 2010.

Certeau, M. *The Practice of Everyday Life*. Berkeley: University of California Press, 1988.

Chion, M. *Audio-Vision: Sound on Screen*. New York: Columbia University Press, 1994.

Church, F. "Aspects of a Religious Analysis of Culture." In *The Essential Tillich: An Anthology of the Writings of Paul Tillich*, 101–11. Chicago: University of Chicago Press, 1987.

Church of England. *Common Worship: Services and Prayers for the Church of England*. London: Church House, 2000.

———. *Statistics for Mission 2019*. London: Research for Statistics, 2020. https://www.churchofengland.org/sites/default/files/2020-10/2019StatisticsForMission.pdf.

Clarke, E. "Music, Space and Subjectivity." In *Music, Sound and Space. Transformations of Public and Private Experience*, edited by G. Born, 90–111. Cambridge: Cambridge University Press, 2013.

Clarke, J., et al. "Subcultures, Cultures and Class." In *The Subcultures Reader*, edited by K. Gelder and S. Thornton, 100–11. London: Routledge, 2013.

Cobb, K. *The Blackwell Guide to Theology and Popular Culture*. Oxford: Blackwell, 2005.

Cohen, S. *Folk Devils and Moral Panics*. Oxford: Routledge, 2002.

Colman, A. "James-Lange Theory." In *A Dictionary of Psychology*. Oxford: Oxford University Press, 2009.

Colwell, J. *Living the Christian Story: The Distinctiveness of Christian Ethics*. Edinburgh: T&T Clark, 2001.

Constable, C. *Postmodernism and Film: Rethinking Hollywood's Aesthetics*. New York: Wallflower, 2015.

Cooper, L. "Change the Tune: How the Pandemic Affected the Music Industry." *The Guardian*, December 18, 2020. https://www.theguardian.com/music/2020/dec/18/how-the-pandemic-affected-the-music-industry.

Corrigan, J. "Introduction: The Study of Religion and Emotion." In *The Oxford Handbook of Religion and Emotion*, edited by J. Corrigan, 3–13. Oxford: Oxford University Press, 2008.

———. "Religion and Emotions." In *Doing Emotions History*, edited by P. Steams and S. Matt, 143–62. Urbana: University of Illinois Press, 2014.

Csikszentmihalyi, M. *Flow*. London: Rider, 2002.
Cotesta, V. "The Axial Age and Modernity: From Max Weber to Karl Jaspers and Shmuel Eisenstadt." *Protosociology* 34 (2017) 217–40.
Crook, S., et al. *Postmodernization: Change in Advanced Society*. London: Sage, 1992.
Curren, G. *21st Century Dissent: Anarchism, Anti-Globalization and Environmentalism*. Basingstoke: Palgrave Macmillan, 2017.
Damasio, A. *The Feeling of What Happens: Body and Emotion in the Making of Consciousness*. London: Vintage, 2000.
Darwin, C. *The Expression of the Emotions in Man and Animals*. London: Murray, 1872.
Davie, G. *Europe: The Exceptional Case*. London: Darton, Longman & Todd, 2002.
Davie, G., et al. "Secularism and Secularization." In *Religions in the Modern World: Traditions and Transformation*, edited by L. Woodhead et al., 600–79. 3rd ed. London: Routledge, 2016.
Davies, S. "Emotions Expressed and Aroused by Music: Philosophical Perspectives." In *Handbook of Music and Emotion*, edited by P. Juslin and J. Sloboda, 15–43. Oxford: Oxford University Press, 2010.
Davis, M. "Bauman's Compass: Navigating the Current Interregnum." *Acta Sociologica* 54.2 (2011) 183–94.
———. *Freedom and Consumerism: A Critique of Zygmunt Bauman's Sociology*. Farnham: Ashgate, 2008.
Davison, A., and A. Milbank. *For the Parish: A Critique of Fresh Expressions*. London: SCM, 2010.
Dawson, A. *Sociology of Religion*. London: SCM, 2011.
Day, R. *Gramsci Is Dead: Anarchist Currents in the Newest Social Movements*. London: Pluto, 2005.
DeNora, T. *Music Asylums: Wellbeing through Music in Everyday Life*. Burlington, VT: Ashgate, 2015.
———. *Music in Everyday Life*. Cambridge: Cambridge University Press, 2000.
———. "Music Space as Healing Space: Community Music Therapy and the Negotiation of Identity in a Mental Health Centre." In *Music, Sound and Space: Transformations of Public and Private Experience*, edited by G. Born, 259–74. Cambridge: Cambridge University Press, 2013.
Dido. "Dido – You Don't Need a God (Official Audio)." *YouTube*, March 7, 2019. https://www.youtube.com/watch?v=G8HzwSxo80U.
Dissanayake, E. "Root, Leaf, Blossom, or Bole: Concerning the Origin and Adaptive Function of Music." In *Communicative Musicality: Exploring the Basis of Human Companionship*, edited by S. Malloch and C. Trevarthen, 17–30. Oxford: Oxford University Press, 2010.
Dobbelaere, K. *Secularization: An Analysis at Three Levels*. Belgium: Peter Lang International, 2012.
"Does Anyone the Meaning/Story of Ella Henderson's Ghost Video?" Ihttps://uk.answers.yahoo.com/question/index;_ylt=A9mSs2VFKC5YL1QAMOFLBQx.;_ylu=X3oDMTByZm5kMHEyBGNvbG8DaXIyBHBvcwM3BHZoaWQDBHNlYw Nzcg—?qid=20140624020538AANZk3w&p=henderson%20ghost%20lyrics%20 meaning.
Donald, M. "An Evolutionary Approach to Culture: Implications for the Study of the Axial Age." In *The Axial Age and Its Consequences*, edited by R. Bellah and H. Joas, 47–76. Cambridge: Harvard University Press, 2012.

Donovan, V. *Christianity Rediscovered*. London: SCM, 2009.
"Don't Matter Now by George Ezra." https://www.songfacts.com/facts/george-ezra/dont-matter-now.
"Don't Stand So Close to Me: How Social Distancing Has Shifted Spotify Streaming." https://newsroom.spotify.com/2020-03-30/how-social-distancing-has-shifted-spotify-streaming/.
Dowling, W., and D. Harwood. *Music Cognition*. New York: Academic, 1986.
Drake. "Drake – God's Plan." *YouTube*, February 16, 2018. https://www.youtube.com/watch?v=xpVfcZ0ZcFM.
Dyrness, W. *Poetic Theology: God and the Poetics of Everyday Life*. Grand Rapids: Eerdmans, 2011.
Eagleton, T. *Culture and the Death of God*. New Haven: Yale University Press, 2014.
"Ella Henderson: Ghost Meaning." https://www.lyricinterpretations.com/ella-henderson/ghost/2.
Elster, J. *Strong Feelings: Emotion, Addiction and Human Behavior*. Cambridge: MIT Press, 1999.
Eno, B. "Music for Airports Liner Notes." http://music.hyperreal.org/artists/brian_eno/MFA-txt.html.
Ezra, G. "George Ezra – Don't Matter Now." *YouTube*, June 16, 2017. https://www.youtube.com/watch?v=lM5mM-QDg24.
Fackre, G. *The Christian Story: A Narrative Interpretation of Basic Christian Doctrine*. 3rd ed. Grand Rapids: Eerdmans, 1996.
Fairclough, N. *Analyzing Discourse: Textual Analysis for Social Research*. London: Routledge, 2003.
Festinger, L. *A Theory of Cognitive Dissonance*. Stanford: Stanford University Press, 1957.
Fiddes, P. *Seeing the World and Knowing God: Hebrew Wisdom and Christian Doctrine in a Late-Modern Context*. Oxford: Oxford University Press, 2013.
Fishbein, M., and I. Ajzen. *Belief, Attitude, Intention and Behavior: An Introduction to Theory and Research*. Reading, MA: Addison-Wesley, 1975.
Fitzpatrick, C., and J. Sharry. *Coping with Depression in Young People: A Guide for Parents*. Oxford: Wiley, 2004.
florencemachine. "Big God." *YouTube*, June 19, 2018. www.youtube.com/watch?v=rqerPXPwhHM.
———. "Florence + Machine – Big God." *YouTube*, June 21, 2018. https://www.youtube.com/watch?v=_kIrRooQwuk.
Fox, C. "Post-Truth Politics? Don't Be So Patronizing: Why Should People Who Vote with Their Hearts be Dismissed as Delusional?" *The Spectator*, November 12, 2016. https://www.spectator.co.uk/2016/11/post-truth-politics-dont-be-so-patronising/.
Frampton, D. *Filmosophy: A Manifesto for a Radically New Way of Understanding Cinema*. New York: Columbia University Press, 2006.
Fraser, N. *Rethinking the Public Sphere*. London: CreateSpace, 2016.
Freeth, B. "I Felt More and More Isolated." *Daily Mail*, November 14, 2016. http://www.dailymail.co.uk/tvshowbiz/article-3934382/Robbie-Williams-describes-roller-coaster-ride-drugs-drink-depression-killed-him.html?ito=social-twitter_dailymailceleb.
Frei, H. *The Eclipse of Biblical Narrative*. New Haven: Yale University Press, 1974.

Frith, S. "Music and Identity." In *Questions of Cultural Identity*, edited by S. Hall, and P. du Gay, 108–27. London: Sage, 1996.

Fritz, J. *Rave Culture: An Insider's Overview*. Victoria, Canada: SmallFry, 1999.

Gabrielsson, A. *Strong Experiences with Music: Music Is Much More than Just Music*. Oxford: Oxford University Press, 2011.

Gaines, D. *Teenage Wasteland: Suburbia's Dead End Kids*. Chicago: Chicago University Press, 1998.

Galston, W. *Liberal Pluralism: The Implications of Value Pluralism for Political Theory and Practice*. Cambridge: Cambridge University Press, 2002.

Gauthier, F. "Rapturous Ruptures: The 'Instituant' Religious Experience of Rave." In *Rave Culture and Religion*, edited by G. John, 65–84. London: Routledge, 2009.

Geddert, T. "Peace." In *Dictionary of Jesus and the Gospels*, edited by J. Green et al., 604–5. Downers Grove, IL: IVP Academic, 1992.

Gerard, M. "Selecting Ritual: DJs, Dancers and Liminality in Underground Dance Music." In *Rave Culture and Religion*, edited by G. John, 167–84. London: Routledge, 2004.

Gibson, C., and J. Connell. *Sound Tracks: Popular Music Identity and Place*. London: Routledge, 2003.

Giddens, A. *The Consequences of Modernity*. Cambridge: Polity, 1990.

———. *Modernity and Self-Identity: Self and Society in the Late Modern Age*. Cambridge: Polity, 1991.

———. *The Transformation of Intimacy: Sexuality, Love, and Eroticism in Modern Societies*. Cambridge: Polity, 1992.

Girlguiding. "Girls' Attitudes Survey: 2016." https://www.girlguiding.org.uk/globalassets/docs-and-resources/research-and-campaigns/girls-attitudes-survey-2016.pdf.

Goffman, E. *The Presentation of Self in Everyday Life*. London: Penguin, 1959.

Goodwin, A. *Dancing in the Distraction Factory: Music, Television and Popular Culture*. Minneapolis: University of Minnesota Press, 1992.

Gorbman, C. *Unheard Melodies: Narrative Film Music*. Bloomington: Indiana University Press, 1987.

Gracyk, T. "The Aesthetics of Popular Music." http://www.iep.utm.edU/music-po/#H6.

Granqvist, P., and L. Kirkpatrick. "Attachment and Religious Representations and Behavior." In *Handbook of Attachment: Theory, Research, and Clinical Applications*, edited by J. Cassidy and P. Shaver, 917–40. 3rd ed. New York: Guilford, 2016.

Grant, J. "Live Aid: Perpetuating the Superiority Myth." *Critical Arts* 29.3 (2015) 310–26.

Gratier, M., and G. Apter-Danon. "The Improvised Musicality of Belonging: Repetition and Variation in Mother-Infant Vocal Interaction." In *Communicative Musicality: Exploring the Basis of Human Companionship*, edited by S. Malloch and C. Trevarthen, 301–27. Oxford: Oxford University Press, 2010.

Greene, C. *Christology in Cultural Perspective*. Grand Rapids: Eerdmans, 2003.

Grenz, S. *Theology for the Community of God*. Carlisle, England: Paternoster, 1994.

Gundersen, E. "Pandemic Songs: The New Music Genre: Songwriters Draw Inspiration from This Challenging Time." https://www.aarp.org/entertainment/music/info-2020/coronavirus-pandemic-song-playlist.html.

Gupta, N. "Singing Away the Social Distancing Blues: Art Therapy in a Time of Coronavirus." *Journal of Humanistic Psychology* 60.5 (2020) 593–603.

Habermas, J. *Between Facts and Norms*. Cambridge: Polity, 2015.
———. *Postmetaphysical Thinking II*. Cambridge: Polity, 2012.
———. "Secularism's Crisis of Faith: Notes on Postsecular Society." *New Perspectives Quarterly* 25 (2008) 17–29.
———. *The Theory of Communicative Action, Volume One: Reason and the Rationalization of Society*. Cambridge: Polity, 1991.
Hailes, S. "A Time to Plant: How the Anglican Church Is Rising Again in Urban Areas." https://www.premierchristianity.com/Past-Issues/2016/July-2016/A-Time-to-Plant-How-the-Anglican-Church-is-rising-again-in-urban-areas.
Hall, J. *Hall's Dictionary of Subjects and Symbols in Art*. London: Murray, 1974.
Hanquinet, L., et al. "The Eyes of the Beholder: Aesthetic Preferences and the Remaking of Cultural Capital." *Sociology* 48 (2014) 111–32.
Hargreaves, D., et al. "How Do People Communicate Using Music?" In *Musical Communication*, edited by D. Miell et al., 1–25. Oxford: Oxford University Press, 2005.
Hargreaves, D., and A. North. "Experimental Aesthetics and Liking for Music." In *Handbook of Music and Emotion*, edited by P. Juslin and J. Sloboda, 515–46. Oxford: Oxford University Press, 2010.
Hawkins, G., and P. Parkinson. *Reveal: Where You Are?* Barrington, IL: Willow Creek Resources, 2007.
Healey, K., and L. Fraser. "A Common Darkness: Style and Spirituality in Goth Subculture." *Journal of Popular Music Studies* 29.3 (2017) 1–14.
Hebdige, D. *Into the Light*. London: Routledge, 1988.
Heelas, P., and L. Woodhead. *The Spiritual Revolution: Why Religion Is Giving Way to Spirituality*. Oxford: Blackwell, 2005.
Hendershot, H. *Shaking the World for Jesus: Media and Conservative Evangelical Culture*. Chicago: University of Chicago Press, 2004.
Henderson, E. "Ella Henderson – Ghost (Official Video)." *YouTube*, April 22, 2014. https://www.youtube.com/watch?v=tA8AfQaUnXM.
Hervieu-Leger, D. *Religion as a Chain of Memory*. Cambridge: Blackwell, 2000.
Hesmondhalgh, D. *Why Music Matters*. Oxford: Blackwell, 2013.
Hick, J. "Religious Pluralism and Islam." Lecture delivered to the Institute for Islamic Culture and Thought, Tehran, Iran, February 2005. www.johnhick.org.uk/article11.pdf.
Hjelm, T. *Social Constructionisms: Approaches to the Study of the Human World*. Basingstoke, England: Palgrave Macmillan, 2014.
Hillsong Church. "Hillsong United – Oceans (Live)." *Vimeo*, July 25, 2013. https://vimeo.com/71070693.
Hodges, D. "Human Musicality." In *Handbook of Music Psychology*, edited by D. Hodges, 30–68. 2nd ed. San Antonio: IMR, 1996.
Hodkinson, P. *Goth: Identity, Style and Subculture*. Oxford: Berg, 2002.
Hogan, M. "Decoding the Politics in Radiohead's 'Burn the Witch' Video." http://pitchfork.com/thepitch/1133-decoding-the-politics-in-radioheads-burn-the-witch-video/.
Hoover, S. *Religion in the Media Age*. London: Routledge, 2006.
Hopps, G. "Byron and the Post-Secular: Quia Impossibile." *The Byron Journal* 43.2 (2015) 91–108.

———. "Theology, Imagination and Popular Music." In *The Bloomsbury Handbook of Religion and Popular Music*, edited by C. Partridge and M. Moberg, 77–89. London: Bloomsbury Academic, 2017.

Houston, J. *Sources of the Christian Self: A Cultural History of Christian Identity*. Grand Rapids: Eerdmans, 2018.

Houtman, D., and S. Aupers. "The Spiritual Turn and the Decline of Tradition: The Spread of Post-Christian Spirituality in 14 Western Countries, 1981–2000." *Journal for the Scientific Study of Religion* 46.3 (2007) 305–20.

Howard, J., and J. Streck. "The Splintered Art World of Contemporary Christian Music." *Popular Music* 15.1 (1996) 37–53.

Hughes, D. *Attachment-Focused Family Therapy Workbook*. London: Norton & Co., 2011.

Hughes, D., et al. "Dyadic Developmental Psychotherapy (DDP): The Development of the Theory, Practice and Research Base." In *Adoption and Fostering* 39.4 (2015) 356–65.

Huq, R. *Beyond Subculture*. London: Routledge, 2006.

Hutchinson, A. "Ella Henderson Explains the True Meaning of Her Smash-Hit Single 'Ghost.'" https://web.archive.org/web/20180222014355/http://www.metrolyrics.com/news-story-ella-henderson-ghost-lyrics-song-explanation.html.

iamOTHER. "Pharrell Williams – Happy (Official Music Video). *YouTube*, November 21, 2013. https://www.youtube.com/watch?v=y6Sxv-sUYtM.

Ingalls, M. "Singing Heaven down to Earth: Spiritual Journeys, Eschatological Sounds, and Community Formation in Evangelical Conference Worship." In *Ethnomusicology* 55.2 (2011) 255–79.

Ingham, T. "The Global Recorded Music Industry Grew By $1.5bn in 2020, despite the Pandemic (Report)." https://www.musicbusinessworldwide.com/the-global-recorded-music-industry-grew-by-1-5bn-in-2020/.

Istudent, O. "Grime Music Is Now the Sound of British Youth – and Things Are Only Beginning." *Independent*, November 24, 2015. https://www.independent.co.uk/student/student-life/music-film/grime-music-is-now-the-sound-of-british-youth-and-things-are-only-beginning-a6747216.html.

James, W. *The Principles of Psychology*. New York: Dover, 1890.

Jaspers, K. *The Origin and Goal of History*. Translated by M. Bullock. Abingdon, England: Routledge, 2010.

Jenkins, H. *Textual Poachers: Television Fans and Participatory Culture*. London: Routledge, 1992.

John, G. "The Difference Engine: Liberation and Rave Imagery." In *Rave Culture and Religion*, edited by G. John, 19–45. Oxford: Routledge, 2004.

———. "Electronic Dance Music Culture and Religion: An Overview." *Culture and Religion* 7.1 (2006) 1–25.

———. "Electronic Dance Music: Trance and Techno-Shamanism." In *The Bloomsbury Handbook of Religion and Popular Culture*, edited by C. Partridge and M. Moberg, 278–85. London: Bloomsbury Academic, 2017.

———. *Global Tribe: Technology, Spirituality and Psytrance*. Sheffield: Equinox, 2012.

———. *Tecnomad: Global Raving Countercultures*. London: Equinox, 2009.

Johnston, R. *Reel Spirituality*. Grand Rapids: Baker Academic, 2009.

JonasBlueVEVO. "Jonas Blue – Fast Car ft. Dakota." *YouTube*, January 15, 2016. https://www.youtube.com/watch?v=5yXQJBU8A28.

Jones, D. *The Eighties: One Day, One Decade.* London: Windmill, 2014.
Jordan, P. *The Modern Fairy Tale: Nation Branding, National Identity and the Eurovision Song Contest in Estonia.* Tartu: University of Tartu Press, 2014.
Juslin, P. "From Mimesis to Catharsis: Expression, Perception, and Induction of Emotion in Music." In *Musical Communication*, edited by D. Miell et al., 85–115. Oxford: Oxford University Press, 2005.
Juslin P., and J. Sloboda. *Handbook of Music and Emotion: Theory, Research, Applications.* Oxford: Oxford University Press, 2010.
Juslin, P., and D. Vastfjall. "Emotional Responses to Music. The Need to Consider Underlying Mechanisms." *Behavioral and Brain Sciences* 31.5 (2008) 559–621.
Kahn-Harris, K., and M. Moberg. "Religious Popular Music: Between the Instrumental, Transcendent and Transgressive." *Temenos* (2012) 87–106.
Kaplan, A. *Rocking around the Clock: Music Television, Postmodernism, and Consumer Culture.* London: Routledge, 1987.
Kaufman, G. "Radiohead 'Burn the Witch' Animator on the Sleepless Nights behind New Video." http://www.billboard.com/articles/news/7356875/radiohead-animator-burn-the-witch-video.
Keuss, J. *Blur: A New Paradigm for Understanding Youth Culture.* Grand Rapids: Zondervan, 2014.
———. *Your Neighbor's Hymnal.* Eugene, OR: Cascade, 2011.
Kiirla, J. "Emotional Energy, Humility and Systems Intelligence in Leadership" in *Systems Intelligence in Leadership and Everyday Life,* edited by R. Hämäläinen and E. Saarinen, 117–29. Helsinki: Helsinki University of Technology, 2007.
Knowles, S. "Signs of Salvation: Insecurity, Risk and the End of the World in Late Modernity." In *Alternative Salvations,* edited by H. Bacon et al., 172–182. London: Bloomsbury, 2015.
Koen B. "Music-Prayer-Meditation Dynamics in Healing." In *The Oxford Handbook of Medical Ethnomusicology,* edited by B. Koen, 93–120. New York: Oxford University Press, 2008.
Konečni, V. "Does Music Induce Emotion? A Theoretical and Methodological Analysis." *Psychology of Aesthetics, Creativity, and the Arts* 2.2 (2008) 115–29.
Koyzis, D. "Imagining God and His Kingdom: Eastern Orthodoxy's Iconic Political Ethic." *The Review of Politics* 55.2 (1993) 267–89.
Kur, M. "Quality in Reflective Thinking: Elicitation and Classification of Reflective Acts." *Quality & Quantity* 52 (2018) 247–59.
"Lady GaGa – Born This Way." https://songmeanings.com/songs/view/3530822107858844306/.
"Lady Gaga – Shallow." https://songmeanings.com/songs/view/3530822107859576904/.
Laing, R. *The Divided Self.* London: Penguin, 1968.
Lakoff, G., and M. Johnson. *Metaphors We Live By.* Chicago: University of Chicago Press, 1980.
Landau, J. "The Flesh of Raving: Merleau-Ponty and the 'Experience' of Ecstasy." In *Rave Culture and Religion,* edited by G. John, 107–24. London: Routledge, 2009.
Langford, B. *Film Industry, Style and Ideology since 1945.* Edinburgh: Edinburgh University Press, 2010.
Lanigan, R. "Director Autumn de Wilde Reveals the Witchcraft in Florence's New Video." https://i-d.vice.com/en_uk/article/xwm3bj/director-autumn-de-wilde-reveals-the-witchcraft-in-florences-new-video.

Lash, S., and J. Friedman. "Introduction: Subjectivity and Modernity's Other." In *Modernity & Identity*, edited by S. Lash and J. Friedman, 1–30. Oxford: Blackwell, 1992.
Lasch, C. *The Culture of Narcissism*. London: Sphere, 1980.
Laski, M. *Ecstasy: A Study of Some Secular and Religious Experiences*. London: Cresset, 1961.
Lawler, S. *Identity: Sociological Perspectives*. 2nd ed. Cambridge: Polity, 2014.
Layard, R. *Happiness: Lessons from a New Science*. London: Penguin, 2011.
Lee, R. "Modernity, Solidity and Agency: Liquidity Reconsidered." *Sociology* 45.4 (2011) 650–64.
Lehman, E. "Washing Hands, Reaching Out: Popular Music, Digital Leisure and Touch during the COVID-19 Pandemic." *Leisure Sciences* 43.1–2 (2020) 273–79.
Levitin, D. *The World in Six Songs: How the Musical Brain Created Human Nature*. London: Aurum, 2010.
Lipscomb, S. "The Cognitive Organization of Musical Sound." In *Handbook of Music Psychology*, edited by D. Hodges, 133–75. San Antonio: IMR, 1996.
Longhurst, B., and D. Bogdanovic. *Popular Music and Society*. Cambridge: Polity, 2014.
Loughlin, G. "A Theological Introduction." In *Cinéma Divinité: Religion, Theology and the Bible in Film*, edited by E. Christianson et al., 1–12. London: SCM, 2005.
Lyden, J. *Film as Religion*. New York: New York University Press, 2003.
Lynch, G. *After Religion: 'Generation X' and the Search for Meaning*. London: Darton, Longman & Todd, 2002.
———. "The Role of Popular Music in the Construction of Alternative Spiritual Identities and Ideologies." *Journal for the Scientific Study of Religion* 45.4 (2006) 481–88.
———. *The Sacred in the Modern World: A Cultural Sociological Approach*. Oxford: Oxford University Press, 2013.
———. *Understanding Theology and Popular Culture*. Oxford: Blackwell, 2005.
Lynch, G., and E. Badger. "The Mainstream Post-Rave Club Scene as a Secondary Institution: A British Perspective." *Culture and Religion* 7.1 (2006) 27–40.
Lyotard, J. *The Postmodern Condition: A Report on Knowledge*. Manchester: Manchester University Press, 1979.
MacDonald, R., et al. "Talking about Music: A Vehicle for Identity Development." In *Musical Communication*, edited by D. Miell et al., 85–115. Oxford: Oxford University Press, 2005.
Machin, D. *Analyzing Popular Music: Image, Sound, Text*. London: Sage, 2010.
Macintyre, A. *After Virtue: A Study in Moral Theory*. Guildford, England: Duckworth, 1985.
Maffesoli, M. "The Return to Dionysus." In *Constructing the New Consumer Society*, edited by P. Sulkunen et al., 21–37. London: Palgrave MacMillan, 1997.
Malloch, S., and C. Trevarthen. "Musicality: Communicating the Vitality and Interests of Life." In *Communicative Musicality: Exploring the Basis of Human Companionship*, edited by S. Malloch and C. Trevarthen, 1–11. Oxford: Oxford University Press, 2010.
Marcuse, H. *The Aesthetic Dimension*. Boston: Beacon, 1978.
Marsh, C., and V. Roberts. "Listening as Religious Practice (Part One): Exploring Quantitative Data from an Empirical Study of the Cultural Habits of Music Fans." *Journal of Contemporary Religion* 30.1 (2014) 125–37.

———. "Listening as Religious Practice (Part Two): Exploring Qualitative Data from an Empirical Study of the Cultural Habits of Music Fans." *Journal of Contemporary Religion* 30.2 (2015) 291–306.

———. *Personal Jesus: How Popular Music Shapes Our Souls*. London: Baker, 2012.

Marti, G., and G. Ganiel. *The Deconstructed Church: Understanding Emerging Christianity*. Oxford: Oxford University Press, 2014.

Martin, P. "Music, Identity, and Social Control." In *Music and Manipulation: On the Social Uses and Social Control of Music*, edited by S. Brown and U. Volgsten, 56–73. Oxford: Berghahn, 2006.

Martindale, C., and K. Moore. "Priming, Prototypicality and Preference." *Journal of Experimental Psychology* 14.4 (1988) 661–70.

Martinelli, D. *Give Peace a Chant: Popular Music, Politics and Social Protest*. Cham, Switzerland: Springer International, 2017.

Maslow, A. *A Theory of Human Motivation*. Radford, VA: Wilder, 2013.

———. *Toward a Psychology of Being*. Radford, VA: Wilder, 2011.

Mazokopaki, K., and G. Kugiumutzakis. "Infant Rhythms: Expressions of Musical Companionship." In *Communicative Musicality: Exploring the Basis of Human Companionship*, edited by S. Malloch and C. Trevarthen, 185–208. Oxford: Oxford University Press, 2010.

McCloud, S. "Popular Culture Fandoms, the Boundaries of Religious Studies, and the Project of the Self." In *Culture and Religion* 4.2 (2003) 187–206.

McCormack, D. *Refrains for Moving Bodies: Experience and Experiment in Affective Spaces*. Durham: Duke University Press, 2014.

Melanie C. "Melanie C – Dear Life (Music Video)." *YouTube*, November 23, 2016. https://www.youtube.com/watch?v=CoqeTtdhXEE.

Mendieta, E. "Spiritual Politics and Post-Secular Authenticity: Foucault and Habermas on Post-Metaphysical Religion." In *The Post-Secular in Question*, edited by P. Gorski et al., 307–34. New York, New York University Press, 2012.

Meyer. L. *Emotion and Meaning in Music*. Chicago: University of Chicago Press, 1956.

Middleton, R. "Faith, Hope, and the Hope of Love: On the Fidelity of the Phonographic Voice." In *Sound and Space: Transformations of Public and Private Experience*, edited by G. Born, 292–311. Cambridge: Cambridge University Press, 2013.

———. "Popular Music Analysis and Musicology: Bridging the Gap." In *Reading Pop: Approaches to Textual Analysis in Popular Music*, edited by R. Middleton, 104–21. Oxford: Oxford University Press, 2003.

———. *Studying Popular Music*. Milton Keynes, England: Open University Press, 1990.

Miell, D., et al. "Talking about Music: A Vehicle for Identity Development." In *Musical Communication*, edited by D. Miell et al., 321–39. Oxford: Oxford University Press, 2005.

"Millennials & Teens Sound Off: Their Favorite Music Artists." https://www.ypulse.com/post/view/millennials-teens-sound-off-their-favorite-music-artists.

Miller, M., and K. Strongman. "The Emotional Effects of Music on Religious Experience: A Study of the Pentecostal-Charismatic Style of Music and Worship." *Psychology of Music* 30.1 (2002) 8–27.

Miller, M., et al. *Religion in Hip Hop: Mapping the New Terrain in the US*. London: Bloomsbury, 2015.

Moberg, M. "Popular Music Divine Services in the Evangelical Lutheran Church of Finland: Concept, Rationale, and Participants." *Journal of Religion and Popular Culture* 30.1 (2018) 35–48.

Moynagh, M. *Church for Every Context: An Introduction to Theology and Practice.* London: SCM, 2012.

Mulcock, J. "Creativity and Politics in the Cultural Supermarket: Synthesizing Indigenous Identities for the R/Evolution of Spirit." *Journal of Media & Cultural Studies* 15.2 (2001) 169–85.

Nagel, J. *Melodies of the Mind: Connections between Psychoanalysis and Music.* New York: Routledge, 2013.

Negus, K. *Popular Music in Theory: An Introduction.* Cambridge: Polity, 2003.

Neworder. "New Order – Restless." *YouTube*, August 18, 2015. https://www.youtube.com/watch?v=8c_3Afx9ZGE.

Nicolaou, A. "How Streaming Saved the Music Industry." https://www.ft.com/content/cd99b95e-d8ba-11e6-944b-e7eb37a6aa8e.

Niebuhr, R. *Christ and Culture.* New York: HarperOne, 2001.

Nørgård, R., et al. "Playful Learning in Higher Education: Developing a Signature Pedagogy." *International Journal of Play* 6.3 (2017) 272–82.

North, A., and D. Hargreaves. "Music in Business Environments." In *Music and Manipulation: On the Social Uses and Social Control of Music*, edited by S. Brown and U. Volgsten, 103–25. Oxford: Berghahn, 2006.

———. "Musical Communication in Commercial Contexts." In *Musical Communication*, edited by D. Miell et al., 405–22. Oxford: Oxford University Press, 2005.

Olaveson, T. "Connectedness and Rave Experience." In *Rave Culture and Religion*, edited by G. John, 85–106. London: Routledge, 2009.

Osborne, N. "Music for Children in Zones of Conflict and Post-Convict: A Psychological Approach." In *Communicative Musicality: Exploring the Basis of Human Companionship*, edited by S. Malloch and C. Trevarthen, 329–56. Oxford: Oxford University Press, 2010.

Ostwalt, C. *Secular Steeples.* Harrisburg, PA: Trinity, 2003.

Otto, R. *The Idea of the Holy.* Oxford: Oxford University Press, 1950.

Panzarella, R. "The Phenomenology of Aesthetic." *Journal of Humanistic Psychology* 20.1 (1980) 69–85.

Partridge, C. "Emotion, Meaning and Popular Music." In *The Bloomsbury Handbook of Religion and Popular Music*, edited by C. Partridge and M. Moburg, 23–31. London: Bloomsbury Academic, 2017.

———. *The Lyre of Orpheus: Popular Music, the Sacred and the Profane.* Oxford: Oxford University Press, 2014.

———. *Mortality and Music: Popular Music and the Awareness of Death.* London: Bloomsbury, 2015.

———. "Occulture and Everyday Enchantment." In *The Oxford Handbook of New Religious Movements: Volume II*, edited by J. Lewis and I. Tollefsen, 315–34. Oxford: Oxford University Press, 2016.

———. "Psychedelic Music." In *The Bloomsbury Handbook of Religion and Popular Music*, edited by C. Partridge and M. Moburg, 294–305. London: Bloomsbury Academic, 2017.

———. "Religion and Popular Culture." In *Religions in the Modern World*, edited by C. Partridge et al., 556–99. 3rd ed. Abingdon, England: Routledge, 2016.

Patel, R. "UK Democracy Must Do Better than This: Reflections on the General Election 2017." *RSA* (blog), June 9, 2017. https://www.thersa.org/discover/publications-and-articles/rsa-blogs/2017/06/democracy-general-election-17-UK.
Peddie, I. "Music, Religion and Protest." In *The Bloomsbury Handbook of Religion and Popular Music*, edited by C. Partridge and M. Moburg, 32–42. London: Bloomsbury Academic, 2017.
Peretz, I. "Towards a Neurobiology of Musical Emotions." In *Handbook of Music and Emotion*, edited by P. Juslin and J. Sloboda, 99–126. Oxford: Oxford University Press, 2010.
Peterson, R. "Understanding Audience Segmentation: From Elite and Mass to Omnivore and Univore." *Poetics* 21.4 (1992) 243–58.
Peterson, R., and R. Kern. "Changing Highbrow Taste: From Snob to Omnivore." *American Sociological Review* 61.5 (1996) 900–907.
Pollack, D. "Varieties of Secularization Theories and Their Indispensable Core." *The Germanic Review* 90.1 (2015) 60–79.
Posner, M. "I Took a Pill in Ibiza." www.genius.com/Mike-Posner-i-took-a-pill-in-ibiza-lyrics.
Price, J. "Expressionism and Ultimate Reality: Paul Tillich's Theology of Art." *Soundings* 69.4 (1986) 479–98.
Putman, R. *Bowling Alone: The Collapse and Revival of American Community*. New York: Touchstone, 2000.
Qureshi, R. "Sufism and the Globalization of Sacred Music." In *Cambridge History of World Music*, edited by P. Bohlman, 606–33. Cambridge: Cambridge University Press, 2013.
Radiohead. "Burn the Witch." *YouTube*, May 3, 2016. https://www.youtube.com/watch?v=yI2oS2hoLok.
Raffman, D. *Language, Music and Mind*. Cambridge: MIT Press, 1993.
Raibley, J. "Happiness Is Not Well-Being." *Journal of Happiness Studies* 13.6 (2012) 1105–29.
Railton, D., and P. Watson. *Music, Video and the Politics of Representation*. Edinburgh: Edinburgh University Press, 2011.
Redden, G. "Religion, Cultural Studies and New Age Sacralization of Everyday Life." *European Journal of Cultural Studies* 14.5 (2011) 649–63.
Rendel, J. "Staying In, Rocking Out: Online Live Music Portal Shows During the Coronavirus Pandemic." *Convergence* (2020) 1–20.
Regev, M. *Pop-Rock Music*. Cambridge: Polity, 2013.
Ricoeur, P. *Figuring the Sacred: Religion, Narrative and Imagination*. Minneapolis: Fortress, 1995.
———. *From Text to Action*. London: Continuum, 2003.
Rietveld, H. "Ephemeral Spirit: Sacrificial Cyborg and Communal Soul." In *Rave Culture and Religion*, edited by G. John, 46–62. London: Routledge, 2004.
Riis, O., and L. Woodhead. *A Sociology of Religious Emotion*. Oxford: Oxford University Press, 2010.
Rimmer, M. "Beyond Omnivores and Univores: The Promise of a Concept of Musical Habitus." *Cultural Sociology* 6.3 (2012) 299–318.
Robinson, J. *Deeper than Reason: Emotion and Its Role in Literature, Music, and Art*. Oxford: Clarendon, 2005.

Robinson, P. "Pop, Rock, Rap, Whatever: Who Killed the Music Genre?" *The Guardian*, March 17, 2016. https://www.theguardian.com/music/2016/mar/17/pop-rock-rap-whatever-who-killed-the-music-genre.

Robinson, S. "What Play Therapists Do within the Therapeutic Relationship of Humanistic Non-directive Play Therapy." *Pastoral Care in Education* 29.3 (2011) 207–22.

Rogers, C. *Client-Centered Therapy: Its Current Practice, Implications and Theory*. London: Constable and Robinson, 2012.

Rolls, E. *Emotion and Decision-Making Explained*. Oxford: Oxford University Press, 2014.

Romanowski, W. "Evangelicals and Popular Music: The Contemporary Christian Music Industry." In *Religion and Popular Culture in America*, edited by J. Mahan and D. Bruce, 105–24. California: University of California Press, 2000.

Ross, C. "Pioneering Missiologies: Seeing Afresh." In *The Pioneer Gift: Explorations in Mission*, edited by J. Baker and C. Ross, 20–38. Norwich: Canterbury, 2014.

Rumsey, A. *Parish: An Anglican Theology of Place*. London: SCM, 2017.

Ryzic, M. "'I Never Thought I Would Talk About It.' So Florence Welch Put It in a Song." *New York Times*, June 14, 2018. https://mobile.nytimes.com/2018/06/14/arts/music/florence-and-the-machine-high-as-hope.html.

Salimpoor, V., et al. "Anatomically Distinct Dopamine Release during Anticipation and Experience of Peak Emotion to Music." *Nature Neuroscience* 14 (2011) 257–62.

Sandywell, B. *Reflexivity and the Crisis of Western Reason: Logological Investigations Volume 1*. London: Routledge, 1996.

Sarid, A. "Self-Critical Appropriation: An Assessment of Bauman's View of Education." *Liquid Modernity, Educational Philosophy and Theory* 49.5 (2017) 462–72.

Schäfer, T., et al. "How Music Changes Our Lives: A Qualitative Study of the Long-Term Effects of Intense Musical Experiences." *Psychology of Music* 42.4 (2014) 525–44.

Schleirmacher, F. *The Christian Faith in Outline*. Translated by D. Baillie. London: Leopold Classic Library, 2017.

Schultz, W. "Updating Dopamine Reward Signals." *Current Opinion in Neurobiology* 23.2 (2012) 229–38.

Scruton, R. *The Aesthetics of Music*. Oxford: Oxford University Press, 1997.

Schwobel, C. "Paul Tillich." In *The Blackwell Encyclopedia of Modern Christian Thought*, edited by A. McGrath, 638–42. London: Blackwell, 1993.

"Selena Gomez – Who Says." https://www.lyricsmode.com/lyrics/s/selena_gomez/who_says.html.

Sennett, R. *The Fall of Public Man*. New York: Knopf, 1977.

Sheehan, J. *The Enlightenment Bible: Translation, Scholarship, Culture*. Princeton: Princeton University Press, 2007.

Shepherd, A. "Global Exoticism and Modernity." In *Cambridge History of World Music*, edited by P. Bohlman, 606–33. Cambridge: Cambridge University Press.

Shepherd, J. "Q&A: Irish Musician Hozier on Gay Rights, Sexuality, & Good Hair." http://nymag.com/thecut/2014/03/qa-hozier-on-gay-rights-sex-good-hair.html.

Shuker, R. *Understanding Popular Music Culture*. Abingdon, England: Routledge, 2013.

Sia. "Sia – Cheap Thrills (Lyric Video) ft. Sean Paul." *YouTube*, Februrary 10, 2016. https://www.youtube.com/watch?v=nYh-n7EOtMA.

Silver, D., et al. "Genre Complexes in Popular Music." *PLoS One* 11.5 (2016) 1–23.

Sloboda, J. "Music and Worship: A Psychologist's Perspective." In *Creative Chords: Studies in Music, Theology and Christian Formation*, edited by J. Astley et al., 110–25. Leominster, England: Gracewing, 2000.

SMF. "Meaning of 'Shallow' by Lady Gaga and Bradley Cooper." www.songmeaningsandfacts.com/meaning-of-shallow-by-lady-gaga-and-bradley-cooper/.

Smith, D. *Zygmunt Bauman: Prophet of Postmodernity*. Cambridge: Polity, 1999.

Smith, J. *Desiring the Kingdom: Worship, Worldview and Cultural Formation*. Grand Rapids: Baker, 2009.

Sommer, S. "C'mon to My House: Underground-House Dancing." *Dance Research Journal* 33.2 (2001) 72–86.

Spencer, N. *Doing Good: A Future for Christianity in the 21st Century*. Theos, 2016.

Starr, G. *Feeling Beauty: The Neuroscience of Aesthetic Experience*. Cambridge: MIT Press, 2013.

Stone, A. *The Value of Popular Music: An Approach from Post-Kantian Aesthetics*. London: Palgrave Macmillan, 2016.

Storey, J. *Cultural Theory and Popular Culture: An Introduction*. London: Routledge, 2015.

Stormzy. "Stormzy – Blinded by Your Grace Pt. 2 Ft. Mnek.'" *YouTube*, December 14, 2017. https://www.youtube.com/watch?v=HPuj6UISMhs.

Stratton, A. "David Cameron Aims to Make Happiness the New GDP." *The Guardian*, November 14, 2010. https://www.theguardian.com/politics/2010/nov/14/david-cameron-wellbeing-inquiry.

Sumner, B. *Chapter and Verse: New Order, Joy Division and Me*. London: Penguin, 2015.

Sylvan, R. *Traces of the Spirit: The Religious Dimensions of Popular Music*. New York: New York University Press, 2003.

———. *Trance Formation*. New York: Routledge, 2005.

Tagg, P. "Analyzing Popular Music: Theory, Method and Practice." In *Reading Pop: Approaches to Textual Analysis in Popular Music*, edited by R. Middleton, 71–103. Oxford: Oxford University Press, 2003.

———. *Analyzing Popular Music: Theory, Method and Practice*. http://tagg.org/articles/xpdfs/pm2anal.pdf.

Tallon, J. "Christianity." In *The Oxford Handbook of Religion and Emotion*, edited by J. Corrigan, 111–24. Oxford: Oxford University Press, 2008.

Tay, L., and E. Diener. "Needs and Subjective Well-Being Around the World." *Journal of Personality and Social Psychology* 101.2 (2011) 354–65.

Taylor, C. *A Secular Age*. Cambridge: Harvard University Press, 2007.

———. *Sources of the Self*. Cambridge: Harvard University Press, 1989.

Thomsen, S., et al. "Pop Music and the Search for the Numinous: Exploring the Emergence of the 'Secular Hymn,' in Post-Modern Culture." *Journal of Media and Religion* 15.3 (2016) 146–55.

Thornton, S. *Club Cultures: Music, Media and Subcultural Capital*. Cambridge: Polity, 1995.

———. "The Social Logic of Subcultural Capital." In *The Subcultures Reader*, edited by K. Gelder and S. Thornton, 200–209. Oxford: Routledge, 1997.

Tickle, P. *Emergence Christianity: What It Is, Where It Is Going and Why It Matters*. Grand Rapids: Baker, 2012.

Till, R. *Pop Cult: Religion and Popular Music*. London: Continuum, 2010.

Tillich, P. *Biblical Religion and the Search for Ultimate Reality*. Chicago: University of Chicago Press, 1955.
———. *On Art and Architecture*. New York: Crossroad, 1987.
———. *Systematic Theology: Volume 1*. Chicago: University of Chicago, 1973.
———. *Systematic Theology: Volume 3*. London: SCM, 1963.
———. *Theology of Culture*. New York: Galaxy, 1959.
———. "Theology and Symbolism." In *Religious Symbolism*, edited by F. Johnson, 107–116. New York: Harper and Brothers, 1955.
Toffler, A. *Future Shock*. New York: Random House, 1970.
Tong, P. "Classic House: The Album." http://www.petetong.com/2016/11/25/classic-house-the-album.
Toubiana, S. "The Brain Is the Screen: Interview with Gilles Deleuze on the Time-Image." *Discourse* 20.3 (1998) 47–55.
Tume, S. "Radiohead Send Mysterious 'Burn the Witch' Leaflet to Fans." http://www.rollingstone.com/music/news/radiohead-send-mysterious-burn-the-witch-leaflet-to-fans-20160430.
Vanhoozer, K. *The Drama of Doctrine*. Louisville: Westminster John Knox, 2005.
———. *Pictures at a Theological Exhibition: Scenes of the Church's Worship, Witness and Wisdom*. Downers Grove: InterVarsity, 2016.
Vernallis, C. *Experiencing Music Video: Aesthetics and Cultural Context*. New York: Columbia University Press, 2004.
———. *Unruly Media: YouTube, Music Video and the New Digital Cinema*. Oxford: Oxford University Press, 2013.
The Verve. "The Verve – Bitter Sweet Symphony (Official Music Video)." *YouTube*, February 28, 2009. https://www.youtube.com/watch?v=1lyu1KKwC74.
Vila, P. "Introduction." In *Music and Youth Culture in Latin America: Identity Construction Processes from New York to Buenos Aires*, edited by P. Vila, 1–16. Oxford: Oxford University Press, 2014.
Viper, M., et al. "Music as Consolation: The Importance of Music at Farewells and Mourning." *Journal of Death and Dying* (2020) 1–23.
Volgsten, U. "Between Ideology and Identity: Media, Discourse, and Affect in the Musical Experience." In *Music and Manipulation: On the Social Uses and Social Control of Music*, edited by S. Brown and U. Volgsten, 74–99. Oxford: Berghahn, 2006.
Wagner, T. "Christianity, Worship and Popular Music." In *The Bloomsbury Handbook of Religion and Popular Music*, edited by C. Partridge and M. Moberg, 90–100. London: Bloomsbury Academic, 2017.
Ward, A., and M. Gayo-Calb. "The Anatomy of Cultural Omnivorousness: The Case of the United Kingdom." *Poetics* 37.2 (2009) 119–45.
Ward, A., et al. "Understanding Cultural Omnivorousness: Or, the Myth of the Cultural Omnivore." *Cultural Sociology* 1.2 (2007) 143–64.
Ward, G. *Unbelievable: Why We Believe and Why We Don't*. London: Taurus, 2014.
Ward, P. *Celebrity Worship*. London: Routledge, 2020.
———. *Gods Behaving Badly: Media, Religion and Celebrity Culture*. London: SCM, 2011.
———. *Liquid Church*. Carlisle, England: Paternoster, 2002.
———. *Liquid Ecclesiology: The Gospel and the Church*. Leiden: Brill, 2017.
Warner, R. *Secularisation and Its Discontents*. London: Continuum, 2010.

Weber, M. *The Protestant Ethic and the Spirit of Capitalism*. New York: Oxford University Press, 2009.
"What Is the Meaning behind the Lyrics of 'Wake Me Up' by Avicii?" https://www.quora.com/What-is-the-meaning-behind-the-lyrics-of-Wake-Me-Up-by-Avicii.
"Where Is the Love?" http://www.songfacts.com/detail.php?id=3301.
White. T. *Sword in the Stone*. London: Collins, 1938.
Whitley, O. "Sociological Models and Theological Reflection." *Journal of the American Academy of Religion* 45 (1977) 331–65.
Whitton. N. "Playful Learning: Tools, Techniques, and Tactics." *Research in Learning Technology* 26 (2018) 1–12.
"Who Says." https://www.songfacts.com/facts/selena-gomez-the-scene/who-says.
"Why 'No Religion' Is the New Religion." http://www.lancaster.ac.uk/news/articles/2016/why-no-religion-is-the-new-religion/.
Williams, Robbie. "Robbie Williams | Love My Life (Official Video)." *YouTube*, November 13, 2016. https://www.youtube.com/watch?v=j4ggyO-OFXU.
Willis, P. *Common Culture: Symbolic Work at Play in the Everyday Cultures of the Young*. Boulder, CO: Westview, 1990.
Winters, J. "Rap and Hip Hop." In *The Bloomsbury Handbook of Religion and Popular Music*, edited by C. Partridge and M. Moberg, 306–15. London: Bloomsbury Academic, 2017.
Woodhead, L. "The Rise of 'No Religion' in Britain: The Emergence of a New Cultural Majority." *Journal of the British Academy* 4 (2016) 245–61.
Woodward, K. "Introduction." In *Identity and Difference*, edited by K. Woodward, 1–6. London: Sage, 1997.
Wright, M. "Christmas Cathedral Congregation Numbers Swell Thanks to Spiritually Inquisitive Festival-Going Millennials." https://uk.news.yahoo.com/christmas-cathedral-congregation-numbers-swell-230100880.html.
Wright, N. *The Epistles of Paul to the Colossians and to Philemon: An Introduction and Commentary*. Tyndale New Testament Commentaries. Leicester: InterVarsity, 1986.
Wyatt, T. "Welby's 'War on Wonga' Credited with Turning Tide on Payday Lending." *Church Times*, February 12, 2016. https://www.churchtimes.co.uk/articles/2016/12-february/news/uk/welby-s-war-on-wonga-credited-with-turning-tide-on-payday-lending.
Yang, M. "Resilience and Meaning-Making Amid the COVID-19 Epidemic in China." *Journal of Humanistic Psychology* 60.5 (2020) 662–71.
Young, A. "New Order Unveil 'Restless', Their First New Song in 10 Years—Listen." http://consequenceofsound.net/2015/07/new-order-unveil-restless-their-first-new-song-in-10-years-listen/.
Youngs, I. "The Orchestra That Won a Top Classical Music Award—for Raving." *BBC*, May 9, 2017. http://www.bbc.co.uk/news/entertainment-arts-39856183.
"Your Own Personal Jesus: Online Services Swell the Church of England's Congregations." *The Economist*, July 4, 2020. https://www.economist.com/britain/2020/06/04/online-services-swell-the-church-of-englands-congregations.
Žižek, S. *Looking Awry: An Introduction to Jaques Lacan through Popular Culture*. Cambridge: MIT Press, 1991.

Discography

Aqua, 1997, 'Barbie Girl,' Universal Music.
Ariana Grande and Justin Bieber, 2020, 'Stuck with U,' Republic Records.
Avicii, 2014, 'Wake Me Up,' Universal Music.
Beyoncé, 2008, 'Video Phone,' Columbia Music.
Brian Eno, 1978, 'Music for airports,' Polydor.
Candi Staton, 1986 and 1991, 'You've got the love,' Island.
Christina Aguilera, 2018, 'Twice,' RCA Records.
Dido, 2019, 'You don't need a God,' BMG Rights Management (UK) Ltd.
DMX, 2006, 'Lord, give me a sign,' Columbia Music.
Drake, 2018, 'God's Plan,' Republic Records.
Ella Henderson, 2014, 'Ghost,' Syco Music.
Fleet Foxes, 2011, 'Helplessness Blues,' Bella Union.
Florence and the Machine, 2018, 'Big God,' Virgin EMI.
George Ezra, 2017, 'Don't Matter Now,' Columbia Music.
George Harrison, 1969, 'My sweet lord,' UMC.
Gloria Gaynor, 1978, 'I will Survive,' Polydoor.
Grace Jones, 1985, 'Slave to the rhythm,' Island Records.
Hillsongs, 2013, 'Oceans,' Hillsongs Music.
Home Made Kazoku, 2008, 'Tsubaki,' Ki/oon.
Hozier, 2014, 'Take me to Church,' Universal-Island Records.
Jay-Z, 2006, 'Empire State of Mind,' Atlantic.
Jonas Blue (featuring Dakota), 2015, 'Fast Car,' Virgin EMI.
Kanye West, 2004, 'Jesus Walks,' Roc-A-Fella.
Lady Gaga, 2011, 'Born this way,' Interscope.
Lady Gaga, 2018, 'Shallow,' Interscope.
Lily Allen, 2009, 'The Fear,' Parlophone.
Los Del Rio, 1993, 'Macarena,' RCA Records.
Maria Carey, 1991, 'Emotions,' Columbia Records.
Max Richter, 2015, 'Sleep,' Deutsche Grammophon Classics.
Mel C, 2016, 'Dear Life,' Red Girl Records.
Metallica, 1986, 'Leper Messiah,' UMC.
Mike Posner, 2015, 'I took a pill in Ibiza,' Monster Mountain/Island.
Monty Python, 1979, 'Always Look on the Bright Side of Life,' Charisma.
Neil Diamond, 1969, 'Sweet Caroline,' Uni Records.
New Order, 2015, 'Restless,' Mute.

Norah Cyrus, 2018, 'Sadness,' Columbia.
OneRepublic, 2013, 'Counting Stars,' Interscope Records.
Pete Tong, 2017, 'Classic House,' Universal.
Peter Gabriel, 1980, 'Biko,' Charisma.
Peter Gabriel with Youssou N'Dour, 1986, 'In your eyes,' Charisma.
Pharrell Williams, 2014, 'Happy,' Columbia.
Radiohead, 2016, 'Burn the Witch,' XL.
Robbie Williams, 2005, 'Angels,' Chrysalis.
Robbie Williams, 2016, 'I love my life,' Chrysalis.
Rush, 1991, 'Digital Man,' Anthem.
St Vincent, 2017, 'Fear the future,' Loma Vista.
Savage Garden, 1999, 'Affirmation,' Columbia.
Stormzy, 2017, 'Mr Skeng,' Warner.
Stormzy, 2017, 'Blinded By Your Grace,' Warner.
Selena Gomez, 2011, 'Who Says,' Hollywood.
Shawn Mendes, 2018, 'In my blood,' Island Records.
Sia, 2016, 'Cheap Thrills,' RCA.
The Blackeyed Peas, 2003, 'Where Is the love?,' Interscope.
The Blackeyed Peas, 2016, '#WhereIsTheLove,' Interscope.
The Icicle Works, 1982, 'Nirvana,' Beggars Banquet.
The Libertines, 2003, 'Can't stand me now,' Rough Trade Records.
The Police, 1979, 'Canary in a Coal Mine,' A&M.
The Police, 1980, 'Don't stand so close to me,' A&M.
The Sex Pistols, 1977, 'Never mind the Bollocks, Here's the Sex Pistols,' Virgin.
The Stooges, 2007, 'The end of Christianity,' Columbia.
The Verve, 1998, 'Bittersweet Symphony,' Hut.
Trent Reznor/ Nine Inch Nails, 1994, 'Hurt', Interscope.
Twenty One Pilots, 2020, 'Level of Concern,' Elektra Records.

www.ingramcontent.com/pod-product-compliance
Lightning Source LLC
Chambersburg PA
CBHW051054230426
43667CB00013B/2290